The Political Classics

GREEN TO DWORKIN

EDITED BY

MURRAY FORSYTH
AND
MAURICE KEENS-SOPER

OXFORD UNIVERSITY PRESS

1996

Oxford University Press, Walton Street, Oxford OX2 6DP
Oxford New York
Athens Auckland Bangkok Bombay
Calcutta Cape Town Dar es Salaam Delhi
Florence Hong Kong Istanbul Karachi
Kuala Lumpur Madras Madrid Melbourne
Mexico City Nairobi Paris Singapore
Taipei Tokyo Toronto
and associated companies in
Berlin Ibadan

Oxford is a trade mark of Oxford University Press

Published in the United States
by Oxford University Press Inc., New York

British Library Cataloguing in Publication Data
Data available

Library of Congress Cataloging in Publication Data
The political classics : Green to Dworkin / edited by Murray Forsyth
and Maurice Keens-Soper.
Includes bibliographical references (p.   ).
1. Political science—History—19th century.   2. Political
science—History—20th century.   I. Forsyth, Murray Greensmith.
II. Keens-Soper, H. M. A.
JA83.P555   1996   320'.9—dc20   95–49644

ISBN 0–19–878094–x
ISBN 0–19–878095–8 (Pbk)

1 3 5 7 9 10 8 6 4 2

Typeset by Graphicraft Typesetters Ltd., Hong Kong
Printed in Great Britain on acid-free paper by
Bookcraft (Bath) Ltd.
Midsomer Norton, Avon

In memoriam
Peter Savigear

Contents

Introduction

Political Reasoning in a Time of Upheaval
THE EDITORS

THE texts chosen for inclusion in this third and final volume of The Political Classics span a hundred years. T. H. Green's *Lectures on the Principles of Political Obligation* were first delivered in 1879, twenty years after the publication of J. S. Mill's *On Liberty*, with which the preceding set of essays in this series concluded. Ronald Dworkin's *Taking Rights Seriously* first appeared in 1977. With the exception of T. H. Green's work, all the books discussed in the following essays were published in this century.

Selecting the Texts

The problem of selecting the appropriate texts for inclusion has been far more acute and challenging in the case of the present volume than in the case of the previous ones. The reasons for this are plain. We are still very close to the political writers of the past century; we cannot see them in full perspective; and posterity has not had time to make its judgement. The example of T. H. Green, the first writer in this volume, is instructive. Since Green's death in 1882 a quiet consensus has formed which places him firmly among the classic political theorists. With most of those that follow him in this volume, however, such a consensus has not yet crystallized. As a result we, as editors, should perhaps admit that our selection is largely conjectural, and that the best we can hope to have done is to have hit upon the works from the past century that have a lasting, outstanding quality. If it turns out that our expectations have been misplaced, that in itself will tell a tale and stir future editors to ponder our judgement.

This, however, is a shade too evasive. In the Introduction to our first collection of essays, *The Political Classics: Plato to*

Rousseau, we tried to put into words what announces and marks off a work of political philosophy that has acquired the status of a classic, and thereby still demands our attention no matter what may be the differences of time and circumstance that separate its composition from its subsequent readers. It is perhaps worth repeating what we confidently asserted when the authors in question had long-established claims as constituent contributors to the canon of Western reasoning about the political condition of mankind.

The peculiarity of political philosophy [we wrote] is the assumption that it is possible, and indeed in some sense necessary, to respond to the fact of rule or government by exercising our reason. Reason is more than curiosity, and once engaged it is as relentless in its search for 'right rule' and 'right order' as is our need for rule on which it dwells . . . What distinguishes the finest, the enduring works (of political philosophy) is precisely that they succeed in bringing the fact of rule or government into reasoned connection with the nature and ends of men. They unify our experience.

These are the qualities we have had in mind in judging which books suggest themselves for inclusion here. We may have detected, qualities that others fail to recognize, and overlooked books that fulfil these demanding requirements, and whose omission appears odd and perhaps perverse. It is one thing, however, to dispute whether a particular book meets the standards outlined, and another to disavow the existence of any such standards and hence the existence of a tradition of reasoning based upon them which continues to the present. We should also make mention of the workaday fact that in a book of this or any length there is inevitably much shuffling for place and that many fine works have been omitted more for reasons of space than anything else. Were we to seek to justify in detail our choice of some and our exclusion of others, the resulting argument might interest those whose task it is to induct students into the manner and preoccupations of political reasoning, but would probably be of less interest to students in need of introductory essays designed to illuminate sometimes difficult texts and to stimulate engagement with them. From the start it has been the prime purpose of the series to provide students with such guidance, and, in pursuing this goal, it scarcely seems necessary to take them behind the scenes (as it were) to where we as editors have argued about whom to put on the stage.

We will limit ourselves, therefore, to a few general remarks. We did not think it appropriate to include works produced by political leaders and activists as part of their struggle to achieve political power or to hold on to it—not because such works are unimportant but because they almost inevitably lack the reflective distance that characterizes a genuine work of political theory. The reader will thus not find an analysis of the writings of leaders such as Lenin, Hitler, Stalin, or Mussolini in this book. We have also restricted ourselves to texts that are explicitly concerned with politics, and have not sought to include texts that illuminate the spiritual or intellectual evolution of the world during the twentieth century, or that focus broadly on 'society', however much these works may have exercised an influence on politics. For this reason there are no chapters on, for example, works by Nietzsche and Freud, while there is a chapter devoted to Georges Sorel, a political writer influenced by Nietzsche.

Mention of Sorel brings us to the inevitable question of cultural bias. The great bulk of the works chosen were written in English by British or American authors, though it is worth noting that three of these—Hannah Arendt, Isaiah Berlin, and Friedrich von Hayek—were emigrants from Central or Eastern Europe. When one casts a glance at recent French books on classic political texts, one is acutely conscious of a cultural chasm. Dominique Colas, for example, in *La Pensée politique: Textes essentiels* (Paris, 1992), chooses as modern texts works by Nietzsche, Freud, Weber, de Gaulle, Sartre, and Foucault. Gérard Mairet, in *Les Grandes Œuvres Politiques* (Paris, 1993), selects Nietzsche, Lenin, Luxemburg, Weber, Scheler, Schmitt, Ferrero, Arendt, Weil, and Patocka. The dearth of British and American writers in both these lists provides a sharp corrective to Anglo-Saxon complacency. One does not have to accept either list as satisfactory to recognize that we have, in our own selection, almost certainly been too indulgent to the Anglo-American tradition with which we are, by background, most familiar.

None the less we have made a deliberate effort to look beyond this tradition and to bring into view thinkers of a very

different background—in particular, Sorel, Gramsci, and Schmitt
—whom we consider to have made substantial contributions
to political theory, and to have sometimes been unjustifiably
ignored. We also consider that the strong American note on
which our selection ends—the chapters on Rawls, Nozick,
and Dworkin—is in no sense a product of bias but a recognition of an exceptionally vigorous contribution to modern
political theory from the other side of the Atlantic.

Our intention throughout has not been to provide a history
of political thought but to draw attention to individual works
of exceptional quality. The result, however, is that twelve
works now appear together giving the impression perhaps that
they are peaks on a single range. If the result of any selection
is to single out and highlight, it also invites one to ask what
those chosen have in common and to comment on those
divergences of argument and interest which suggest that they
share nothing much at all. This is the task to which we shall
now turn.

Common Themes

Philosophical reasoning about politics rarely occurs in a vacuum
and there are grounds for saying that the best in political
theory is prompted by historical upheavals. In the Introduction
to the second volume in this series we suggested, for example,
that what presided over political argument during the late
eighteenth and early nineteenth century was the accelerating
popular demand for representative government and the simultaneous transformation of the body politic by nascent industrialization. Is it possible to offer something similar with respect
to the period covered by the present set of essays? A plausible
generalization that offers the right setting in which to examine
the separate texts?

There is, of course, no shortage of suggestions. 'The rise of
ideology and ideological struggle.' 'The revolt of the masses.'
'The advent of totalitarianism.' 'The emergence of world communism.' 'The assault on liberalism.' 'The decline and renaissance of liberalism.' All have a certain plausibility. Perhaps the
most appropriate framework is, however, that already implicit
in the European world of the early nineteenth century and

symbolized by the two writers with which our previous volume ended—Marx, with his cataclysmic view of the future evolution of the Western world, and Mill, still at heart a liberal optimist, but with anxieties about the consequences of the progress of democracy. In other words, the late nineteenth and early twentieth century mark an extension and intensification of the tensions already present in the earlier period. On the one hand, there is the spread and intensification of the dislocation caused by the growth of what Marx called 'great industry'. The nature of the 'social problem' thrown up by this dislocation is so well known as scarcely to require elaboration here. What needs more emphasis is the spiritual problem: the spreading anxiety amongst intellectuals about the growth of a mechanical, materialist civilization with no values beyond the economically acquisitive. On the other hand, there is the steady expansion of representative, parliamentary government, and the gradual widening of electorates—unmistakable signs of progress and maturity to many liberals and democrats, but frequently failing to fulfil their promise in practice.

The successors of Marx and Mill set their minds to resolve these issues. Liberals agonized over how far they could or must embrace democracy and socialism and an activist state; socialists debated fiercely how much of the 'bourgeois ideology' of liberal parliamentary institutions and practices was compatible with their cause, and necessary to the creation of a new society beyond capitalism. In the wings, political thinkers arose who doubted whether either conventional socialism or conventional liberalism was capable of resolving the radical malaise of a corrupted civilization.

T. H. Green was, for example, alert to how vulnerable the liberalism of his time had become to the charge that it served primarily the material interests of the economically strong. He did not, however, conclude that the situation could best be improved by retaining the prevalent 'negative' view of liberty and making it the basis of a more broadly based representative system. If the prevailing liberal view of liberty was wrong nothing could be expected from a mere extension of the suffrage. A state whose purpose was limited to holding the ring so that a free-for-all could take place under a canopy of law was, in Green's opinion, morally defective. It was not the job of liberalism to justify either capitalism or democracy. His is unmistakably the voice of a moralist who discusses the state from the angle of someone exploring the conditions necessary for the full development of individual personality. Although the state could not make people moral, in establishing the right conditions for the good life it was implicated in more than material concerns. In keeping with the Aristotelian tradition, Rousseau, and Hegel, Green saw the state as closely associated with the accomplishment of the ultimate ends pursued by mankind. This conception is plainly far removed from the view of the state that has been propounded at the end of the twentieth century by such liberals as Hayek or Nozick.

With Green we can see liberalism striving to provide itself with deeper roots in order to confront more adequately the social and spiritual problems of the day. With the French writer Georges Sorel, a generation later, we encounter a pessimistic radicalism that goes far beyond such efforts at liberal reconstruction, and points the way towards the anti-liberal revolutionary movements from both the right and the left that erupted in Europe during and after the First World War. Sorel's observations of the political workings of the Third Republic left him disillusioned with liberal parliamentarianism and all who contaminated themselves with it. Influenced by Marx, his criticism of the Marxists of his day was precisely that they had either passively (the Kautskyan orthodoxy) or actively (the revisionists) accommodated themselves to existing political institutions, and had thus transformed Marx's original summons to spiritual rejuvenation through revolution into a mere policy of replacing one set of rulers by another. They had robbed Marxism of its heroic grandeur. More than this, they had misconstrued what it takes to move men towards an 'ethics of sublimity'. It was not the misplaced scientism of cause-and-effect thinking that inspires action but the energizing force of myth. To act, men have first to be moved, and what moves man is the summons to play a role in some ennobling fable. The myth of the general strike which Sorel expounded has more to do with Nietzschean heroics in the face of a decadent civilization than with the emancipation of the proletariat. His purpose has little to do with the establishment of 'rightful government' or with politics understood in the liberal sense as the conciliation of interests. His contempt for both is boundless. So, too, is his related hostility to the doctrine of historical progress, for so long in the nineteenth century the underpinning of liberal optimism. Following Nietzsche, Sorel regarded faith in historical progress as a curse of the Enlightenment because it substituted mean-minded confidence in a benign providence for the generative if risky powers of human will and imagination. Belief in progress left no room for truly creative action, and any view of civilization based on the banishment of conflict endangered civilization.

Sorel placed his faith in a new ethics derived from the productive energies of *homo faber*, man the maker of things, who with industrialization now finds the world at his disposal. Creative energy lay with the new industrial workers whose mission it was to sweep away not only liberal parliamentarianism but the state itself by violent revolutionary action. Sorel was in a sense calling for an end to politics, as Jeremy Jennings points out. However, in another sense he was calling for the thoroughgoing politicization of the working class, its transformation from a social category represented by a parliamentary party into a separate warring totality dedicated to the defeat and overthrow of a total enemy. We are here using the concept of the political elaborated by Carl Schmitt in a later essay discussed in this volume to illuminate the political nature of Sorel's doctrine. Sorel wanted to transmute the relatively peaceful sparring of French political life into an intense 'friend–enemy' antithesis. It is precisely the paradox of the revolutionary totalitarian party or 'movement' that it aims typically at going beyond conventional politics and indeed at ending them, but that in attempting to do so it politicizes life as never before.

It is perhaps the main significance of Antonio Gramsci's political theory that he attempts to resolve this particular paradox, and in doing so reveals the nest of political problems that confront revolutionary anti-state movements. As a Marxist revolutionary—more orthodox than Sorel—Gramsci regarded a political party not as one of the organizational components of a liberal parliamentary state, but rather, in the words cited by John Hoffman, as itself 'an embryonic state structure', the seed from which a new state, a new political order, is to emerge. As such it had to be able to defend itself against enemies, it had to exercise a 'policing function'. The political struggle was not a gentlemanly debate conducted within a parliamentary chamber, nor a periodic competition to decide the majority in such a chamber. It was, as for Sorel, a war, a class war. Marxism, however, sought to use such an embryonic state structure to bring about a world where the state was redundant. How could this be achieved? Gramsci's answer is that the new Marxist party-state must be based not—or not exclusively, for there is ambiguity here—on force, but must be organized primarily on the principle of 'hegemony'. This meant that the 'spontaneous', 'ethical', 'organic', and 'unitary' relationship of 'leaders' and 'led' must progressively replace the artificial, political, inorganic, and dual relationship of 'rulers' and 'ruled'. This, in turn, meant that the party must be less exclusive in its outlook, be less openly belligerent, place greater reliance on education and persuasion, and show a greater recognition of national and cultural traditions. In this way an 'ethical state' or 'civil society' would emerge which would not be a 'state' in the conventional sense of the term. By positing a state that is not a state as the final end of Marxist revolutionary activity, Gramsci thus squares the circle, but at a tremendous cost to credibility.

In their sharply different ways, Green, Sorel, and Gramsci were all preoccupied with ethics or morality. Carl Schmitt, by contrast, in the essay discussed in this volume, focuses remorselessly on the political, and seeks not to subordinate it to other categories of human existence, but to allow its own specific characteristics to appear. He was acutely sensitive to all the new political tendencies at work in Europe during the early part of the twentieth century and from his critical engagement with them he was led to define the political as pivoted on the friend–enemy antithesis. This provocative thesis was not, however, conjoined to a revolutionary or bellicose world-transforming programme. On the contrary, Schmitt used his fresh definition of the political as a basis for reauthenticating and reasserting the beleaguered traditional concepts of the state and the states-system. Not surprisingly, in view of the shackles placed on Germany at the end of the First World War and the patent inadequacies of Weimar's parliamentary system, the main target of Schmitt's critique was not the new revolutionary movements of right and left but rather the liberalism that they too attacked.

With its non-political and anti-political presuppositions, liberalism was incapable, in Schmitt's view, of conceiving, founding, or sustaining a genuine state, or of providing an effective framework of international order. Schmitt had in mind here, of course, the formal, agnostic, neutral constitutionalism that characterized German liberalism in the Weimar period, as well as the moralizing liberalism characteristic of Woodrow Wilson and the supporters of the League of Nations. Liberalism, he wrote, typically approaches the field of politics from either a moral standpoint or an economic standpoint; it fails to face squarely the political in and for itself. The state, as the quintessential manifestation of the political, was not a mere association of individuals who have agreed to regulate their activities by a common set of laws; it was a community of 'friends' united under a sovereign authority capable of identifying and taking action against internal and external 'enemies'. This was the primordial unity that underpinned the moral and economic worlds and it reflected in turn the dangerous character of the human species. Where these political truths were ignored or evaded by politicians and statesmen or constitution-makers then the state concerned was in grave danger of dissolution or overthrow. Schmitt's attack on liberalism has sometimes given the misleading impression that he belonged to the ranks of the ideological radicals, but at heart he was a conservative.

Michael Oakeshott was also a conservative drawn to diagnose the follies of his time, and like Schmitt he admired Hobbes. His milieu was very different, however, and his appeal to traditional modes of thought and action followed a different path. For Oakeshott the liberal, democratic system of government, which in the United Kingdom had weathered successfully the ideological onslaught from right and left, had become infected with errors of understanding about the scope of political action which were not unlike those that characterized totalitarianism. In particular, he detected a pervasive impatience with human experience and inherited ways of doing things and a corresponding overestimation of the benefits of detached, self-conscious, ends–means reasoning. He identified both with the rapid pace of modern historical change and found their influence pernicious. When men are constantly in a hurry, time itself comes to be seen as an obstacle, and when that occurs reason is made to serve as a reservoir of techniques, an instrument for the design and implementation of blueprints. This short-cut approach is justified by the supposed transparent clarity and value of the ends in question and by the ensuing confidence that there is no point in wasting time. The consequence for politics is a jettisoning of well-tried practices and a trust in the mechanics of problem-solving. Morality, too, is disfigured as it comes to be treated as the self-conscious pursuit of ideals that are susceptible to precise formulation. Nothing is to be valued until it is made clear, distinct, precise. This holds true as much for liberal programmes of individual rights as for socialist programmes of equality. The gradual adjustments to change which conduct steeped in experience allows for and indeed encourages is replaced by the clash of inflexible doctrines which readily become murderous. Rationalism in politics, in sum, disrupts its practice by seeking to reduce (or raise) it to the fancied rigours of logical exposition and systematic application. Whether we— in the West or elsewhere—any longer inhabit a world of indicative historical continuities of the kind that Oakeshott explores and endorses may now be seriously doubted, and, if this is so, it leaves unresolved what kind of politics is compatible with conditions where change is so volatile that experience has insufficient time to become the ballast of settled conduct.

Oakeshott detected in the liberal doctrine of Friedrich von Hayek the kind of rationalism he opposed, and there is not a little irony in this, given Hayek's constant endorsement of the benefits that flow from the unplanned and spontaneous activities of individual human beings. Hayek preceded Oakeshott to the London School of Economics, but he did so as a refugee from Austria. His turn from economics to the study of politics was connected with what he regarded as a threat to the highest achievement of Western civilization—the advancement of prosperity through the maintenance of the widest possible freedom from constraint for the individual. The threat that animates all Hayek's political reasoning is that of collectivism, which he subsumes under the name of socialism. For him the century from 1848 was the century of European socialism and his fear was that, having withstood the onslaughts of the Nazi and Soviet brands of socialism, the liberal democracies might inadvertently, in the name of democracy, and using its methods, introduce a 'welfare-state' or 'social-democratic' variety of socialism, as pernicious as all the others. The nub of Oakeshott's comment is that Hayek's unremitting endeavour to defend individual economic freedom against socialism leads him to draft a blueprint for preventing the state from making even the slightest move towards upholding common ends or interests. The political—to revert to the terms of our earlier discussion— must, according to Hayek's *The Constitution of Liberty*, be placed in a strait-jacket to enable the evil of socialism to be kept permanently in check and to permit economic interchange between individuals to flourish unhindered. This is not to dispute that economic productivity may be hindered by certain forms of state intervention. It is rather to suggest that Hayek's liberalism is as thin and brittle as it is dismissive of the autonomy of the political.

Hannah Arendt, like Hayek, was a refugee from fascism, though unlike him she came to the study of politics via philosophy rather than economics. Her sense of something catastrophically vile at work in Western civilization comes out in her exploration of how difficult it has become to feel fully at home in the world. The powers of modern man, set free by science and technology, have produced first hubris and then nemesis. The same intoxication with the idea of recasting human kind that marks the inhumanity of twentieth-century totalitarianism is, in her reckoning, also present in the liberal democracies of the West. In exalting our productive powers and then hoping to find happiness in consumption—that is, in focusing so exclusively on the very activities in which Hayek finds hope— we have forsaken our humanity. In Arendt's view, we have lost an item of understanding that the Greeks of antiquity found essential to self-knowledge. In the life of the *polis* it was action and not production or consumption that was valued as uniquely human, and by action Arendt means something like the open, direct, and continuous participation of citizens in the determination of their public affairs. It is in political action that human individuality finds both its opportunity to shine and to win recognition, and the means to set common limits to its performance. It is by action in the world, and by acting together to 'house' its ramifications, that we come to be at home in the world. This is a defence of individuality directed equally against homogenization and liberal individualism—or at least against the liberal suspicion of the state and its predilection for the activities of the private world over those of politics and the public realm. Arendt's is a 'republican' view of politics which finds the idea of 'representative democracy' as ontologically shallow as is the translation of private desires into public issues. It is open to the criticism that it treats with disdain exactly those 'activities' which constitute the stuff of party politics in mass democracies.

Isaiah Berlin's *Two Concepts of Liberty* was published in the same year as Arendt's *The Human Condition*, and, although they differ in their estimate of the domain of politics and the virtues associated with it, what they share is also revealing. Like Arendt, Berlin seeks to account for the decline into barbarism of a civilization at the height of its powers. In both cases their trawl of history and thought is impressively wide-ranging and discovers at the centre of our tribulations intellectual errors giving rise to political perversity. Whereas Arendt emphasizes that politics should take its cue from the valuable 'plurality' of human re-beginnings, Berlin stresses the importance of the multiple ends that human beings discern and value. The fact of this kind of diversity is of importance, because our rival and often incompatible values raise the matter of how human beings thus constituted are to live together. This becomes of direct political significance when one version of what is to be valued tries to impose itself on others.

In the modern European world the worst examples of political barbarism have arisen, according to Berlin, where power has been mobilized to impose a single, because rational, concept of liberty. It may be questioned whether this is true in relation to the various fascist movements in Europe which, in Sorelian fashion, did not express much respect for reason. Antirational assertions of freedom surely have their terrors no less than rational ones. The intolerant, rational concept of liberty grew, in turn, according to Berlin, out of the notion of liberty as 'positive', that is, as involving the notion of individual self-realization. This raises the interesting question whether the political doctrine of T. H. Green, who clearly *did* believe in liberty as self-realization, leads *necessarily* to the forcible political homogenization of individuals. It is surely possible to argue that it does not, in which case an important link in Berlin's argument is snapped.

Be that as it may, Berlin's vigorous defence of 'negative' liberty carries with it the undeniably important reminder that the normal state, as distinct from its totalitarian distortion, secures and implies a space where privacy exists and individuality can flourish. In his idiosyncratic way, Gramsci seems to have been trying to communicate this same message to his fellow Marxists thirty years earlier when he argued that the Marxist party-state must strive to give birth to a non-state arena or civil society. Hayek, of course, goes much further than this and accords complete primacy to the non-state arena. Berlin's position is less clear, as he makes surprisingly little effort, in his essay, to elucidate the nature and role of the state.

John Rawls's *A Theory of Justice* is another exemplar of the reinvigoration of liberalism which has been so marked a feature in the West over the past few decades. On its publication in 1971 it was greeted as a vindication of theory in the grand manner at a time when it was thought to have expired. The confidence that the book exudes in the power of reasoning to construct an entire edifice of principled politics may owe something to its country of origin, and in particular to the relatively peaceful history of American domestic politics during this century. Whereas much of the most acute thinking of writers of European origin is seldom free from doubts over the capacity of reason to govern politics, and is preoccupied often with civilization's self-inflicted wounds, Rawls and the other two American writers discussed in the last chapters of this book do not suffer from qualms of this kind. It is as if the optimistic and progressive beliefs identified with the founders of liberalism still flourished with undiminished vigour in American political thinking. Rawls, Nozick, and Dworkin are not poring over the Enlightenment seeking to discover what in its legacy contributed to the political turmoil of the twentieth century. Most noticeably there is a lack of fear in respect of human powers and propensities.

Regarded as the most fertile of Rawls's critics, Robert Nozick shares with his academic colleague one crucial characteristic: both assume that the right way to philosophize about politics is not to ask what it is or what necessities inhere in it, but to set out the principles which should direct it. These principles are at once moral and rational: in Rawls's case they are those of social or distributive justice, in Nozick's those of natural individual rights. Rawls elaborates a hierarchy of norms and axioms which will allow those who govern to read off, so to speak, the correct answers to the problems of wealth distribution. His approach presents a striking example of the 'rationalism in politics' that Oakeshott was concerned to denounce. In contrast to Rawls, who at least allows the state some scope for social action, Nozick disputes whether the state has any business beyond providing a basic security system for the protection of pre-political rights. The public order of law on which freedom from government ultimately depends appears— as in most utopias—stripped of political substance, and this banishment of politics is seen by Nozick as something brought about by the free and rational consent of individuals.

The primary importance which Nozick assigns to rights is shared by his fellow countryman, Ronald Dworkin, but he displays a far greater sensitivity to the complexities of any political order, and a far greater reluctance to subject it to abstract, rationally deduced, external rules, than either Nozick or Rawls. His stress on the presence of immanent rather than external guidelines for the resolution of hard judicial cases is reminiscent of Oakeshott's position, and his refusal to sever the political, legal, and moral, while acknowledging their relative autonomy, is reminiscent of Hegel. His theory focuses on the nature of law, which has always been a principal concern of political theory, and it is best studied in conjunction with the work he is at pains to rectify, Herbert Hart's *The Concept of Law*. This is in turn analysed and discussed at an earlier point in the present volume. Hart's book represents a subtle and sustained attempt to renovate the positivist interpretation of law that has its roots in the writings of Bentham and Austin, refining the crude definitions of the earlier thinkers and showing a certain sensitivity to other traditions. Like all positivists, however, Hart is seeking, in conceptualizing law, to provide certainty and clarity by separating the phenomena of the social

world into self-contained compartments external to one another. (Schmitt and Arendt, in their works already mentioned,
can perhaps also be charged with this tendency, with the all-
important reservation that Schmitt emphasizes the capacity of
non-political categories to become political rather than their
mutual incompatibility.) Hart concentrates on separating law
from morality, defining the former as a hierarchy of rules
which culminates as a matter of empirical fact in a 'rule of recognition'. Dworkin considers that this definition, however clear,
does not go to the root of the matter. He is aware of how little
at both its core and borders law can be insulated from the political and moral and he develops a richer and more comprehensive theory, stressing continuities rather than disjunctions.

Open Questions

When Croce wrote that all history is contemporary history he
was emphasizing how present-day preoccupations cannot fail
to influence our view of the past. Just as the military defeat of
Nazi Germany in 1945 mocked the pretensions that the future
lay with fascism, so the collapse of the Soviet Union suggests
that the Russian 'experiment' with collectivist planning and
one-party rule was a wasteful exercise in ideological zeal and
oppressive mendacity. In the aftermath of the Cold War we
are busy trying to decide whether the failure of these massive
political attempts to leap beyond conventional politics are a
conclusive vindication of liberal principles, representative democracy, and capitalism. Can we now claim to *know* that states
in which constitutions protect individual rights and restrain
governments, in which mass electorates possess the power pe-
riodically to dismiss rulers, and in which the operations of the
competitive market are actively maximized provide the sure
expression of good government? Have the respective claims of
the political, the moral, and the economic at last been adequately reconciled? Are we—to use Arendt's phrase—'at home'
in the world that we have created and which has outlived its
rivals? Is liberalism an unproblematic and self-evident political
ideal? The texts discussed in this volume perhaps provoke us
to be less confident in answering these difficult questions.

The gaps or omissions in the texts are also instructive. The growth of the global economy and the sense that the world is becoming rapidly foreshortened impels us now to pay ever increasing attention to events and actions beyond the individual state, and to pose the question whether new structures are arising that will transcend or replace the state. The writings considered in this selection, however, with one exception, tend to look at the state in isolation from its neighbours, as if the existence of a multiplicity of states in a mixed setting of war and diplomacy did not go to the very heart and centre of a state's *raison d'être*. Although long established as a habit of reasoning, theorizing about the state as if other states did not exist or did not impinge directly on its existence may yet come to be seen as one of the more implausible oddities of a century whose public events were steeped in the consequences of war and international conflict.

The contributors to this volume have been drawn from a wide variety of academic institutions in the United Kingdom. The direct link with Leicester is not so strong as in the earlier volumes, but, on the other hand, the link with the University of Wales Swansea, with which the Department of Politics at Leicester has had a long and fruitful connection, is relatively stronger. We would like to thank all the contributors for their patience during the often frustrating time of preparing the book for publication, the frustrations being caused mainly by the departure of one of the editors for Hong Kong.

I

Thomas Hill Green: *Lectures on the Principles of Political Obligation*

PETER NICHOLSON

THE ideas of Thomas Hill Green mark a significant change of direction in the evolution of British political thought in the latter part of the nineteenth century. Green rejected what he considered to be the wholly inadequate individualism and materialism popular at the time. He returned to an earlier tradition, drawing on the Greeks, particularly Aristotle as revitalized by Hegel, to create a new synthesis. This is notable for its emphasis on the social nature of the individual and therefore of politics, and on the spiritual side of human life and correspondingly a moral role for society and for the state. His ideas were extremely influential among philosophers for two generations or so; and in politics they were taken up by New Liberals and some socialists. His thought has been out of fashion for much of the twentieth century, but remains important. Green offers a version of liberalism which makes substantial moral claims and which retains its radical political edge. It is also highly relevant to the contemporary debate about the proper sphere of the state. Green poses a powerful challenge to the doctrine of rights advanced by some of the writers who appear towards the end of this volume, notably Nozick and Rawls.

Born in 1836 and educated first at home and then at Rugby and Balliol College, Oxford, Green spent most of his adult life in Oxford. As a Fellow at Balliol, he was a powerful and effective teacher, quickly recognized as the exponent of fresh ideas. In 1878 he became Whyte's Professor of Moral Philosophy, and in the four years before his early death he gave several series of lectures on the subject. In an innovatory step, he designed them so as to interest graduates as well as undergraduates. Among the professorial lectures were those later published from his papers as the *Lectures on the Principles of*

Political Obligation. It must always be borne in mind that Green examines politics in the wider context of moral philosophy.

My aim in this chapter is to use the *Lectures* to exhibit Green's basic approach to politics and to outline the main principles of his political philosophy together with some of his applications of them. That text suffers from certain limitations: this course of lectures is unfinished, because Green ran out of time (see sect. 247)[1]; it is not complete in itself because it is part of a larger cycle of lectures; and it is a little disorganized and slightly repetitious because Green never revised it for publication. Accordingly I have not always felt obliged to observe Green's order of topics, and occasionally I have drawn on his *Prolegomena to Ethics*, based on his other professorial lectures.

The Main Principles of Politics

Green's central idea is that the state, by enforcing a system of legal rights and obligations, serves a moral function. It maintains the conditions under which individual human beings can be morally good.

Being morally good means acting for the sake of the goodness of what one does, rather than for any satisfaction that the act may bring. Obviously, one cannot live one's life by the principle 'do what is good, because it is good' alone, since that does not specify *what* one should do. There must also be 'a prior morality', consisting of rules about which acts are good. These rules are part of the institutions of one's society, some forming its conventional morality and some embodied or reflected in the law of the state. One is morally good, on Green's view, if two conditions are met: first, that one does the act because it is good; and, secondly, that the act really is good. Over the course of human history it has come to be understood that true moral goodness is this attribute of character, so that it is now possible and necessary to use this criterion to criticize the prior morality, asking whether its rules actually are good. Do the ways they require us to act in fact contribute to our developing morally good characters?

---

[1] Thomas Hill Green, *Lectures on the Principles of Political Obligation*; references in the text are to sections number so that any edition may be used.

In the *Lectures* Green undertakes the most important part of this enquiry. Confining himself to the states of modern Europe, he asks how and to what extent the legal rules in force in those 'civilized societies' contribute to the moral development of individuals. Thus political institutions are scrutinized from the moral point of view: how far are they contributing as they should to individual human beings' opportunities to live a moral life? Above all, how far do they allow and help them to exercise their wills freely and rationally, and act upon the idea of self-perfection (sects. 2–6, 19)?

The value of political institutions is that they generally do make it possible for people to act morally. So far as they do, they are morally justified, and hence have a moral claim upon us to support them loyally and to conform with their rules. However, the question of the moral duty to obey the law is a very live issue for Green, because he acknowledges that no state is wholly adequate. 'No one would seriously maintain that the system of rights and obligations, as it is anywhere enforced by law . . . is all that it ought to be' (sect. 9). People may actually have legal rights which they ought not to; conversely, they may not possess as enforceable legal rights, rights which are morally valid and in that sense 'really exist'. The latter are rights which people ought to have as legal rights because they are necessary for them to develop fully as moral persons.

The state's business is to use law 'to maintain certain conditions of life—to see that certain actions are done which are necessary to the maintenance of those conditions, others omitted which would interfere with them' (sect. 13). Green is absolutely clear and explicit that the state can only provide people with the conditions under which they can act morally; it cannot *make* them good. The state operates through law, law rests ultimately on force, and it is impossible to force people to act from the right disposition and with the right motive. Moreover, 'the enforcement of the outward act, of which the moral character depends on a certain motive and disposition, may often contribute to render that motive and disposition impossible' (sect. 10)—for example, 'legal requirements of religious observance and profession of belief' (sect. 17).

These considerations set the limits to the proper province of law: it should enjoin those acts of which the performance is found to produce conditions favourable to action proceeding from a moral disposition, and it should not enjoin any action if the injunction interferes with actions proceeding from that disposition (sect. 16). The only exception to the latter, negative part of this general rule is if the performance of the actions 'is so necessary to the existence of a society in which the moral end stated can be realised that it is better for them to be done or omitted from that unworthy motive which consists in fear or hope of legal consequences than not to be done at all' (sect. 15).

Rights and the State

The true function of government, then, is 'to maintain conditions of life in which morality shall be possible'; and, since morality consists in 'the disinterested performance of self-imposed duties', the state should maximize the room for the self-imposition of duties and for the play of disinterested motives (sect. 18). To achieve this, the state operates principally by providing the individual with legal rights, and placing other individuals under corresponding legal obligations. The notion of a right thus needs careful analysis.

Green has a theory of rights which covers rights in all types of society, not only legal rights enforced in states. He views a right as a power to act which is recognized by the society as a power which individuals ought to have. They ought to have it because they need it in order to fulfil effectively their vocation as moral beings; which they do by devoting themselves to developing the perfect character in themselves and in others (sect. 23). He observes that, as a matter of fact, in every kind of society certain powers (e.g. to possess things, or to raise a family) 'are recognised by men in their intercourse with each other as powers that *should be* exercised, or of which the possible exercise *should be* secured' (sect. 24). These powers are recognized as rights, and their exercise is protected by the society. A number of presuppositions are involved in this, according to Green. First, the idea of a right presupposes that the person to whom it is given is capable of conceiving himself or herself as morally better, and of taking that as an ideal end which they have an unconditional moral duty to realize. Secondly, it presupposes that those who give the right regard it as in some way a means to the recipient's realizing that ideal end. Thirdly, it presupposes that those who give the right, do so because they see the ideal end as a good which is good for themselves too. Fourthly, it presupposes that the holder of the right takes the same view, understanding that the right can contribute to a good for him or for her, that it is granted for that reason by others, and that those others see that same good as a good for them too (sects. 6, 25).

In other words, the idea of a right is irreducibly moral. Exercising rights, and acknowledging the rights of others, is a way of acting morally, and of being treated as a moral being. Hence the idea of a right is also, necessarily, social. No one can have a right, Green claims, except as a member of a society in which some common good is recognized by its members as their own ideal good and as a good which each of them should have (sect. 25). On this way of looking at it, we have to think in terms of a social system of interlocking rights and obligations. Each person has rights, with other people under the corresponding obligations; and, reciprocally, others have the same rights, with the corresponding obligations owed to them. The key idea is that the good which justifies the rights of any member of the society—namely, having secured to one the opportunity to develop, in some form, one's moral capacity—is the same good which justifies those rights for every member: it is a common good. In this way, my conception of good necessarily includes a conception of your good, because I have to understand that what I take as a good I accept is a good for you, and you have to understand that what is a good for you is a good for me. That people do think this way is 'an ultimate fact of human history' (*Prolegomena to Ethics*, sect. 201).[2]

This view of rights produces a principle of fundamental political importance. The capacity to conceive a common good and pursue it is what constitutes a moral person; so every moral person is capable of rights, 'i.e. of bearing his part in a society in which the free exercise of his powers is secured to

---

[2] Thomas Hill Green, *Prolegomena to Ethics* (henceforth *Prolegomena*); references in the text are to sections so that any edition may be used

each member through the recognition by each of the others as entitled to the same freedom with himself' (sect. 25). Every moral person is capable of holding rights and recognizing them in others, understanding their moral function: therefore every moral person ought to possess the rights which are the necessary conditions for their realizing their moral capacity. Green sums up this part of his argument:

There ought to be rights, because the moral personality—the capacity on the part of an individual for making a common good his own—ought to be developed; and it is developed through rights; i.e. through the recognition by members of a society of powers in each other contributory to a common good and the regulation of those powers by that recognition. (sect. 26)

This analysis gives Green a criterion for determining which rights are justified and which are not. No right is justifiable or should be a legal right unless, directly or indirectly, it enables the individual to conceive a good the same for himself and others, and to act on that conception; and, conversely, 'every power should be a right, i.e. society should secure to the individual every power, that is necessary for realising this capacity' (sect. 29). The analysis also gives Green a criterion for setting the limits to the exercise of each right.

Green is clear that a society should secure these powers to *everyone* in it, explicitly including women (*Prolegomena*, sect. 267). He is well aware that not everyone in his day agrees with him, and that past societies have treated many human beings as inferior members or excluded them completely, allowing them fewer rights or none at all (the poor, women, slaves, outsiders). He is also aware that in the past the view of what counts as morally good has often been much narrower than the modern civilized world's. Over the course of human history, people's conceptions of what is good (and so their idea of which powers should be rights, and who should have them as rights) have become wider and fuller, and mankind has made moral progress (sects. 6, 91, 148, 239; *Prolegomena*, sects. 199–285). That is to say, more people have been given greater opportunities to develop morally—opportunities which, he realizes, they may not make the most of (sects. 25, 221).

Green contrasts his theory with those of Spinoza, Hobbes,

Locke, and Rousseau. He makes some of the standard criticisms against them, formulated in his own language. For example, he rejects the view of rights he finds in Spinoza and Hobbes. They contend that, whatever one is able to do in the pre-social state of nature, one has the right of nature to do. But such 'rights' cannot be rights at all, according to Green; they are merely powers. Without 'a consciousness of common interest on the part of members of a society . . . there might be certain powers on the part of individuals, but no recognition of these powers by others as powers of which they allow the exercise, nor any claim to such recognition, and without this recognition or claim to recognition there can be no right' (sect. 31). Having failed to explain rights properly, such writers also fail to explain the true nature of law and of the state (which they see in terms of power alone), and consequently cannot account for political obligation as a moral duty. More generally, the great objection to social-contract theory is not that it is a fiction, but that it is a fiction which conveys a false notion of rights. It 'implies that individuals have certain rights, independently of society and of their functions as members of a society, which they bring with them' to the contract which forms society: but outside society, individuals can only have powers, not rights (sect. 49).

Green himself denies that there is any major break between political society and the preceding condition of man. In the state, society is regulated by written law and by officers with defined powers; what came before it was not a 'state of nature' but an earlier form of society, 'regulated by customs and tacitly recognised authority' (sect. 52; see also sects. 49—55). To a large extent, the state does not create rights, but simply provides a more effective way of protecting the rights which individuals already possessed. Characteristically it carefully defines, reconciles, and harmonizes those rights of different individuals; it provides more extensive rights; and it provides them to a larger number of persons (sects. 91, 132—4). Once a state is established, all kinds of new rights arise in it, as other communities are drawn in, new social forms grow up, and the state's own administration requires new powers. In these ways, the state 'leads to a development and moralisation of man beyond the stage which they must have reached before it could be possible' (sect. 135). The older forms of community (such as the family) are carried on into it, 'supporting its life and in turn maintained by it in a new harmony with each other' (sect. 141). The state is a 'more highly developed form of society', 'the society of societies' (sect. 141), and is plainly regarded by Green, in a very Aristotelian manner, as the final layer of social organization, coming last in history and constituting a definite advance in moral development because it provides opportunities for the extension and deepening of all rights (e.g. sects. 218–19). It is, in Green's eyes, one of the major errors of contract theory that it takes no account of these earlier forms of community and their place in the development of man through society (sect. 113).

Green's theory of rights has difficulties of its own, of course. Critics have been alarmed at the way Green ties rights to social recognition, especially since he explicitly accepts the corollary that the individual can have no rights against his or her state (sects. 99, 141). If one's rights are only those one's state recognizes, what of the basic and inalienable human rights of individuals which natural-rights theorists have asserted we all possess, whether or not our state acknowledges them? Is not Green leaving the individual unprotected and at the mercy of his society, exposed to tyranny and social oppression?

This objection rests largely on a misunderstanding of Green's position, and it can be met. Green fully acknowledges that the powers which individuals should have secured to them as rights, because necessary for their moral development, may not be secured in a particular state. These powers really are rights, and are recognized by at least some of those among whom they live, but because they are not legal rights they are 'implicit rights'. The individual has a moral claim to implicit rights being made legal rights. In such a case, the individual's position is the same as under a natural-rights theory. At the same time, Green is able to avoid the drawback of the natural-rights approach, that people often claim rights which they should not have, or try to retain privileges which have become outdated. The idea of natural rights which the individual possesses on his own account before and independently of the state encourages people to think they have an unconditional right to freedom which the state should not invade (sect. 50). For instance, in his own day, Green faced claims that a man had a right to drive at any speed he liked through the streets, or build houses without any reference to sanitary conditions, or send his children out to work uneducated (sect. 142). But on Green's view one has to justify a claim to legal protection for the exercise of a particular power on the basis that its exercise is necessary to one's acting as a full member of one's society considered as a moral community, necessary to 'the work of developing the perfect character in himself and others' (sect. 21)—which rules out certain alleged rights of the individual which carry no corresponding duty to the other members of the society. There are no absolute rights of the individual: all rights are limited by and conditional upon the moral purpose for which the society recognizes them. It is only in society that men can have rights, so that by their very nature they are limited by the rights of others and by the acknowledged common good of the society. There can be no such thing as a right to do as one likes, for the condition of having a right is that one exercise the power it guarantees 'within the limits necessary to the like exercise by all the other members' of the society (sect. 138). People are granted rights 'conditionally upon their allowing a like freedom in others' (sect. 91).

It is true that Green's approach means that argument about rights is relative and historically conditioned (which is not, of course, to say it is 'subjective'). Exactly which rights are considered necessary for one to develop morally, and who should have them, have been questions answered differently in different societies and states, and one should regard our own answers, as well as Green's, as subject to historical change. But on this point Green's approach is surely sounder than any natural-rights theory, since it is more realistic and accurate about what happens. It is flexible and allows for development, whilst always requiring claims to rights to satisfy a demanding moral test. Some more recent theories seem inferior in their accounts of rights: Nozick's for merely asserting that 'individuals have rights', and Rawls's in so far as it extracts individuals from their actual social relations.

The General Will and Political Obligation

Green accepts a positivist legal analysis of what sovereignty in a state is, taken from John Austin (who in turn drew considerably from Hobbes). There is a determinate person or body of persons with the ultimate power of making, interpreting, and applying law, and having habitual obedience from the people. Green stresses, however, that the reason the sovereign receives habitual obedience is not because the people fear it and its ultimate sanction of force. It is obeyed because it 'is regarded as expressing or embodying what may properly be called the general will', as acting for what is in the subjects' general interest, and the obedience is conditional upon that (sect. 84). The sovereign is the agent of the general will (sect. 93).

Green accordingly applauds Rousseau for introducing morality, in the form of the general will, into his account, and for seeing that the state rests a moral claim to obedience on its representing the general will (sect. 77). But Green thinks that Rousseau is confused because he emphasizes what the people actually wills rather than the 'impartial and disinterested will for the common good' (sect. 69). This diverts Rousseau into looking for the general will where it can never be found, in majority votes, and into pursuing a hopeless attempt to found government on consent (sects. 77, 98). Instead, he should have tackled the far more important question of 'what really needs to be enacted by the state in order to secure the condition under which a good life is possible' (sect. 69). Green calls the general will 'that impalpable congeries of the hopes and fears of a people bound together by common interests and sympathy' (sect. 86), and believes it is to be found in their 'organised common life' (sect. 89). The general will lives in and throughout the whole range of the institutions, practices, judgements, aspirations, and ideals of a society—in the same moral and institutional framework (*Sittlichkeit*) that Hegel had emphasized. Thus the state and its laws, by which equal rights are guaranteed to the members of society, 'are an expression of, and are maintained by, a general will', and are regarded by the people as something they have an interest in supporting (sect. 93). Once again Green has provided a moral analysis, turning upon the common ideas of good in a society:

an interest in common good is the ground of political society, in the sense that without it no body of people would recognise any authority as having a claim on their common obedience. It is so far as a government represents to them a common good that the subjects are conscious that they ought to obey it, i.e. that obedience to it is a means to an end desirable in itself or absolutely. (sect. 98)

The state, then, is in principle or 'idea' a moral institution which by maintaining rights plays an important role in the activities through which individuals develop their moral character together. Accordingly I have a duty to submit to the power of the state, because it is morally necessary: it is what holds together 'that complex of institutions without which I literally should not have a life to *call my own*'. Through the state and its constituent institutions, I can count on the freedom of action I need to achieve my moral ends, and thereby *be* a moral person, which is a good common to me and to the other members of society (sects. 114–17). Correspondingly, Green emphasizes, conscious acceptance that the restraints of law are imposed for a good reason must always be an element in political obedience (though not always the sole element—fear of sanctions may enter too), if it is to be a 'political'—i.e. free—society at all (sect. 118). The crucial factor is that the citizens can and do recognize the legal system of rights and duties, and the particular laws, as morally justified. Green concedes that, historically, laws have often been made and states controlled by sectional interests which have not put the common good first; however, moral factors have also been at work, and they predominate (sects. 120–1, 124–31). Indeed, unless coercive power is exercised under law and for the maintenance of rights, there is not a state at all—so that 'we only count Russia a state by a sort of courtesy on the supposition that the power of the Czar, though subject to no constitutional control is so far exercised in accordance with a recognised tradition of what the public good requires as to be on the whole a sustainer of rights' (sect. 132).

Contrary to the social-contract theorists (and in line with Kant) Green does not think consent is necessary for the existence of a true state, fulfilling its primary function of maintaining law equally in the interest of all. Rather, the law must

represent an idea of common good, which each member of the society can make his own so far as he is rational, or capable of the conception of common good, however much particular passions may lead him to ignore it and thus necessitate the use of force to prevent him from doing that which, so far as influenced by the conception of common good, he would willingly abstain from. (sect. 118; see also sect. 62)

Whether or not a given state will be true to the idea of common good without 'popular control', and whether that requires 'active participation of the people in legislative functions' (as Rousseau thought) or simply a representative system (as Hegel thought), is 'a question of circumstances which perhaps does not admit of unqualified answer' (sect. 119). However, Green is confident that, if its citizen is to be not just a 'loyal subject', but an 'intelligent patriot' who 'so appreciates the good which in common with others he derives from the state . . . as to have a passion for serving it', then 'he must take part in the work of the state'. 'He must have a share, direct or indirect, by himself acting as a member or by voting for the members of supreme or provincial assemblies, in making and maintaining the laws which he obeys' (sect. 122). This kind of moral patriotism will be most active in nation-states (sect. 123; see also sects. 170–3, 182).

Law expresses the general will; and every state, by definition, by enforcing the law fulfils a moral role to a greater or lesser extent. Consequently the state and its laws merit the citizen's obedience. But what of laws which conflict with the general will, tending to thwart those powers of free action and self-development which law should sustain and extend (sect. 94)? Green is explicit and adamant that the individual must judge for himself whether a law is for the common good or not. That he does so 'is the measure of his intelligent, as distinguished from a merely instinctive, recognition of rights in others and in the state' (sect. 100). In other words, part of being an intelligent patriot, a morally good and active citizen, is conscious assessment of the moral adequacy of the laws one lives under.

However, whether and when the individual citizen is entitled to disobey a law which he decides is not for the common good is a separate question. Normally the answer is clear:

In a country like ours, with a popular government and settled methods of enacting and repealing laws, the answer of common sense is simple and sufficient. He should do all he can by legal methods to get the command cancelled, but till it is cancelled he should conform to it. The common good must suffer more from resistance to a law . . . than from the individual's conformity to a particular law . . . that is bad, until its repeal can be obtained. (sect. 100)

Green recognizes there can be hard cases—for instance, if the authority of the law is disputed, as in a civil war, or if there are no legal means for obtaining the repeal of the law. His detailed discussions take full account of the complexities of the kind of difficult situation which can arise. He refuses to lay down any precise rules of conduct beyond the injunction to look to 'the moral good of mankind, to which a necessary means is the organisation of the state' (sect. 106). But he refuses to say that it is never right to resist the law. Under certain conditions, there might be a moral duty to resist it (sects. 107–9). He examines one contemporary example carefully: was a citizen of the United States before the Civil War whose state prohibited him by law from teaching slaves to read or from harbouring runaway slaves justified in breaking that law and instructing and assisting slaves? As a general rule, Green concludes, even bad laws should be obeyed pending repeal, but not in this case. The decisive factors are that the public conscience had come to acknowledge slaves' capacities for rights, alteration of the law was being resisted by a powerful class in its own selfish interest, the law-breaker acted on behalf of the slave and not in his own interest, and there was no danger to the law-abiding habits of the people (sect. 144; see also sects. 143–6). However, even in this example, in other circumstances the duty to obey the law might be paramount: if, for instance, disobedience would lead to the destruction of the state, because that 'would mean a general loss of freedom . . . that would outweigh the evil of any slavery under such limitations and regulations as an organised state imposes on it' (sect. 147).

The primary duty of the citizen, then, is to examine his state's laws and to ensure that his state is true to the idea of the state. When it is not, his duty is to reform it. Green can give him little practical guidance in this complicated task. Green views it as his role as a philosopher to highlight the moral principles the citizen should follow; their actual application is a matter of political action not philosophical reflection and must be in the hands of the citizen. This seems a reasonable position for Green to take. It is none the less sometimes criticized, on the ground that Green's moral principles give no guidance at all. I shall return to this.

Particular Rights and State Action

Up to this point, Green has considered the most general principles of politics, discussing what a right is and how the state maintains rights, but not considering which rights in particular we have or which actions states should take. Next he turns to the details of the function of the state, examining which rights it maintains or should maintain, and enquiring whether it has any 'further office . . . in the moralization of man' (sect. 136).

Green begins with the right to life and liberty, or to 'free life' (sect. 151). This right is 'the condition of [one's] exercising any other rights—indeed, of all manifestation of personality' (sect. 150). It is founded on the 'capacity on the part of the subject for membership of a society—for determination of the will . . . by the conception of well-being as common to self with others'. In principle this right belongs to every human being and should be accorded to him or her by every other human being, 'but actually, or as recognised, it only gradually becomes a right of a man, as man, and against all men' (sect. 151; see also *Prolegomena*, sects. 205–17, 286, 370). Logically it implies the conception of humanity as a single society, with a common good. In practice, it is effected to a limited extent. We act on the universal right to free life in a negative way, condemning slavery and treating life as sacred. But we do not act positively. We do not apply it to our international dealings at all, where we accept killing in war; and Green has a long discussion of the immorality of war and the duty of a true state to avoid it, stressing that war is not inevitable (sects. 157–75). Again, in our own society we do very little positive to secure the right to free life. We enact 'that no man shall be used by other men as a means against his will, but we leave it to be pretty much a matter of chance whether or no he shall be qualified to fulfil any social function' or be able to use himself for any social end at all (sect. 155; also *Prolegomena*, sect. 245). Green aims to spell out the full implications of the idea which society partially recognizes, so that the state will begin to make the potential or implicit right fully actual for everyone.

In the case of the state's maintenance of rights in its own society, Green looks closely at punishment. On what principle does the individual forfeit the right to free life, and is it ever forfeited absolutely so that capital punishment is justified (sects. 156, 176–206)? He gives the Hegelian answer, that punishment is justified as a necessary part of the process of securing the rights which it is the principal task of the state to maintain (including the suspended rights of the criminal). Punishment is for the moral good of the community and of the criminal. The kind and amount of penalty will depend on the importance of the right; the extent of the threat to it; and the degree of terror necessary as a deterrent, subject to the limits set by the moral purpose of punishment and the goal of reforming the criminal. Green allows that under certain exceptional conditions capital punishment or perpetual imprisonment are justified, but not in a state which is doing its job properly (sect. 205).

In the course of his discussion of punishment, a very important principle emerges:

The justice of the punishment depends on the justice of the general system of rights—not merely on the propriety with reference to social well-being of maintaining this or that particular right which the crime punished violates, but on the question whether the social organisation in which a criminal has lived and acted is one that has given him a fair chance of not being a criminal. (sect. 189)

This criterion of being 'given a fair chance' of abiding by the law widens the issue, since it is clear that law-abidingness can be weakened by poverty and other deprivation. If part of the state's function in maintaining the conditions of free life is to ensure that every member of society has a fair chance not to act criminally, Green is assigning the state a large role.

It leads him to consider what positive steps the state can take to promote morality (sects. 207–10). Each member of the community has a claim on it 'to be enabled positively to realise that capacity for freely contributing to social good which is the foundation of his right to free life' (sect. 207). The question is the extent of that claim, and how the state should meet it. Green's general principles have already established that there are limits to what the state can do. It cannot force the individual to do what he ought to do spontaneously for a common good. Hence state action seems 'confined to the removal of obstacles' (sect. 209). However, there is much more that the state might do than it does—for example, in the field of education. Again, the state ought to restrict freedom of contract in order to protect the health and housing of the people (sect. 210).

Next Green tackles the controversial topic of property, which is obviously closely connected. For Green the opportunity to acquire and bequeath property is essential to the development of one's moral capacity, since it is required for the independence and self-expression which are part of the free life. What grounds the right to the free life also grounds 'the right to the instruments of such life' (sect. 216). So it is a critical question whether it is possible under a capitalist economy for all members of society effectively to exercise their right to acquire property? Green admits the inadequacies of the property rights which have actually grown up in modern Europe, where 'the free play given to powers of appropriation' has meant that many people, a proletariat, are virtually denied the moral benefits of property altogether (sect. 220). The law is not what it should be, but secures possession to some at the expense of others (sect. 221). Yet he argues that this is not inevitable, and certainly not the fault of capitalism (sects. 226–30). If certain laws, particularly regarding the ownership of land, were changed (laws which have no basis in common good but favour selfish interests), the means to the free life would be available to all. There would still be inequality, and rightly so (sect. 223); but that would be morally acceptable when everyone could acquire for themselves 'such ownership as is needed to moralise a man' (sect. 222).

Finally Green examines the law concerning the family, and once again compares the moral ideal of how the family should provide all its members with opportunities for moral action with the actual position under English law in his day. He concentrates on explaining how the family is a moral institution, and marriage a moral education. To achieve its purposes, marriage must be monogamous, and men and women must be equal under the law: this requires revision of the English divorce laws.

In the context of the popular politics and political thought of the time, Green's position on the scope of state action is strikingly positive. The popular rallying cry against social and economic legislation to limit the powers of employers or land-owners in the interest of protecting workers and tenants, for instance, was that such laws interfered with the liberty of the individual 'to do as he likes'. This reaction was defended the-oretically by writers such as Herbert Spencer; even J. S. Mill, while he supported certain reforms, had laid down that the general rule should be *laissez-faire* and that the individual's liberty should be restricted only to prevent him harming others. Green, however, espoused the 'Constructive Liberalism' which favoured a greater role for the state. The state's province is not limited to securing the individual from violent interference by other individuals. Green asserts that the state has, beyond that bare protection of the individual and his property against force and fraud, a moral end to serve. To achieve it, the state must make positive reforms to promote conditions favourable to moral life, even though this 'brings with it more and more interference with the liberty [*not* the right] of the individual *to do as he likes*' (sect. 18). This is the direction in which civil-ization is advancing.

Conclusion

Green's *Lectures* are an unusually sustained and single-minded effort to examine politics as a moral phenomenon. His prin-ciples are sometimes condemned as unrealistic, and as provid-ing none of the guidance in practical politics he thought they did. It is charged that he directs the citizen to seek the com-mon good of the members of the society, but he never suf-ficiently explains what that is. Moreover, the typical experience in politics is that people have different and conflicting interests and that they compete for goods. So how can his principles pos-sibly tell the citizen what to do? At one level, Green accepts this. He admits he can lay down no precise rules of action on such matters as when the law should be resisted, or how much to punish a specific offence, or exactly which restrictions to impose on freedom of contract. All such questions must be considered pragmatically, case by case and in the light of the particular circumstances.

However, Green would deny that his principles are empty or useless for political practice. He does not make large or controversial substantive moral claims. He starts simply from the idea that all human beings are capable of being moral agents and developing their character, and on this grounds the principle, which he thinks is generally accepted in the modern world, that they should all be enabled to become moral agents. Thus what is good for one is good for all; and this common good can be achieved by all, since it is non-competitive and non-exclusive—indeed, since the goods of all individuals are interdependent, it can be achieved by any only if it is achieved by all (sect. 216; for details, *Prolegomena*, sects. 206–17, 240–7, 286–8, 370). Only then are people truly free. This may seem very general and vague; but, as Green's examination of the law and political institutions of his day has shown, it can have radical implications. It means that no claim to a right is justified unless account is taken of all others' good too, unless all have a fair chance of perfecting their character, and unless none gains at the expense of others. If the right is justified for one person by the moral end the state upholds, the perfection of character, then it is justified for every member of the society and, ultimately, for every human being.

Green's moral principles of politics still have a sharp cutting edge. For example, although they do not prescribe the precise form, institutions, and extent of the welfare state, they do tell us that the state must make some provision for all the members of society to have access to the material basis of the free life, and in such a way that they remain independent and responsible for their lives so that their moral capacity is strengthened not weakened. Again, Green's principles do not lay down whether a state should belong to the European Union, or whether that should have a single currency or a stronger parliament; but they do tell us that membership of the Union is morally worthwhile only if it increases the moral opportunities of all the citizens of all the member states and ultimately of all mankind. Because Green works with fundamental moral principles making universal claims, and because he is conscious of the way forms of social life and human ideals constantly change historically, it is possible to transfer his principles to the problems which have developed since his time (to 'globalization', or to multicultural societies, for instance).

It is for the citizen to do the hard work of actually applying the principles. That is why Green's first objective is to encourage the emergence and activity of trained and devoted citizens. On them, and their critical review of how far their state is performing its moral function, depends the advance of their society and, ultimately, of humanity. They—that is, we—are charged with the duty of checking that for the 'less favoured members of society' it does not happen that 'the good things to which the pursuits of society are in fact directed turn out to be no good things for them' (*Prolegomena*, sect. 245).

Bibliographical Note

The best edition of Green's principal work of political philosophy, the *Lectures on the Principles of Political Obligation*, is in P. Harris and J. Morrow (eds.), *T. H. Green: Lectures on the Principles of Political Obligation and Other Writings* (Cambridge, 1986). References in the text have been given to the section numbers, not the pages, so any edition may be used. Some of Green's political ideas are developed with reference to contemporary politics in his important 1881 lecture, 'Liberal Legislation and Freedom of Contract', also in Harris and Morrow. The main source for Green's moral philosophy, which is closely linked with his political philosophy and indispensable for a full understanding of it, is the posthumous *Prolegomena to Ethics*, ed. A. C. Bradley (Oxford, 1883); extracts appear in Harris and Morrow (including most of the sections, or selections from them, which I cite). Also very informative is a lecture of 1879 'On the Different Senses of "Freedom" as Applied to Will and to the Moral Progress of Man', again in Harris and Morrow.

The main incidents of Green's life are related, and the whole range of his thinking is expounded, by his close friend and colleague R. L. Nettleship, in a long 'Memoir' prefixed to the third volume of his edition of the *Works of Thomas Hill Green* (London, 1888; printed separately, 1906). A more recent biography, including a major reassessment of Green's thought and an attempt to explain the great contemporary impact of his ideas, is M. Richter, *The Politics of Conscience: T. H. Green and his Age* (London, 1964); he summarizes the main lines of his interpretation in 'T. H. Green and his Audience: Liberalism as a Surrogate Faith', *Review of Politics*, 18 (1956), 444–72.

There are sympathetic accounts of Green's political ideas by those who knew him and were deeply influenced by him in D. G. Ritchie, *The Principles of State Interference* (London, 1891), ch. 4; B. Bosanquet,

The Philosophical Theory of the State (London, 1899), *passim*; and J. H. Muirhead, *The Service of the State: Four Lectures on the Political Teaching of T. H. Green* (London, 1908).

For good general discussions of Green's political philosophy, see: A. J. M. Milne, *The Social Philosophy of English Idealism* (London, 1962); A. C. Cacoullos, *Thomas Hill Green: Philosopher of Rights* (New York, 1974); I. M. Greengarten, *Thomas Hill Green and the Development of Liberal-Democratic Thought* (Toronto, 1981); A. Vincent and R. Plant, *Philosophy, Politics and Citizenship: The Life and Thought of the British Idealists* (Oxford, 1984); and A. Vincent (ed.), *The Philosophy of T. H. Green* (Aldershot, 1986). The fullest examination of Green's moral philosophy is G. Thomas, *The Moral Philosophy of T. H. Green* (Oxford, 1987).

On particular aspects of Green's political philosophy, see: P. Hansen, 'T. H. Green and the Moralization of the Market', *Canadian Journal of Political and Social Theory*, 1 (1977), 91–117; J. Morrow, 'Property and Personal Development: An Interpretation of T. H. Green's Political Philosophy', *Politics*, 18 (1981), 84–92; J. Roberts, 'T. H. Green', in Z. A. Pelczynski and J. Gray (eds.), *Conceptions of Liberty in Political Philosophy* (London, 1984), 243–62; P. Harris, 'Moral Progress & Politics: The Theory of T. H. Green', *Polity*, 21 (1988/9), 538–62; R. Bellamy, 'T. H. Green and the Morality of Victorian Liberalism', in Bellamy (ed.), *Victorian Liberalism* (London, 1990), 131–51; A. Simhony, 'T. H. Green's Theory of the Morally Justified Society', *History of Political Thought*, 10 (1989), 481–98; A. Simhony, 'On Forcing Individuals to be Free: T. H. Green's Liberal Theory of Positive Freedom', *Political Studies*, 39 (1991), 303–20; O. Anderson, 'The Feminism of T. H. Green: A Late-Victorian Success Story?', *History of Political Thought*, 12 (1991), 671–93; R. Bellamy, 'T. H. Green, J. S. Mill, and Isaiah Berlin on the Nature of Liberty and Liberalism', in H. Gross and R. Harrison (eds.), *Jurisprudence: Cambridge Essays* (Oxford, 1992), 257–85; J. Horton, *Political Obligation* (London, 1992), 70–8; and A. Simhony, 'T. H. Green: The Common Good Society', *History of Political Thought*, 14 (1993), 225–47.

In *The Political Philosophy of the British Idealists: Selected Studies* (Cambridge, 1990), I have examined the main charges brought against Green, and set out to defend him, especially his views on the common good, rights, property, freedom, and state action. Its bibliography contains many further references.

2

Georges Sorel: *Reflections on Violence*

JEREMY JENNINGS

WRITING in *Literature and Western Man*[1] the critic and novelist
J. B. Priestley argued that, if one could understand why a
retired and respectable former civil servant had written a book
like *Reflections on Violence*, then the modern age would not
remain a complete mystery. Born in 1847 into the provincial
bourgeoisie, Georges Sorel spent his earliest years in Cherbourg,
before being sent to Paris to complete his education at the
École polytechnique, France's premier scientific academy. Photo-
graphs taken at the time show a young man proudly sporting
the military uniform worn by students of this prestigious institution. Upon graduation Sorel began a career as a government engineer, loyally serving the newly established Third
Republic as he travelled throughout France before coming to
rest in Perpignan close to the Pyrenees. Here he remained
quietly until his retirement in the early 1890s, whereupon the
Republic awarded him the red ribbon of the Legion of Honour, a decoration he wore upon his lapel until the last days of
his life in 1922. Yet for all this sober personal existence the
principal theme of *Reflections on Violence* was the radical transformation through the use of violence of what Sorel saw as a
decadent bourgeois society resting upon a decaying capitalism.
How can this be explained and what is it that has made *Reflections on Violence* one of the most widely read and controversial books of our century?

Background

Sorel had begun to publish his first articles in the mid-1880s
and even prior to his retirement he had published two books,
one a study of the Bible, the other an unconventional analysis

[1] J. B. Priestley, *Literature and Western Man* (London, 1972), 301–4.

of the trial of Socrates. It was, however, after his return to Paris that he began directly to write about politics. With remarkable speed he established himself as an expert on Marx, then hardly known in France. Quickly distancing himself from the orthodox 'scientific' Marxism associated with Engels, he came to see socialism principally as an ethical doctrine, with Marxism cast in the role of 'social poetry'.

In the first instance this meant agreement with the revisionism then advocated by Édouard Bernstein in Germany and an endorsement of social democracy.[2] Significantly this encouraged Sorel to support the movement seeking to secure the release of Captain Alfred Dreyfus, a Jewish army officer falsely imprisoned for high treason. Arguably the most famous legal case in history, the Dreyfus Affair turned into a monumental clash between the forces of reactionary nationalism and those of progressive republicanism, with the continued existence of parliamentary democracy itself in the balance. It is these events that form the political backdrop to *Reflections on Violence* and from which are drawn the innumerable minor (and mostly forgotten) figures that litter the text.

In short, the victory of the Dreyfusards and their speedy incorporation into the conventional structures of political power met with Sorel's profound disapproval. Where then was he to turn for inspiration? The answer came in the form of the revolutionary syndicalist movement then entering a period of intense militancy. Here appeared to be an alternative that was genuinely committed to working-class self-emancipation and which had no time for either the intrusions of bourgeois intellectuals or the parliamentary route to reform. It was, moreover, the prior existence of the syndicalist movement that allowed Sorel to state in *Reflections on Violence* that he had 'invented nothing at all', only described what was already there, and hence to refute the charge that he himself was playing the role of the intellectual in politics.

The Origins of the Text

The earliest version of *Reflections on Violence* appeared as a series of articles during the first half of 1906. These were

[2] On this see especially the recently published letters of Sorel to Bernstein written between 1898 and 1902 in *Mil neuf cent: Revue d'histoire intellectuelle*, 11 (1993), 141–97.

published in *Le Mouvement socialiste*, a review edited by Hubert Lagardelle and in which the so-called 'new school' of socialism associated with Sorel's admirers occupied pride of place. It was, however, the former Dreyfusard Daniel Halévy who, in May 1907, convinced Sorel that *Reflections on Violence* should be republished in book form. The outcome was not merely its publication by *Pages libres* in 1908 but the addition of a thirty-page introduction in the form of a 'Letter to Daniel Halévy'. Four subsequent editions appeared before Sorel's death, with the result that three appendices were added (the most significant of which is 'In Defense of Lenin' written in 1919).[3]

Quickly established as Sorel's 'standard work',[4] *Reflections on Violence* displays all the stylistic features associated with his writing. Sorel could never leave a completed text alone. His voracious intellectual appetite and curiosity meant that new reading and ideas always had to be incorporated into the new edition, with the consequence that the reader is often perplexed by the apparent disorder of the argument. Sorel felt no embarrassment at this. 'I am', he wrote in his introduction to the text, 'a self-taught man exhibiting to other people the notebooks which have served for my instruction. That is why the rules of the art of writing have never interested me very much' (p. 27).[5] Into those notebooks, he claimed, went only those things he had not met elsewhere, all idle commonplaces and points of transition being left to one side. Indeed, nothing appalled Sorel more than the idea of producing a perfectly symmetrical and coherent body of knowledge. 'Philosophy', Sorel went on, 'is after all perhaps only the recognition of the abysses which lie on each side of the footpath that the vulgar follow with the serenity of somnambulists' (p. 30). The aim, therefore, was 'to stir up' the world. As we shall see, there is plenty of evidence to suggest that *Reflections on Violence* was well suited to the task.

[3] The most complete edition of *Réflexions sur la violence* was published by Éditions du Seuil in 1990. Extracts of Sorel's letters to Halévy are published at the end of the text, pp. 309–16. A new English edition is soon to appear from Cambridge University Press.

[4] This was Sorel's own description: see 'Lettere di Georges Sorel a B. Croce', *La critica*, 28 (1930), 194.

[5] G. Sorel, *Reflections on Violence* (New York, 1972). References in the text are to this edition, although on some occasions where necessary I have made minor alterations to the translation.

The 'Letter to Daniel Halévy'

The explicit purpose of this long introductory essay is to clarify some of the central ideas of *Reflections on Violence* for what Sorel perceived to be a 'wider public' beyond the original specialist readership of *Le Mouvement socialiste*. Typically Sorel introduces several new features into his argument. One is an unlikely reference to the ideas of Cardinal John Henry Newman, one of the most controversial Catholic converts of the nineteenth century, and his text *Grammar of Assent*, newly translated into French. This work, Sorel believed, did much to explain the nature of religious faith. Secondly, Sorel made use of a key image given to him by Halévy. 'The Wandering Jew', he writes, 'may be taken as the symbol of the highest aspirations of mankind, condemned as it is to march for ever without knowing rest' (p. 37). The idea here is that true moral grandeur is only attained when action is undertaken with no thought for its utilitarian or prudential consequences. This is the starting-point of *Reflections on Violence*.

Sorel begins by establishing a dichotomy between optimism and pessimism in politics, his clear preference being for the latter. Optimism, he argues, always underestimates the difficulties in securing fundamental change, with the result that the optimist is not only naïve but dangerous. 'During the Terror,' he comments, 'the men who spilt most blood were precisely those who had the greatest desire to let their equals enjoy the golden age they had dreamt of' (p. 32). The pessimist, by contrast, considers social transformation as a *march towards deliverance* (a phrase Sorel takes from the seventeenth-century religious philosopher Blaise Pascal) that is narrowly conditioned both by the immense obstacles that we face and 'by a profound conviction of our natural weakness'. The former are such that they 'cannot disappear except in a catastrophe which involves the whole', whilst our natural weakness is sufficient to ensure that we will only engage in the heroic acts that are required if we are convinced that we will secure our complete salvation and if we have the 'help of a whole band of companions'. Sorel's prime (and frequently repeated) example of such 'a fully developed and completely armed pessimism' is that of the early Christian communities, but the implication is that the French working class requires such a mentality if it is to fulfil its historic mission. Sorel's next controversial point is to argue that it does not in fact matter whether salvation is ever attained: the result will in any case be 'considerable moral progress'. It is the journey and not the arrival that matters.

This leads Sorel to consider how individuals conceive of the struggle in which they are to participate. We see the 'coming action', he argues, as a 'battle' in which our 'cause is certain to triumph'. And in this, he asserts crucially, we are sustained by a form of knowledge that takes the form of myth. Here is one of Sorel's most controversial ideas.

'People who are living in the world of "myths"', Sorel writes, 'are secure from all refutation' (p. 52). In the main body of the text it is the proletarian general strike that figures as the most important example of myth, but at this stage Sorel restricts himself to making several general points. First, myths should not be confused with utopias. A utopia is an 'intellectual product' whilst a myth is 'identical to the convictions of a group'. This explains not only why a myth cannot be broken down into its constituent parts but also how it is able to inspire action. No failure proves anything against it. Secondly, myths exist as part of what is described as 'the profounder region of our mental life'. The reference here is to the philosophy of Henri Bergson, then the most celebrated philosopher of the day. There is no need to explore the full complexity of Bergson's ideas, but it is important to realize that both he and Sorel shared a hostility towards the prevailing scientism inherited from the nineteenth century. What Bergson tried to do in such books as *Time and Free Will* was to explore the possibilities of moving towards a more 'integral' knowledge of reality and being than that obtained by conventional linguistic categories and analysis. This new form of comprehension he identified as 'intuition', the internal and empathetic understanding of phenomena, both human and natural, as movement and duration. Drawn from the 'inner depths of the mind', myths, in Sorel's opinion, provided precisely this form of intuitive understanding, so much so that in the contemporary working class they were 'capable of evoking as an undivided whole the mass of sentiments which corresponds to the different manifestations of the war undertaken by socialism against modern society'. Thirdly, Sorel's recognition of the importance of myths allowed him to reject what he dubbed the 'intellectualist philosophy' and which he associated most of all with the great nineteenth-century critic and philologist Ernest Renan.[6] A sceptic like Renan, Sorel argues, could not understand what motivated human beings to perform heroic and unselfish acts. In Sorel's view we did so in those few moments when, inspired by myth, we were 'creating an imaginary world ahead of the present world'. This, too, Sorel equated with acting freely. As he concluded: 'as long as there are no myths accepted by the masses, one may go on talking of revolts indefinitely, without ever provoking any revolutionary movement' (p. 149).

All of this figures by way of introduction to the main body of the text. In effect, Sorel is laying bare the methodological and philosophical assumptions that underpin his argument. Sorel is, however, being slightly disingenuous when he implies overmodestly that the aim of his enquiry is limited to 'attacking middle-class thought in such a way as to put the proletariat on its guard against an invasion of ideas and customs from the hostile class' (p. 53). What this conceals is the underlying subject of the book, which Sorel himself defined as 'the historical genesis of morality'. This, he readily acknowledged, was the 'great preoccupation of my entire life'.[7]

Class War and Violence

Sorel did not create the syndicalist movement in France. Nor was he behind the wave of violent strike activity that rocked French society in the first decade of the twentieth century. But their existence did mean, according to him, that any serious discussion of socialism 'must first of all investigate the functions of violence in actual social conditions' (p. 57). He also knew that the conventional wisdom dispensed by 'middle-class philosophers' was that violence was a relic of barbarism that was bound to disappear under the impact of enlightenment. In this, Sorel believed, they were profoundly mistaken. What he therefore seeks to show in the first chapter is that 'the

---

[6] For Sorel's most extensive treatment of Renan, see *Le Système historique de Renan* (Paris, 1906).

[7] 'Lettere di Georges Sorel a B. Croce', *La critica*, 26 (1928), 100.

revolutionary and direct method' is not on the point of disappearing. Where formerly workers thought of military battles,
they now thought of strikes, each one a 'vanguard fight' preparing the way for 'the general strike in which the capitalist
regime will be annihilated' (p. 78). What makes this stance
controversial (and so shocking for many) only becomes fully
evident with Sorel's conclusion to the second chapter. 'Proletarian violence', he writes, 'carried on as a pure and simple
manifestation of the sentiment of class war, appears thus a very
fine and very heroic thing; it is at the service of the immemo-
rial interests of civilization. It is not perhaps the most appropriate method of obtaining immediate material advantages but
it may save the world from barbarism' (p. 98).

How could violence *save* the world from barbarism?[8] To
answer this Sorel had to decide what Marxism was. His answer
was that it was essentially 'Manchesterianism' (i.e. classical liberal economics) plus an emphasis upon the self-development of
the proletariat. This implied (1) that the workers were held to
possess a purely financial and non-social relationship with their
bosses, (2) that the state had only limited powers to direct the
economy, and (3) that, left to its own devices, the capitalist
economy would surmount all obstacles placed before it. The
sting in Marxism's tale was that it assumed that the proletariat
would eventually take over the wealth created by capitalism,
but apart from this the only thing it added to 'Manchesterianism'
was a stress upon the moral, technical, and intellectual formation of the workers.

So how did this help to answer Sorel's question? Sorel now
realized that capitalism was no longer being allowed to run as
either classical liberalism or Marxism dictated. The state was
coming to exercise a control over the economy and this in
turn was being justified by reference to new doctrines pro-
claiming the virtues of 'social peace' and 'solidarity'. There
were no class interests, only social duties shared by all. Worse

---

[8] For the background to this reassessment of Marxism by Sorel, see *Social Foundations of Contemporary Economics*. This was first published in Italian as *Insegnamenti
sociali dell'economia contemporanea* (Palermo, 1907) but is now available in an edition
edited and translated by John L. Stanley and published by Transaction Books (New
Brunswick, NJ, 1984). The text has never been available in French. For a commentary on the evolution of this text, see Jeremy Jennings's review article in *Cahiers
Georges Sorel*, 4 (1986), 166–70.

still, the result of this would be 'the simultaneous ruin of the capitalist and revolutionary spirits'. The warrior-like captains of industry that had formerly driven the industrial system forward were being replaced by a 'timorous humanitarian middle class' whilst the 'civilized socialism of our professors' was leading to an 'intermingling' of employers and producers in what Sorel describes contemptuously as 'the democratic bog'.

Consequently, the capitalist economy was not developing in a manner appropriate to the needs of the future socialist society but had rather entered a period of 'economic decadence'. And here, Sorel believed, we had a clear historical precedent to demonstrate what occurred when social transformations took place at a time of economic decadence. The victory of Christianity over the Roman Empire, he argued, showed that 'at least four centuries of barbarism had to be gone through before a progressive movement showed itself: society was compelled to descend to a state not far removed from its origins' (p. 97).

To avoid such a descent into barbarism it was indispensable that socialism distance itself from the processes of democracy and abandon the doctrines of social peace in favour of those of class war. 'To repay', Sorel proclaimed, 'with black ingratitude the benevolence of those who would protect the workers, to meet with insults the homilies of the defenders of human fraternity, and to reply by blows to the advances of the propagators of social peace—all that is assuredly not in conformity with the rules of fashionable socialism—but it is a very practical way of indicating to the middle classes that they must mind their own business and only that' (p. 91). The representatives of democracy and of government, Sorel goes on, should be under no illusions about the character of acts of violence. They were meant to be 'the clear and brutal expression of class war'. Proletarian violence would thus serve to confine capitalists to their role as producers and would restore the separation of classes, thereby making possible the development both of capitalism and of the working class. 'If', Sorel writes, 'a united and revolutionary proletariat confronts a rich middle class, eager for conquest, capitalist society will have reached its historical perfection' (p. 92). It was in this way that the revolutionaries would save civilization.

In Sorel's next chapter, 'Prejudices against Violence', he

gives his argument a further paradoxical twist. It is assumed, he remarks, that, because today's syndicalists call themselves revolutionaries, their actions will reproduce the bloodthirsty events of the Revolution of 1789: 'instinctively, people start thinking of the committees of revolutionary inspection, of the brutalities of suspicious agents . . . of the tragedies of the guillotine' (p. 103). Yet, Sorel contends, the imagined parallel is mistaken and this because the violence of the French Revolution, and specifically that of Robespierre's Committee of Public Safety in 1793, was the work of the middle classes. Moreover, the latter's 'ferocity' derived from the fact that they had remained imbued with the 'detestable practices' of the pre-revolutionary *ancien régime*. Under the monarchy, Sorel argued, the legal system's 'essential aim was not justice but the welfare of the State'. It was this that justified the destruction of any obstacle that stood in the monarch's way and it was the same mentality that during the Revolution had given rise to 'police operations, proscriptions, and the sittings of servile courts of law' (p. 103).

To conclude this chapter Sorel turns this argument against the critics of syndicalism. It would, he remarks, 'be strange if the old ideas were quite dead'. Indeed, the Dreyfus case demonstrated that there were still a large number of people who were prepared to interpret justice in terms of *reasons of state*. And these, Sorel makes plain, were to be found in the Dreyfusard camp, as their enthusiasm for 'political persecution' after their victory showed. Specifically Sorel argues that this criticism extends to the parliamentary socialists. They, he writes, 'preserve the old cult of the State: they are therefore prepared to commit all the misdeeds of the old regime and of the Revolution' (p. 113). This allows Sorel to reach the novel conclusion that, if ever the parliamentary socialists succeeded in gaining power, 'political courts will be at work on a large scale'. They would show themselves to be the 'worthy successors' of the Inquisition and of Robespierre! 'We might again see', Sorel comments, 'the State triumphing by the hand of the executioner.'[9]

---

[9] For a broader consideration of Sorel's views on the French Revolution, see Jeremy Jennings, 'Syndicalism and the French Revolution', *Journal of Contemporary History*, 26 (1991), 71–96.

It was, therefore, the parliamentary or *civilized* socialists who would be the most likely to resort to 'the abominations which sullied middle-class revolutions'. Proletarian acts of violence were of an entirely different character: they were 'purely and simply acts of war', carried out without hatred and without the desire for revenge. It is hard to know exactly what Sorel means by this—it is only later in the text that he explores more fully what he takes to be 'the ethics of violence'—but crucial to the argument that proletarian violence can be differentiated from middle-class violence is the claim that the syndicalists do not wish to preserve or reform the state but to destroy it. The clearest evidence of this, Sorel argues, lies in their endorsement of anti-patriotism, a doctrine which entailed irreconcilable opposition to 'the clearest and most tangible of all possible manifestations of the State', the army.[10] Upon this basis Sorel is able to conclude that syndicalist violence would not imitate the 'acts of savagery' typical of the French Revolution, parliamentary socialism, and, more generally, the bourgeoisie. But what form would these syndicalist acts of violence take?

The General Strike

Sorel's disillusionment with social democracy in the wake of the Dreyfus Affair coincided with the emergence of a French labour movement committed to the tactics and the goals of revolutionary syndicalism. Taking its name from the word *syndicat* or trade union, syndicalism saw itself as both an instrument of working-class resistance and the vehicle of revolutionary change. This was deemed to be the case for the simple reason that the *syndicat*, as opposed to the political party, was said to embody the permanent and real (i.e. economic) interests of its members, who, by definition, had to be drawn from the world of labour. Moreover, the future society was itself to be rebuilt around the trade union as the nucleus of production, consumption as well as social life. These ideas figured as part of a wider rejection of politics which placed little faith in the benefits of universal suffrage. The preferred strategy, therefore,

---

[10] On anti-patriotism, see Jeremy Jennings, *Syndicalism in France* (London, 1990), 39–41.

was *direct action*. This took a variety of forms (including an advocacy of sabotage that never met with Sorel's approval) but concentrated upon strikes both as the best means of hitting the capitalist where it most hurt and as the means of preparing the working class for the final struggle to remove capitalism in the shape of the general strike. Whilst there was no undisputed conception amongst syndicalists about either its duration, the numbers to be involved, or its form, there was agreement that the general strike was to be seen not as a prelude to revolution but as the revolution itself.[11] It is in Sorel's next two chapters, 'The Proletarian Strike' and 'The Political General Strike', that he explores what he regards as the originality and merits of this strategy.

Again it is important to realize that intrinsic to Sorel's argument is the attempt to turn the tables upon his opponents. Having cast them as the harbingers of barbarism and the guillotine, he now seeks to show that it is they who are out of touch with both modern science and modern philosophy. The core of this position relates back to what Sorel has already told us about myth in his introductory 'Letter to Daniel Halévy', and it is here that myth is again central in the argument.

Sorel's assault is now directed at what he describes as 'the middle class conception of science'. This conception, he argues, sees science as 'a mill which produces solutions to all the problems we are faced with'. It was science, in this view, that could remedy the defects of society. Moreover, the prestige of science—and especially astronomy—had led the purveyors of this 'little science' to believe that the 'aim of all science was to forecast the future with accuracy'. This led them to believe that 'truth' was attained by 'clarity of exposition' and that everything that was 'mysterious' or 'obscure' had no place in scientific explanations or solutions. This was taken to be part of the wider 'progress of enlightenment' that, as Sorel had commented earlier, decreed that violence too was soon to disappear.

Yet, Sorel argues, the 'errors' of these 'sham scientists' were all too evident. In philosophy, metaphysics had lost none of its

---

[11] For a brief summary of the main features of the syndicalist movement, see Jeremy Jennings, 'Syndicalism', *Modern History Review*, 4 (1992), 8–12.

ground; religion was not about to wither away, despite the attempt to provide 'a perfectly rationalistic exposition of Christian theology'; no 'science of art' had been developed and it was still acknowledged that the best art flourished on 'mystery'. Ethics—especially with regard to sexual relationships—still remained impossible to codify, and much the same could be said of social life. In short, this 'useless pseudo-science' was fundamentally mistaken in believing that 'eventually everything will be explained rationally'.

For Sorel this conclusion had at least three important implications. First it indicated that the future could not be 'predicted scientifically'. Secondly, 'thorough psychological analysis' showed that in the 'genesis of action' we 'do nothing great without the help of warmly coloured and clearly defined images which absorb the whole of our attention' (p. 148). These images Sorel here equates with myths. Thirdly, and most importantly, the doctrine of socialism is 'necessarily very obscure', since it deals with what Sorel defines as 'the most mysterious part of human activity', the realm of production. Its meaning could, therefore, only be attained by 'intuition', and as such 'we obtain it as a whole, perceived instantaneously'. Reference to the 'real revolutionary movement', Sorel concludes, demonstrates that it is in the myth of the general strike that 'socialism is wholly comprised'. Strikes, he writes, 'have engendered in the proletariat the noblest, the deepest, and most moving sentiments that they possess; the general strike groups them all in a coordinated picture, and, bringing them together, gives to each of them its maximum of intensity; appealing to their painful memories of particular conflicts, it colours with an intense life all the details of the composition presented to consciousness' (p. 127). To accept the idea of the general strike, even if we know it is a myth, was therefore to 'proceed scientifically'.

There is another important dimension to Sorel's attempt to wrest the authority of science from his opponents. Writing in *The Decomposition of Marxism*,[12] a seventy-page pamphlet also published in 1908, Sorel argued that Marx 'had always

---

[12] The full text in English translation is printed as an appendix to I. L. Horowitz, *Radicalism and the Revolt against Reason* (London, 1961).

described revolution in mythical form'. Rather than being a weakness (as Marx's critics claimed), it was precisely this that constituted 'the definite value of his work'. Marx's 'catastrophic conception' of the end of capitalism was not intended to explain and predict the development and subsequent demise of capitalism but was rather meant to inspire the proletariat to action and to 'total revolution'. Following on from this Sorel argues in *Reflections on Violence* that it is his own 'new school' of socialism rather than Marxist orthodoxy that is closest to 'the spirit of Marx' and therefore that no better proof of 'Marx's genius' can be provided than the agreement that exists between his views and those of revolutionary syndicalism. 'Thus,' Sorel writes, 'the fundamental principles of Marxism are perfectly intelligible only with the aid of the picture of the general strike and, on the other hand, the full significance of the picture . . . is apparent only to those who are deeply versed in Marxist doctrine' (p. 131).

What then were the strengths of this picture? Marx speaks of a society divided into two mutually hostile classes, capitalists and proletarians. Strike activity served to preserve this separation through all levels of the 'economic–judicial structure' to 'the summit of perfection'. Secondly, it would be impossible to conceive of the disappearance of capitalism 'if we did not suppose an ardent sentiment of revolt' in the soul of the worker. The idea of the general strike served to keep this sentiment alive. Thirdly, the strategy of compromise and social reform pursued by middle-class politicians posed a very real threat to the maintenance of class war. The partisans of the general strike correctly showed that even the 'most popular reforms' had a middle-class character and therefore justly placed before us 'the other picture of complete catastrophe'. Fourthly, as Sorel puts it, 'Marx wishes us to understand that the whole preparation of the proletariat depends solely on the organization of a stubborn, increasing and passionate resistance to the present order of things' (p. 135). This is precisely what the myth of the general strike is designed to stimulate. Fifthly, both Marx and the advocates of the general strike recognized that the success of the revolution depended upon 'the constant and rapid progress of industry'. This emphasis upon technological continuity, implying that the working class would simply take up where the capitalists left off, also meant that there would be no room 'for the intellectuals who embraced the position of thinking for the proletariat'. Finally, Marx believed that the revolution 'would mark an absolute separation between two historical eras'. Syndicalism recognized therefore the need for 'serious, formidable and sublime work' on the part of the proletariat.

What should be clear from this is that Sorel pays scant attention to the organizational detail of the general strike and of the syndicalist movement. He does, however, give us one awesome summary of what it all means.

The proletariat [he writes] organizes itself for battle, separating itself distinctly from the other parts of the nation, and regarding itself as the great motive power of history, all other social considerations being subordinated to that of combat: it is very clearly conscious of the glory which will be attached to its historical role and of the heroism of its militant attitude; it longs for the final contest in which it will give proof of the whole measure of its valour. Pursuing no conquest, it has no need to make plans for utilizing its victories: it counts on expelling the capitalists from the productive domain, and on taking their place in the workshop created by capitalism. (p. 167)

Before we move on to consider the final part of *Reflections on Violence*, some mention should be made of what Sorel describes as the political general strike. This is used by Sorel as a form of comparison with the proletarian general strike and is intended to illustrate how a general strike should *not* be organized. In effect, this is a general strike led by politicians. Conceived thus, it entails no more than the transfer of power among politicians, uses the proletariat in the interests of the middle class, occurs in a time of economic decadence, and would be motivated not by the sentiment of revolt but by 'violent jealousy'. In brief, Sorel tells us, 'it shows us how the State would lose nothing of its strength, how the transmission of power from one privileged class to another would take place, and how the mass of producers would merely change masters' (p. 177). There is every chance, Sorel adds, that those new masters, the parliamentary socialists, would show themselves less able and more exploitative than their capitalist predecessors.

The Ethics of Violence

It is only now—towards the end of chapter five and into chapter six—that Sorel makes a more concerted effort to clarify just what he means by violence. Following on from his discussion of the two types of general strike, he now argues that the differences between them become more obvious when we consider the existence of two rival conceptions of war. War, he argues, can be considered from its 'noble side'. Seen in this light—by the poets of antiquity, for example—it embodies the idea that the carrying of arms is the supreme profession, the sense that 'the sentiment of glory' is 'one of the most singular and most powerful creations of human genius'. Conversely, the other 'aspect of war' is one deprived of nobility, in which 'the object is to allow politicians to satisfy their ambitions' and to secure material advantages. The proletarian general strike, Sorel tells us, draws upon the first conception of war.

More importantly Sorel makes a distinction between violence and force. The object of force is 'to impose a certain social order'; the object of violence is 'the destruction of that order'. Force sought to secure obedience to authority, violence sought to smash that authority. Force, in other words, was the work of the state; violence was the proletariat's act of revolt.

Sorel's next argument is more surprising. 'It may be conceded', he comments, 'to those in favour of mild methods that violence may hamper economic progress and even, when it goes beyond a certain point, that it is a danger to morality' (p. 182). Too much violence would therefore represent a threat to civilization. But there is, Sorel now argues, little danger of this from the proletariat. In the same way that there were few Christian martyrs but their martyrdom served to prove the absolute truth of the new religion, so too for syndicalism there would in reality be 'only a few short conflicts' yet these would be sufficient to evoke the idea of the general strike as being 'perfectly revolutionary'. It might be accomplished by 'means of incidents which would appear to middle-class historians as of small importance'. Described in this way, Sorel's violence does not look very violent at all and appears strictly limited to a few heroic gestures. The emphasis, as Sorel makes clear, falls on 'the minimum of brutality' (p. 188). Yet this minimal level of violence will nevertheless be able to secure an ethics of 'sublimity'. Sorel here paints a pretty dismal picture of the state of contemporary political morality. In the Third Republic everything had been done to reduce democracy to a competition between 'politico-criminal associations'. Confirming all that he had earlier said about the need to preserve the separation of classes, Sorel now argues therefore that what he describes as 'lofty moral convictions' never depend upon reasonableness but on 'the competition of communions, each of which regards itself as the army of truth fighting the armies of evil' (pp. 209–10). It is upon this 'battle-field' that it is 'possible to find sublimity'.

The Ethics of the Producers

Even if we accept Sorel's word that the number of acts of violence he envisages in the course of the proletariat's struggle will be limited, it would be natural to conclude that the motivating force for that struggle would be a product of a blind and irrational will. This is undoubtedly the impression left by a superficial reading of *Reflections on Violence* and one that has been fuelled by the false supposition that Sorel was deeply influenced by the Bergsonian notion of an *élan vital*. What this ignores is Sorel's own admission (cited earlier) that his real subject was 'the historical genesis of morality'. Violence for Sorel was quite definitely of value not for its own sake but for the morality it was capable of engendering. It is with this theme of ethical rejuvenation that Sorel completes his final chapter.

Sorel's question therefore is straightforward: 'upon what conditions is regeneration possible?' (p. 224). His answer (partly already revealed) is that regeneration is being brought about by a class working 'subterraneously' within society and which is 'separating itself' from the modern world. This class, the proletariat, is responsible for 'the birth of a virtue', a virtue capable of saving civilization. But what is still unclear is the precise nature of that virtue. What, as Sorel phrases it, will be 'the ethic of the producers of the future?'

It is here that Sorel makes his only extended reference to the ideas of Friedrich Nietzsche. Citing *The Genealogy of Morals* and *The Origins of Tragedy*, Sorel now praises 'Homer's Archean type, the indomitable hero', as a model for the future. But he also sees something of great value in the ascetic ideal pilloried by Nietzsche as part of the morality of the weak. 'True ethical values', Sorel argues, are to be found in the modern equivalent of Nietzsche's reviled 'sacerdotal castes': the family. 'Respect for the human person, sexual fidelity and devotion to the weak', Sorel writes, 'constitute the elements of morality of which all high-minded men are proud' (p. 233). Love too can produce the sublime. A third element of morality that Sorel wishes to emphasize is, he accepts, not touched upon by Nietzsche. In contemporary society, Sorel argues, 'we are on the level of an ethics adapted to consumers'. This is necessarily immoral as well as decadent and has to be replaced by its opposite, an ethic of producers. The transformation—'turning the men of today into the free producers of tomorrow working in factories where there are no masters' (p. 224)—will be attained through the educational action and beneficial influence of the *syndicats*. But for Sorel there is a deeper point to this argument. For Sorel not only are industrial work and economic progress the great intellectual and scientific challenges of our day—demanding supreme skill and dedication from the workers—but it is also man the maker, *homo faber* rather than *homo politicus* and *homo academicus*, that is the source of our moral values. It is, for example, in the factory that will be found an 'economic epic' to rival the Homeric virtues formerly found on the battlefield. There, too, art will achieve its finest form. Yet the 'entirely epic state of mind' required to make possible this dedication of free men to industrial production will only occur through sentiments aroused by the myth of the general strike.

This is where Sorel stops. What in his view had he achieved?

I have [Sorel writes] established that proletarian violence has an entirely different significance from that attributed to it by superficial scholars and by politicians. In the total ruin of institutions and of morals there remains something which is powerful, new and intact, and it is that which constitutes, properly speaking, the soul of the proletariat. Nor will this be swept away in the general decadence of our moral values, if the workers have enough energy to bar the road to the middle-class corrupters, answering their advances with the plainest brutality. (p. 249)

Conclusion

For a writer so imbued with pessimism it is not surprising to discover that, not long after the publication of *Reflections on Violence*, Sorel became disillusioned with the syndicalist movement, believing that it too had been corrupted. He did not, however, relinquish his faith in 'the value of this philosophy of violence', as he made plain in a note appended to the third edition in February 1912. In Lenin and the Bolshevik Revolution he saw a new incarnation of his beliefs, casting Russia as 'the Rome of the proletariat' at war with the 'New Carthages' of Europe's 'plutocratic democracies'. Later still he glimpsed beyond Europe the possibility of revolt against Western bourgeois civilization.[13] He went to his grave, no doubt, an unhappy man.

Yet *Reflections on Violence* remains a profoundly disturbing book. This most obviously derives from the fact that Sorel takes violence as his subject. More importantly, he is prepared to equate it with life, creativity, and virtue. In this he knew that he was challenging one of the fundamental beliefs of society. Moreover, this included challenging the notion of progress that, he believed, underpinned and informed his own society's very conception of itself. With supreme self-confidence it was held that as science progressed and wealth increased so progress was assured and man's irrationality would disappear, giving way to a positivistic and secular ethic that would guarantee peace and prosperity. If the nineteenth century was littered with texts that disputed this picture of sure and rectilinear progress, it is Sorel's *Reflections on Violence* that declared its death-knell. And, in this sense, the First World War only served to confirm his prognosis. Synthesizing the conclusions of contemporary philosophy and psychology, Sorel paints a picture of people who are frequently not guided by their reason and whose highest aspirations and dreams are captured in myths. From this emphasis is derived the charge that Sorel celebrates the power of the irrational and is thereby implicated in the rise of fascism.[14]

[13] See Jeremy Jennings, 'Georges Sorel and Colonialism', *History of Political Thought*, 8 (1987), 325–33.
[14] See e.g. Z. Sternhell, *The Birth of Fascist Ideology* (Princeton, 1994).

Beneath the façade of bourgeois respectability and ascendency Sorel saw mediocrity, corruption, cowardice, and moral decadence. If this tone of revulsion expressed a sentiment that led 'the generation of 1914' to go off gaily to war, it has also been one of the principal themes of Europe's intellectual avantgarde in the twentieth century.[15]

Sorel's criticism, however, goes beyond the bourgeoisie to the very heart of democracy. For over a century progressive movements had sought to extend the franchise and to make democracy a reality for the working class. After just thirty years of male universal suffrage under France's Third Republic—the most advanced political system of its day—Sorel boldly proclaimed that it was nothing more that a cynical exercise in bourgeois domination that would only further enslave and degrade the proletariat. Schism and confrontation were much to be preferred. Here, too, is a voice that has found frequent echo in our century: witness today the rhetoric of black and female separatism. But what Sorel realized—and as the twentieth century has confirmed—was that a radical transformation of society directed by intellectuals and politicians and achieved largely through the mechanisms of the state would only serve to produce a new tyranny and oppression. For Sorel the revolution had to be, above all, an act of moral transformation and it is for this reason that he chose to use Nietzsche's call for a transvaluation of all values as a description of what should be the proletariat's aim.

Sorel did not underestimate the difficulty of the task. All along he recognized that our natural instincts drew us towards the easy life: hence the need for an epic state of mind and for heroism. Sorel is one member of the so-called left who cannot be accused of having entertained a faith in human perfectibility.

Sorel's *Reflections on Violence* may contain a yet more contentious argument. Ever since the Greeks there has existed a powerful philosophical tradition that has placed politics at the centre of our lives and which as a consequence has established a hierarchy of social utility and value designating, at its summit, the statesman or politician, followed by the artist and intellectual, with at the bottom the labourer, who is thought

---

[15] See R. Wohl, *The Generation of 1914* (Cambridge, Mass, 1979).

to provide nothing more important than life's material necessities. It is there in Pericles' funeral speech, permeates the Renaissance tradition of civic republicanism, and in the twentieth century was restated in Hannah Arendt's *The Human Condition*. In a much-bastardized form it informs the presuppositions of liberal democracy. Sorel turns this table of merit upside-down. The politician and the intellectual are deemed to be mere parasites purveying cynicism and corruption. It is rather the world of labour that is the source of all worth—intellectual, moral, and aesthetic—and the basis upon which civilization should be built. Accordingly it is the factory, and not the public debating space, that is the location of our freedom and creativity. What is being envisaged, in other words, is nothing less than the end of politics.

Bibliographical Note

In English an authorized translation (by T. E. Hulme) of *Reflections on Violence* was first published in 1915. It was subsequently reprinted in the USA by Peter Smith in 1941 and then by The Free Press in 1950 and Collier Books in 1961. The Collier edition was last reprinted in 1972 with two appendices newly translated by J. Roth. Just over thirty pages of the text have also been reprinted in John Stanley's edited volume, *From Georges Sorel* (New York, 1976). A new edition is presently in preparation by Cambridge University Press.

A wide selection of Sorel's work is now available in English, mostly translated by the indefatigable John Stanley: see *The Illusions of Progress* (Berkeley and Los Angeles, 1969); *From Georges Sorel: Essays in Socialism and Philosophy* (New York, 1976; New Brunswick, NJ, 1987); *Social Foundations of Contemporary Economics* (New Brunswick, NJ, 1984); and *Hermeneutics and the Sciences* (New Brunswick, NJ, 1990). Selections of Sorel's writings are also available in R. Vernon, *Commitment and Change: Georges Sorel and the Idea of Revolution* (Toronto, 1978).

With regard to secondary literature, my own *Georges Sorel: The Character and Development of his Thought* (London, 1985) can be read alongside John L. Stanley, *The Sociology of Virtue: The Political and Social Theories of Georges Sorel* (Berkeley and Los Angeles, 1982). The wider intellectual and political context in which Sorel operated is examined in J. Roth, *The Cult of Violence: Sorel and the Sorelians* (Berkeley and Los Angeles, 1980); my own *Syndicalism in France: A Study of Ideas* (London, 1990);

P. Mazgaj, *The Action Française and Revolutionary Syndicalism* (Chapel Hill, NY, 1979); and Z. Sternhell, *Neither Right nor Left* (Berkeley and London, 1986) and *The Birth of Fascist Ideology* (Princeton, NJ, 1994). Sternhell's volumes provide a controversial and stimulating misreading of Sorel's ideas.

Of the many articles and chapters written in English on Sorel over the last few decades there are a limited number that stand out, most notably: I. Berlin, 'Georges Sorel', *Against the Current: Essays in the History of Ideas* (London, 1979), 296–332; L. Kolakowski, 'Georges Sorel: A Jansenist Marxist', in *Main Currents of Marxism* (Oxford, 1981), ii. 151–74; and K. Steven Vincent, 'Interpreting Georges Sorel: Defender of Virtue or Apostle of Violence', *History of European Ideas*, 12 (1990), 239–57. For Sorel's relationship with both the left and the right, see L. Wilde, 'Sorel and the French Right', *History of Political Thought*, 7 (1986), 361–74, and D. Schecter, 'Two Views of Revolution: Gramsci and Sorel, 1916–1929', *History of European Ideas*, 12 (1990), 637–53.

Finally, mention must be made to the most valuable source of recent Sorel scholarship, the *Cahiers Georges Sorel*, published annually since 1983 and from 1987 onwards under the title *Mil neuf cent: Revue d'histoire intellectuelle*. Not only have these volumes contained numerous articles and book reviews on aspects of Sorel scholarship but they have also made available previously unpublished material. Of greatest interest are Sorel's letters to his closest associate Édouard Berth and to Édouard Bernstein between 1898 and 1902.

3

Antonio Gramsci: *The Prison Notebooks*

JOHN HOFFMAN

GRAMSCI is one of the most tantalizing and interesting Marxist theorists of the twentieth century. He has been hugely influential not only on the Italian left but in radical circles generally. In the 1970s and 1980s he was dubbed the father of Euro-communism.

Gramsci was a founder member of the Italian Communist Party who died in 1937 as a result of being incarcerated by Mussolini's fascists for eleven tormenting years. His leadership of the Italian party was backed by the Comintern based in Moscow, and, generally speaking, Gramsci remained loyal to its official policies during the inter-war period. To understand how a protagonist of the Comintern could come to be regarded as the creator of a relatively liberal movement like Euro-communism, we need to get to grips with the curious quality of Gramsci's Marxism.

Gramsci's commitment here was both a strength and a weakness. He felt passionately that Marxist theory had been all too frequently interpreted as a form of economic determinism, and he was particularly concerned to develop a Marxist science of politics. As a committed Marxist, he identified with the vision of an emancipated society which is not only classless, but stateless as well. At the same time his political allegiances meant that he embraced authoritarian arguments for revolution, class war, and party organization. The question inevitably arises: how was a stateless end to be realized through statist means?

Gramsci sought to resolve this problem by incorporating into his Marxist framework the ethical–political concepts of the Italian humanist, Benedetto Croce. This made it possible to raise questions of morality, culture, and freedom which he believed that a fatalistic form of Marxism had suppressed. At the same time, this attempt at a synthesis was unsuccessful and undermined a coherent argument for emancipation, since the abstract idealism of Croce coexists uneasily in Gramsci's work with authoritarian arguments for class war, revolution, and the proletarian state.

The Ambiguous Relationship to Liberalism

In seeking to understand what I have described as the curious quality of Gramsci's Marxism, a study of the *Prison Notebooks* is essential. But this task in turn requires that we take account of what have been called his 'pre-prison writings'.[1] While he was in prison, Gramsci told his sister-in-law Tatiana that he wanted to write 'something *für ewig*' (p. xcii).[2] There is a tendency in the *Notebooks* to stand back from the immediate political concerns which are vigorously emphasized in his earlier work.

Although the young Gramsci won a scholarship to the University of Turin in 1911 (at the age of 20), he had been born and brought up in Sardinia. By 1913 he had become convinced that Sardinia's problems of underdevelopment could only be solved in the context of a regeneration of Italy's political life as a whole. Deeply influenced by the liberal idealism of Croce, Gramsci was, like many students of his generation, particularly preoccupied with the problem of nation-building and state-formation. As a Sardinian, it was clear to him that Italy was a pre-modern country on the periphery of the industrial world. He took the view that the Italian bourgeoisie were too divided and corrupt to unify the country around robust parliamentary institutions so that liberalism, as the apparent ideology of the middle classes, seemed impotent. Only a movement led by the proletariat could regenerate the nation.

By 1915 Gramsci was writing regularly for the socialist press on cultural questions, and he welcomed the Russian Revolution as the dramatic act of a popular collective will. Gramsci's

[1] The term is used in an excellent edition recently published by Cambridge University Press. See R. Bellamy (ed.), *Pre-Prison Writings* (Cambridge, 1994).

[2] For purposes of this analysis, I have used the *Selections from the Prison Notebooks*, ed. and trans. Q. Hoare and G. Nowell-Smith (London, 1971). References in the text are to this edition.

commitment to militant revolution became particularly clear when his weekly *L'ordine nuovo* vigorously supported the workers' councils and factory occupations which mushroomed in Turin and other northern industrial cities during the turbulent red years of 1919–20. Although it is true that Gramsci's sharp attacks on the passivity and reformism of the Italian Socialist Party won the approval of Lenin, there is little doubt that his fervent support for workers' councils owed more to traditional syndicalism—with its belief in the 'producers'' organization as the instinctive and organic substitute for conventional politics—than it did to classical Marxism. It is only as Gramsci began to see in the council movement the nucleus of the future dictatorship of the proletariat that he started to stress the need for a communist party to provide leadership and vision for the insurgent workers. With the collapse of councils, Gramsci took the view that this party must unite workers and peasants around a strategy for renewing the nation as a whole.

His early view of socialism as 'an integral vision of life with its own philosophy, mysticism and morality'[3] exemplifies the wider contextual point which is essential for an understanding of the *Notebooks* themselves. Where liberalism and the bourgeoisie are weak, political polarization, it might be argued, will generate conditions in which socialism (especially in its Marxist form) is likely to be strong. Both the anti-politics of Gramsci's syndicalist writing and the support he subsequently expressed for the revolutionary party and state reflected a view held by many intellectuals in Italy at the time that liberalism was an exhausted political tradition. In this kind of climate it was relatively easy for a fervent protagonist of workers councils in 1919 to become a founder member and subsequent leader of a communist party—with (as we have already noted) the backing of the Comintern.

Hegemony as the Leitmotiv of the *Notebooks*

Gramsci began work on his masterpiece in February 1929 nearly three years after he had been arrested and brought to trial.

---

[3] Quoted by R. Bellamy and D. Schecter, *Gramsci and the Italian State* (Manchester, 1993), 25–6.

Consisting of over 2,848 pages in thirty-three notebooks, it was smuggled out of prison by his devoted sister-in-law, Tatiana, and taken to Moscow via the Soviet diplomatic bag. The *Notebooks* were first published in Italy in 1948–51. When his work was rediscovered in the 1960s by new-left theorists in general and in the 1970s by Eurocommunists in particular, a significant portion of the *Notebooks*—along with his other writings—was translated into English.

Despite the enormous prestige they came to acquire, the *Notebooks* are not easy to read. They were written as rough drafts, often in notes and fragments, and were not intended for publication. Gramsci felt it necessary to employ a terminology which would not arouse the suspicions of the prison censor,[4] and English translations of the Italian pose particular problems with words like *dirigente* and *directivo*, where Gramsci's own notion of leadership is innovative and ambiguous. Moreover, it has to be said that the influence of Crocean idealism gives Gramsci's work a rather abstract philosophical flavour which English-speaking readers can find daunting.

The *Notebooks* contain sharply perceptive analyses of Italian history, Marxist philosophy, education, literature, economic development, linguistics, the theatre, and political science. In a 'Note on Method' (written about Marx but equally applicable to the *Notebooks*), Gramsci stresses the importance of seeking out the 'essential aspects', the leitmotiv, of a thinker's work (pp. 383–4). It is generally agreed that what threads the formidable breadth of topics covered in the *Notebooks* together is the concept of hegemony. Gramsci defines hegemony as 'intellectual and moral leadership' (p. 57), and an exposition and critique of this most distinctive and seminal of concepts is perhaps the best way to understand this classic political text.

---

[4] Thus e.g. Lenin and the Bolsheviks become Ilich and the 'the majoritarians', and Trotsky is 'Bronstein'. The problem is that sometimes these terms have a critical bite to them. Thus the celebrated reference to Marxism as the 'philosophy of praxis' helps to convey Gramsci's disapproval of the materialist content of Marxist philosophy, while the term 'group' also has an anti-reductionist thrust to it since, while it usually refers to classes, it does not always. See P. Ransome, *Antonio Gramsci* (Hemel Hempstead, 1992), 3; Hoare and Nowell-Smith, *Selections*, p. xiii.

Hegemony, Intellectuals, and the Political Party

The Hoare and Nowell-Smith selection of the *Notebooks* (which runs to nearly 500 pages) begins with Gramsci's discussion of intellectuals. What he makes clear is that, while all activities involve the expression of ideas, intellectuals are best defined as those who elaborate 'a new and integral conception of the world' (p. 9). In addition to traditional intellectuals like writers, artists, teachers, priests, and lawyers, there are the organic intellectuals who have a specialist and professional relationship to the fundamental group or class which they represent. In the modern world these organic intellectuals (who need to absorb and conquer the traditional intellectuals) provide the functionaries who run political parties. It is their particular role to project the interests of the economic group or class they represent in national and international terms. This function ties in directly with the notion of hegemony.

The concept of hegemony normally denotes domination. With Gramsci, the term has a very different meaning. Identifying hegemony as a moral and intellectual leadership, Gramsci contrasts it with force and what he calls 'direct domination'. Hegemony is characterized as the expression of 'consent' in political relationships, and he conceptualizes the 'superstructural level' in which this hegemony is exercised as a sphere of 'civil society'. Civil society in Gramsci's terminology is opposed to 'political society', where we encounter the direct domination or force of the state (p. 12). On the one hand, hegemony is the work of political parties and intellectuals in general. On the other hand, it has a particular relationship to the development of democracy and working-class power.

In his comments on education, Gramsci links learning as a creative process with the development of 'spontaneous assent' (p. 34), and argues that education should encourage people to think independently. In this it advances the cause of democracy by equipping people to govern themselves. If the creation of working-class intellectuals is the responsibility of the mass political party, it is also the function of a democratized educational system to work towards 'the transcendence of class divisions' (p. 41), since the consolidation of hegemony—

government based upon consent—implies breaking down the division between rulers and ruled.

Forging the National–Popular Will

Hegemony is central to Gramsci's 'Notes on Italian History', where he is preoccupied with the failure of the Italian bourgeoisie in the nineteenth century to move beyond the 'narrow egoism' of their immediate or corporate interests, and unify a national–popular movement for change. Like their forebears during the period of the medieval communes, the bourgeoisie were an economic class unable to create their own category of intellectuals. As a consequence they proved powerless to exercise an effective 'hegemony' over society as a whole (p. 56; see also p. 249).

Gramsci not only identifies hegemony as one of the most realistic and concrete meanings of democracy (p. 56), but asserts that no group or class can win political power unless it also succeeds in exercising hegemonic leadership (p. 58). The bourgeoisie have never been able to exercise this kind of leadership in Italy because the country's intellectuals have lacked 'a national–popular character' (p. 56). Hence Gramsci argues that only the working class and its intellectuals are capable of realizing a genuine hegemony. It is true that, during the Renaissance, Machiavelli had sought to promote the hegemony of the city over the country as the 'first Italian Jacobin' (p. 56), but in this he was unsuccessful. Only the communists can continue the radical legacy of the Jacobins, and, like Lenin, Gramsci characterizes the Jacobins as French revolutionaries who had succeeded in winning the consent of the peasant masses to the project of national unification. They were, he says at one point, 'a group of extremely energetic and determined men driving the bourgeoisie forward with kicks in the backside' (p. 77). By breaking up feudal estates and mobilizing the peasantry, they made the bourgeoisie the hegemonic class of the nation (p. 79).

By contrast, the Risorgimento—the Italian national movement which led to unification in 1860-1—was unable to embrace the expansive hegemony which Gramsci identifies with French Jacobinism. The Action Party linked to Mazzini and Garibaldi failed to take up peasant demands, while the Moderates around Cavour adopted a policy of what Gramsci calls 'transformism'. 'Transformism' involved a process of absorbing the opposition parties (including the socialists after 1900) into the ranks of a conservative élite anxious to prevent mass hegemony and democratic rule (p. 98). Transformism, like the cognate concepts of 'passive revolution' and 'Caesarism', designates a mode of government which at best limits and at worst eliminates hegemony as rule by consent. In the case of a passive revolution, political leadership becomes an aspect of the function of domination rather than leadership (p. 59) so that what exists is dictatorship without hegemony (p. 106). With Caesarism (as in Marx's analysis of Bonapartism), a stalemate between contending political forces brings into play a 'great personality' (p. 219) as arbitrator of the conflict.[5]

Gramsci's preoccupation with the concept of hegemony was stimulated by his Sardinian background. 'Intellectual and moral leadership' must, he insisted, demonstrate sensitivity to local, regional and national identities if it is forge a 'national-popular collective will' (p. 133). This is why Gramsci was so hostile to Amadeo Bordiga, the powerful leftist figure who dominated the Italian Communist Party in its early days, and whose dogmatic brand of Marxism would, Gramsci feared, turn the party into a sterile sect divorced from ordinary people. For the same reason, Gramsci (though no admirer of Stalin) was implacably opposed to Trotsky's 'literary and intellectualistic' internationalism (p. 85), which ignores the national and cultural factors central to the struggle for hegemony.

Class, Party, and the Critique of Economism

Gramsci's notion of hegemony is tied, as we have already seen, to a concept of democracy. Gramsci believed that democracy implied not merely that class divisions had to be transcended. He also took the view that democracy embraced a notion of self-government which would break down the very division between ruler and ruled. At the same time, he treats this

---

[5] For Gramsci's analysis of fascism itself as a passive revolution, see D. Forgacs (ed.), *A Gramsci Reader* (London, 1988), 247–8; on Caesarism, see *Selections*, 206.

division as the 'primordial fact' upon which 'the entire science and art of politics is based' (p. 144). Politics is not only unavoidable, but—and here he dissents from Croce—it cannot be defined merely in terms of 'passion' since it is linked to 'permanent political formations' like parties and armies.

However, Gramsci was interested in the political party not as 'a sociological category' but as the institution which forges the collective will of the nation and thus seeks to found the state (pp. 123, 131; also p. 253). In rooting his analysis in what he calls the 'precocious Jacobinism' of Machiavelli, Gramsci argues that in the modern world the prince can no longer be a heroic individual—he has to be a political party. The 'superstructural' characteristic of this 'modern' or 'new' prince derives from the fact that the party exists as 'the expression and the most advanced element' of a particular social group (i.e. class). Indeed Gramsci states that 'every party is only the nomenclature for a class' (p. 152), but he believes that politics can enjoy autonomy when we recognize that parties are not simply the mechanical or passive expression of classes, but react energetically upon these classes 'in order to develop, solidify and universalise them'. Parties represent classes as 'the living realities of national life' (pp. 227–8).

How then does this concept of the party as an organizational expression of class relate to the realization of hegemony and democracy? In noting the division between rulers and ruled as the basic fact of politics, Gramsci also poses the question as to whether conditions can be created in which a division between leaders and led would no longer be necessary (p. 144). Since the political party is the state in microcosmic form—it is 'an embryonic State structure' (p. 226)—this division is evident in the party itself. Although political parties are primarily concerned with forging consent, they also carry out what Gramsci calls a 'policing function' in order to safeguard a particular political and legal order (p. 155). The crucial question, however, is whether this policing function is 'reactionary'—in which case the party seeks to hold back 'the vital forces of history'—or whether it is 'progressive'—in which case the party raises the masses to a new level of legality. The revolutionary or 'progressive' party functions democratically, whereas the reactionary or 'regressive' party functions bureaucratically.

However, democracy is conceived as a political force which is both statist and anti-statist at the same time. To be democratic, as we have seen, is to work to overcome the division between rulers and ruled. Because parties express classes, the party which proposes to put an end to class divisions will, Gramsci argues, 'only achieve complete self-fulfilment when it ceases to exist' (p. 152). To see how the revolutionary party, the modern prince, can work to secure this kind of self-annulling hegemony, we need to note Gramsci's comments on what he (like Lenin) called 'economism'.

Economism seeks to abstract society from the state and the economy from politics so that (as in Lenin's critique in *What is to be Done?*) it involves identifying working-class interests with mere trade unionism. Gramsci makes a number of important points in his critique here. The first is that economism embraces both syndicalism—which would confine workers' struggles to the factory—and *laissez-faire* liberalism, which naïvely assumes that a capitalist economy can function outside the state (p. 160). His second point extends the notion of economism to embrace a mode of analysis which sees economic reality as the sole determinant of historical events. Here Gramsci reiterates Engels's strictures against those who reduce historical materialism to a simple, easy to assimilate economic formula (see also pp. 427, 437, 472), and he links this kind of theoretical dogmatism to political sectarianism. The belief that objective laws of historical development will always win the day constitutes a 'predetermined teleology like that of a religion' (pp. 168, 336).[6] This predetermined telology encourages leaders to shun the need to compromise, and promotes a tendency to substitute force for persuasion.

On the one hand, economism represents a mistaken theoretical stance. It constitutes a failure to distinguish between what Gramsci calls 'conjunctural' phenomena—particular events as they occur at a particular time—and 'organic movements' as the deep-rooted developments which derive ultimately from the economic 'structure' of society. However, an economism

---

[6] Gramsci develops his critique of vulgar materialist influences in Marxism in some detail in his extended analysis of the Bukharin's *Theory of Historical Materialism*, in *Selections*, 419–72.

which presents indirect causes as though they were 'immediately operative' (p. 178) is not only theoretically deficient. It also undermines the creation of hegemony, since hegemony, in Gramsci's view, can only be forged if political leaders 'transcend the corporate limits of the purely economic class' (p. 181) and take into account the interests of other groups as well. The creation of hegemony involves 'the decisive passage from the structure to the sphere of complex superstructures' so that politics and economics unite; intellectual and moral unity develops and questions are posed on a 'universal' plane. Even though the state still represents the interests of the dominant group, it does so *hegemonically* when the interests of all its allied groups are linked to its own through the continuous formation of 'unstable equilibria' (p. 182).

Gramsci defends the concept of 'democratic' (as opposed to 'bureaucratic') centralism as a political process which requires 'an organic unity between theory and practice, between intellectual strata and popular masses, between rulers and ruled' (p. 190). This 'organic unity' means that 'spontaneous' protest among the masses (as the *Ordine Nuovo* group had earlier demonstrated in relation to the workers' council movement) must not be neglected but 'educated'. The concept of hegemony makes it possible to give spontaneity theoretical depth and vision, so that the eruption of protest engages with people's everyday experiences, and allows the masses to believe that they are 'founders of a State' (p. 198).

War of Position and War of Movement

Hegemony is not only central to the concept of the party, the critique of economism, and the analysis of intellectuals: it is also a concept which provides crucial insights into questions of political strategy. In what he presents as an analysis of military science, Gramsci speaks of three forms of 'war'—a war of movement, a war of position, and underground warfare. In discussing the implications of this analysis for political science, he regards the first two—the war of position and the war of movement (or manœuvre as he sometimes calls it)—as the 'commanding concepts' (p. 233).

Both moments are relevant to political strategy. Gramsci

takes it for granted that political struggle expresses class war. The war of position arises when a social movement gradually consolidates its strength and support, and it passes into a war of manœuvre when revolutionaries are able to launch a sharp 'lightning' attack which rapidly overwhelms the enemy (p. 235). In his notes on Italian history, Gramsci identifies the war of position with Cavour and the war of manœuvre with Mazzini, and asks rhetorically: 'are not both of them indispensable to precisely the same extent?' (p. 108). At the same time there is no doubt that it is the war of position rather than the war of movement which advances the development of hegemony and civil society. If the war of movement involves force, the war of position derives from consent. If the former seems the more revolutionary, it is the latter which demands 'enormous sacrifices by infinite masses of people' so that 'an unprecedented concentration of hegemony is necessary' (p. 238).

What makes Gramsci's analysis particularly interesting here is the way in which he links an emphasis on the war of manœuvre with the kind of economism noted above. Thus he criticizes Rosa Luxemburg for an 'economistic' prejudice in her analysis of the Russian Revolution of 1905. Her stress on the war of manœuvre reflects 'a form of iron determinism', out-and-out historical mysticism, the awaiting of a sort of miraculous illumination (p. 233). We have already noted Gramsci's criticism of Trotsky for a neglect of the importance of hegemony within a national political strategy: here he characterizes Trotsky's impractical theory of permanent revolution as a theory of the permanent character of movement (p. 236). Economism in other words abstracts the war of movement from a wider strategy which involves organizing mass support through 'exceptional qualities of patience and inventiveness' (p. 239).

Gramsci argues that the war of position has become the kernel of an effective political strategy. While he identifies the Bolshevik Revolution as 'the war of manœuvre applied victoriously' in 1917 (p. 237), henceforth, he contends, the war of position is the only form of struggle which will advance hegemony. It is at this point he makes his celebrated contrast between Russia (and the East) as a world in which the state was everything and civil society 'primordial and gelatinous', and the West where the state was 'only an outer ditch' behind which there stood a powerful system of fortresses and earthworks, i.e. the hegemonic institutions of civil society (p. 236).

Indeed Gramsci argues that, in the West, the theory of permanent revolution with its emphasis upon a war of movement has been obsolete since 1870. It belonged to the period in which the great mass political parties and economic trade unions did not yet exist; in which the countryside was backward and state power concentrated in a single city; where national economies largely functioned outside a world system, and where, above all, civil society was fluid and undeveloped. A theory which arose in the context of the revolutions of 1848 must give way to the 'formula' of 'civil hegemony'—a dictum of political science which requires (as Gramsci puts it) that a war of movement 'increasingly becomes' (p. 243) a war of position.

It is an argument which has led some of Gramsci's Marxist critics to complain that he appears to side here with the historic reformism of Kautsky. Was Gramsci suggesting that parliamentary systems in the West owed their legitimacy purely to consent? Lenin had certainly spoken of the importance of proletarian hegemony, as Gramsci acknowledged, but nowhere does he differentiate leadership from domination in the way Gramsci does. In arguing rather cryptically that Ilich (i.e. Lenin) did not 'have time to expand his formula [of hegemony]', Gramsci seems to be suggesting that the Russian Revolution offered no positive political lessons for revolutionaries in the West.[7]

Hegemony and the State

In Gramsci's political theory, the doctrine of hegemony complements 'the theory of the State-as-force' (p. 56). He identifies politics in terms of 'two fundamental levels', which correspond to the dual nature of Machiavelli's centaur, that half-animal and half-human beast of mythology which Gramsci's Renaissance ancestor regarded as an allegory for politics in

---

[7] See e.g. P. Anderson, 'The Antinomies of Antonio Gramsci', *New Left Review*, 100 (1976–7), 5–78, at 65. Also J. Hoffman, *The Gramscian Challenge* (Oxford, 1984), 148.

general. Machiavelli had spoken of two ways of fighting: by law and by force. Every 'prince' must master both. Gramsci concurs. The Communist Party can become a modern prince only when it is able to utilize both 'ways of fighting' (p. 170).

This dual perspective is to be found at every level of Gramsci's political analysis. He uses different terms to convey the same basic duality, referring to hegemony and authority, civil and political society, civilization and violence, propaganda and agitation, strategy and tactics, consent and coercion (p. 170). But since Gramsci believed that it was hegemony rather than force which had been neglected as the 'essential ingredient' of modern Marxism,[8] this is the moment of the Machiavellian centaur that he explores most fully in his prison writings.

The concern with the dual nature of politics leads Gramsci to define the state in both narrow and broad terms. In some of the passages noted above he contrasts hegemony with the state (e.g. p. 12) since hegemony arises in the arena of civil (as opposed to political) society. At the same time, he sees the distinction between the state as political society and hegemony as civil society as 'merely methodological' and 'not organic', and declares that 'in actual reality' civil society and the state 'are one and the same' (p. 160). Hence Gramsci also defines the state broadly as the 'entire complex of practical and theoretical activities with which the ruling class not only justifies and maintains its dominance, but manages to win the active consent of those over whom it rules' (p. 244). Here the state is not merely 'a politico-juridical organisation' but also embraces the private apparatus of hegemony or civil society (p. 261).

These two moments—that of hegemony and force, leadership and domination—are distinct but they cannot be separated. As a result, when the state is defined broadly, it has both a negative and a positive role to play. In its negative role, the state 'punishes', 'dominates', and uses force. But as an 'educator' the state also creates a new level or type of 'civilisation', restructuring the economy and social life in general. Thus Gramsci can refer to the law as 'the repressive and negative aspect of the entire positive, civilising activity undertaken by the State' (p. 247). In the real world the two levels or moments of

---

[8] A. Gramsci, *Letters from Prison* (London, 1975), 235.

politics intertwine. On the other hand, it is crucial to be able to distinguish them.

Transcending the State

The notion of hegemony, as we have already seen, is linked both to the struggle for the state power and to the realization of democracy. However, there is clearly a tension between the two. The formation of a new state involves a class war waged by a political party capable of rising above narrow corporate interests and projecting the interests of the class it represents in universal terms. In this context hegemony forges mass consent in order to win and sustain state power. Given the fact that the political party has a policing as well as an educative role, the concept is organically linked to the notion of force within a broad view of the state itself.

At the same time democracy also implies a movement beyond the very division between ruler and ruled: it necessarily challenges the permanency of classes and the state. It is true that on occasion Gramsci can identify normal democracy with parliamentarism (p. 216), and he characterizes the parliamentary regime as one in which force does not 'predominate excessively' over consent (p. 80). But it seems clear that, as a Comintern Marxist, he took the view that parliament was part of a class-divided state (i.e. an organization of 'bourgeois democracy'), so that, despite its relatively positive features when compared with overtly authoritarian legislative bodies, parliament would need to give way to 'a new type of representative system' (p. 254), presumably of a Soviet kind.

The problem then is this. What relationship does democracy and hegemony as *statist* concepts have to democracy and hegemony as concepts which challenge the need for the state itself? Gramsci rejects the confusion between what he calls the class-state and 'regulated society' (i.e. communism) on the grounds that communism is a classless society which involves the disappearance of the state (pp. 258, 382). If the state is defined narrowly as political society, then a regulated society transcends the state. But what if the state is broadly defined so that (to cite one of Gramsci's oft-quoted formulas) 'the

State = political society + civil society, in other words, hegemony protected by the armour of coercion' (p. 263)?

Gramsci's argument is this. In a theory which conceives the state as 'tendentially capable of withering away', it is possible to imagine the coercive element of the state disappearing by degrees, as 'ever-more conspicuous elements of regulated society (or ethical State or civil society) make their appearance' (p. 263). As this happens, hegemony would cease to be organically linked with force, since political society gradually transforms itself into a regulated or communist society. The ethical state comes to denote what Gramsci calls a state without a state (p. 263), so that a stateless society (in the narrow sense of the term 'state') emerges when civil society is able to displace political society; when force gives way to hegemony.

Clearly there are two levels to Gramsci's own analysis which need to be distingushed here. On the one hand, Gramsci insists (when arguing with liberals and syndicalists) that the distinction between civil and political society is methodological rather than organic. Hence the ethical state is always linked in reality to the state-as-dictatorship, as when Gramsci argues, for example, that every ethical state must raise the population to a cultural and moral level which corresponds 'to the interests of the ruling classes' (p. 258). On the other hand, the ethical state as a democratic hegemony can actually displace the hierarchical and repressive divisions of political society as the state (narrowly defined) begins to wither away. On this argument, the methodological distinction increasingly becomes an organic one, since, as Gramsci puts it, within the husk of political society a 'complex and well-articulated civil society' develops in which individuals can govern themselves without their self-government coming into conflict with political society (p. 268). The state as force is restricted to safeguarding 'the development of the continually proliferating elements of a regulated society' as it progressively reduces 'its own authoritarian and forcible interventions' (p. 263).

The notion that the ethical state is a form of the state ceasing to be a state is a fascinating one. Gramsci argues that the idea arises from the dynamism of the bourgeoisie, which, in contrast to previous ruling classes, poses itself as 'an organism in continuous movement', a class capable of assimilating the whole of society to its own cultural and economic level. How-ever, the universal aspirations of the bourgeois state wither as capitalism itself moves into crisis, so that this mantle has to be taken over by the proletariat as the only class which can per-fect this conception of the state and law. To 'perfect' this conception is to conceive its 'end' (p. 260). Marxism, that is to say, must build upon what is historically a bourgeois vision of a self-governing society—an emancipated world of autono-mous individuals—by insisting that this vision can only be realized if the state itself withers away.

Hegemony is conceptually crucial to analysing this process. It promotes democracy as a form of the state which looks beyond the state, or, to put it in Gramscian terms, hegemony denotes the ethical state which supplants the state as a coercive institution. If the distinction between civil and political society is initially methodological, it comes to acquire an increasingly organic character.

The Plausibility of the Gramscian Project

Gramsci argues that the only way to realize a hegemony with-out force is through the successful prosecution of class struggle by a revolutionary political party. There are, however, a number of problems with this argument.

The first is that Gramsci bases the realization of the ethical state—the state without a state—on the assumption that people are 'capable of accepting the law spontaneously, freely, and not through coercion'. Coercion is identified as a form of class oppression, 'external to consciousness' (p. 263), and indeed throughout the *Notebooks* the terms 'coercion' and 'force' are used synonmyously. This argument makes it impossible to acknowledge the character of coercion as a constraint inherent in all social relationships. It is true that Gramsci himself refers to a 'coercion' in the private zones of civil society which derives from public opinion and a moral climate (p. 196; the quotation marks are Gramsci's; see also p. 247). Elsewhere he refers to 'mechanical coercion' involved in education (p. 37; see also p. 96), but essentially he remains wedded to the view that coercion and force are basically the same.

Yet, as I have argued elsewhere,[9] an effective critique of the state is only possible if we rigorously distinguish between force—as the negation of a subject's capacity to exercise will—and coercion as constraints which compel the freest of subjects to act in one way rather than another. Force as it is institutionalized within the state can be overcome: coercion cannot. It is true that in his analysis of 'Americanism and Fordism' Gramsci speaks of direct and indirect coercion in the production process (p. 301), but he still tends to identify coercion with physical force and not with social pressures in general.[10]

If Gramsci's concept of coercion undermines his argument for statelessness, so too does his repeated identification of the (narrowly defined) state with *government* (e.g. pp. 12, 227, 261, 269). In my view coercion is best understood as a broad social term which can explain how stateless societies secure cohesion, and so too is government. The use of both enable people to resolve their conflicts in a non-violent manner. Without a *social* concept of coercion and government, the stateless world does indeed constitute pure utopia, and the notion of a stateless society as (in Gramsci's words) a 'morally unitary social organism' (p. 259) comes to acquire a somewhat menacing monolithic character.[11]

Gramsci's problem is therefore this. On the one hand, he took the Marxist case for emancipation seriously and saw in the concept of hegemony a notion which could bridge the movement from a class-divided to a classless society. But Marxists

[9] J. Hoffman, 'Capitalist Democracies and Democratic States: Oxymorons or Coherent Concepts?' *Political Studies*, 39 (1991), 347; J. Hoffman, 'Is Political Violence Ever Justified?', Discussion Paper for the Centre for Study of Public Order (Leicester, 1994), 7–9. See also J. Hoffman, *Beyond the State* (Cambridge, 1995), ch. 6.

[10] Like many other Marxists at the time, Gramsci failed to see Marx's analysis of the commodity as a philosophical argument pointing to the social character of coercion. Although Gramsci was familiar with Marx's *Capital*, he appeared to read it superficially. See T. Nemeth, *Gramsci's Philosophy* (Brighton, 1980), 46, 65; J. Femia, *Gramsci's Political Thought* (Oxford, 1981), 62; Hoffman, *Gramscian Challenge*, 84–5, 98, 104–5.

[11] Bellamy and Schecter, *Gramsci and the Italian State*, 161, criticize Gramsci for his lack of concern with pluralism and difference, and this problem is clearly exacerbated by a failure to distinguish between force and coercion, state and government. In the same way, Gramsci was unable to theorize a concept of politics which would embrace a non-violent and thus non-statist resolution of social differences. For a contrary view, see E. Hobsbawm, 'Gramsci and Marxist Political Theory', in A. Showstack-Sassoon (ed.), *Approaches to Gramsci* (London, 1982), 23.

like Lenin also stress the need for hierarchical party organization, revolution, and the formation of a dictatorship of the proletariat, and all this makes it impossible to see how the transition from a state-centred to a stateless society can actually occur. Even Gramsci's war of position is, when all is said and done, a *war* between classes with radically divergent interests.

The Crocean Legacy

Gramsci's distinction between hegemony and dictatorship or civil society and political society is one which he explicitly took from Croce, and he defends Croce's distinction against (for example) Gentile's authoritarian argument that force and consent are indistinguishable (p. 271). But Gramsci is also critical of Croce for ignoring the role of class conflict in historical development, and for treating hegemony as though it constituted the life of the state itself (pp. 119, 271).[12]

But how is it possible to realize an emancipated society through war and revolution? For Gramsci, the only way round the problem was to graft onto Marxism an abstract notion of hegemony. A concept derived from an idealized liberal capitalist society is transferred to an equally idealized classless communist one. As a result the stateless society becomes a utopia in which freedom has vanquished necessity (pp. 366–7); theory and practice have become one (p. 333), and (as we have seen) law ceases to be something external to consciousness (p. 263).[13] In embracing the notion of hegemony in its abstract Crocean form as a consent mystically free from any kind of governmental coercion, Gramsci made it impossible to explain how the methodological distinction between hegemony and force could ever become organic.

A loyalty to Marxism saddled Gramsci with authoritarian concepts that he sought to dilute with Crocean idealism. This explains why his work was received with particular enthusiasm by Eurocommunists who sought to pursue a liberal politics within

[12] See, on this, Anderson, 'The Antinomies of Antonio Gramsci', 47; Hoffman, *Gramscian Challenge*, 62.

[13] For a sustained critique of Gramsci's interpretation of Marxist philosophy, see Hoffman, *Gramscian Challenge*, ch. 5 and esp. 122–3; Bellamy and Schecter, *Gramsci and the Italian State*, ch. 4.

a Marxist framework. If, then, Gramsci's Marxism is tantalizing, it is also incoherent, for he was ultimately unable to develop the concepts necessary for promoting a self-governing world in place of the hierarchical and repressive institutions of the state.

Bibliographical Note

Between 1948 and 1951 the Turin publisher Einaudi produced six volumes of the *Prison Notebooks* edited by Felice Platone. In 1975 the same publisher produced a 'critical' edition of four volumes edited by Valentino Gerratana.

In 1957 an English edition entitled *The Modern Prince and Other Writings* was translated by Louis Marks and published by Lawrence & Wishart. The English edition of the *Notebooks* used here was edited and translated by Hoare and Nowell-Smith in 1971. It is the most comprehensive English edition so far produced, and contains a lengthy and valuable introduction. Additional material in English from the *Notebooks* appears in D. Forgacs and G. Nowell-Smith, *Selections from Cultural Writings* (London, 1985) and in D. Forgacs, *A Gramsci Reader*, (London, 1988). An edition of Gramsci's *Letters from Prison* was published in 1975.

In 1977 *Selections from Political Writings 1910–1920* appeared and the following year *Selections from Political Writings 1921–26*. Some of this material has been retranslated (along with other hitherto untranslated writings) in R. Bellamy (ed.), *Pre-Prison Writings* (Cambridge, 1994). G. Fiori's extremely readable *Antonio Gramsci: Life of a Revolutionary* was translated by Tom Nairn and published by New Left Books in 1970, while Alistair Davidson produced *Antonio Gramsci: Towards an Intellectual Biography* in London in 1977.

The massive Gramsci industry which began in the 1970s has generated a substantial amount of secondary literature in English. In terms of the books produced, particular note should be made of C. Boggs, *Gramsci's Marxism* (London, 1977), and J. Femia, *Gramsci's Political Thought* (Oxford, 1981). A translation of C. Buci-Glucksmann's Althusserian account *Gramsci and the State* was published in London in 1980. Anne Showstack-Sassoon wrote a lively book entitled *Gramsci's Politics* (London, 1982) and edited a useful selection of articles in *Approaches to Gramsci* (London, 1982). A rather different (and equally useful) series of articles was edited by C. Mouffe, in *Gramsci and Marxist Theory* (London, 1979). J. Hoffman's critical *The Gramscian Challenge* appeared in 1984, and was fiercely reviewed by J. Femia, 'Gramsci: Marxism's Saviour or False Prophet?' *Political Studies*, 37 (1989), 282–9. Roger Simon's introductory *Gramsci's*

Political Thought was published in London in 1982, while James Joll wrote the volume on Gramsci for Fontana Collins Modern Masters series in 1977. A classic account of Gramsci and the factory councils' movement was written by Gwyn Williams, *Proletarian Order: Antonio Gramsci, Factory Councils and the Origins of Italian Communism* (London, 1977).

Richard Bellamy and Darrow Schecter have recently sought to take issue with 'canonical' accounts which depict Gramsci as a Eurocommunist in their *Gramsci and the Italian State* (Manchester, 1993) and Paul Ransome has produced a very accessible work, *Antonio Gramsci: An Introduction* (Hemel Hempstead, 1992). Of the torrent of articles which have appeared on Gramsci, note should be made particularly of Perry Anderson's detailed critique of what he calls 'The Antinomies of Antonio Gramsci', *New Left Review*, 100 (1976–7), 5–78.

4

Carl Schmitt: *The Concept of the Political*

MURRAY FORSYTH

THE stream of essays, articles, and monographs produced by the German constitutional lawyer and political theorist Carl Schmitt, during the inter-war years, have a trenchant quality matched by few other works of this genre in the twentieth century. Today, long after the events that generated them have faded into the past, they still possess a remarkable capacity to seize the attention and to open new vistas. What is the explanation of their powerful impact? Why are they still viewed by many with distrust or aversion? Is this continuing distrust justified? These are some of the preliminary questions that must be addressed, if only briefly, before turning to an examination of one of the most significant of Schmitt's essays of this period, *The Concept of the Political* (*Der Begriff des Politischen*).

Carl Schmitt: The problematic background

The arresting character of Carl Schmitt's writings can be attributed to their singular combination of analytical brilliance and expository flair. The incisiveness with which Schmitt distinguishes and defines fundamental political concepts—sovereignty, parliamentarianism, democracy, dictatorship, the state, and, of course, the political—has the effect of throwing the whole arena of politics into unusually sharp relief. Schmitt was drawn to the extreme edges of ideas, to the boundaries at which they contrast and conflict with each other, and he mapped their contours with an etcher's precision. He excelled at the illuminating antithesis.

His style too has a directness that compels attention. Rather than winding cautiously into a subject, Schmitt preferred to strike at once, confronting the reader at the outset with his own terse, epigrammatic expression of the essence of the subject;

only then did he proceed to unfold the reasoning behind the epigram, drawing the reader with him. His style is *Blitzkrieg*.

Finally, for all the range and depth of his knowledge, Schmitt's theorizing is never self-indulgent speculation, as if political theory were a cosy, insulated world of antiquarian enquiry or normative dreaming. Theory was for him interesting in so far as it illuminated, and had implications for, political practice. He never lost sight of what he called the 'subject-matter and the situation'. In this respect Schmitt's writings are not only arresting but liberating too; they cut through all that is merely arcane, or pedantic, or moralizing in political theory, and bring the subject vividly to life before the bar of political actuality.

All these features are superbly illustrated in Schmitt's essay *The Concept of the Political*, which is in many ways the culminating expression or epitome of the ideas that he had put forward in his shorter works during the period of the Weimar Republic. Lest it be thought that Schmitt was only a master of the short tract, mention should also be made of his substantial book on constitutional theory and practice, the *Verfassungslehre* (1928), which is also a classic in its own domain, and of his later book, *Nomos der Erde* (1950), a magisterial survey of the practice and principles of the European states-system.

Why then does Schmitt's name continue to arouse distrust and aversion? Two reasons can be adduced. The first, and by far the more significant, is Schmitt's connection with the National Socialist movement in the 1930s, about which most scholars, in the English-speaking world at any rate, have some kind of vague awareness. The second is the overall tenor of his political philosophy, his unflinching 'realism'. Schmitt himself made some remarks on the unpopularity of realism in his essay on the political, and they will be discussed in due course.

As for the first factor, a few words on Schmitt's career are necessary. As he himself recognized, his life bore an uncanny resemblance to that of his hero and mentor, Thomas Hobbes. Schmitt was born into a Catholic family in Westphalia in 1888, 300 years after Hobbes's birth. Like Hobbes, he lived for an unusually long time, dying in 1985 at the age of 96. Like Hobbes, he lived through a period in which his country was ravaged by revolution, political instability, dictatorship, and war, though unlike Hobbes he did not flee abroad when the critical testing time—in his case 1933—arrived. Like Hobbes, who was treated with revulsion by many of his compatriots during the second half of the seventeenth century and beyond, Schmitt found himself shunned in many circles inside and outside his own country after the collapse of the Third Reich.

During the period from 1919 to 1933 Schmitt pursued the career of an academic jurist, rising rapidly to the level of professor, and then moving from one chair to another until, in October 1933, he secured the ultimate prize of the chair of public law at the University of Berlin. He came into public prominence when he acted as a legal adviser to the national government in the momentous case brought against it by Prussia in 1932 (following the national government's intervention in Prussia earlier in that year).

Schmitt was, from the early 1920s onwards, an outspoken and sophisticated critic, not only of the Versailles Peace Settlement and the League of Nations, but also of the political structure of the Weimar Republic. His theoretical writings during this period are rooted more or less explicitly in Germany's internal and external problems. Where did he stand in the political spectrum? He is probably best characterized as a right-wing critic of the Weimar system, who argued that the country's governing institutions required greater unity, authority, and power if they were to resist the disintegrative and hostile forces within, and the pressures that threatened from without. He wanted a reform of the political system, and he was bitterly critical, as we shall see, of liberalism, and of the effects of democracy on the German state. However, he was not a 'conservative revolutionary' in the sense of one seeking the overthrow of the Republic and a return to the old monarchical order, or the establishment of a corporatist state. Nor was he, before Hitler came to power, in any way associated with the National Socialist movement.

From 1929 onwards Schmitt favoured the concentration of power in the hands of the president, via the emergency powers granted to him under article 48 of the Weimar Constitution, as offering the best means of protecting the political structure from paralysis and overthrow, and of preserving peace, order, and security, until a constitutional revision could be attempted. In this critical period—from 1929 to the first months of 1933—

Schmitt was allied politically with General Schleicher and his entourage. These men, it must be repeated, were not National Socialists. Essentially they wanted to preserve and strengthen the authority of the German state, in broadly the same way that General de Gaulle wished to repair the authority of the French state in 1958. Hitler and his followers were not primarily concerned with elevating the state and its authority, but rather with asserting the demands of the *Volk* as a biologically defined entity. The resignation of Schleicher, following the rejection of his emergency proposals by Hindenburg, in January 1933, destroyed the 'last chance' of the Republic. Two days later it was 'handed over' to Hitler, and the 'legal revolution' was accomplished. Schleicher was subsequently assassinated in the Nazi purge of June 1934.

It was not until the passage of the Enabling Act of 24 March 1933, which in effect destroyed the Weimar Constitution and transformed the whole political system of Germany, that Schmitt, like many hundreds of thousands of his fellow countrymen, adjusted to the new system and joined the National Socialist Party (1 May 1933). This act, in itself, given the time and circumstances, was scarcely reprehensible. It was Schmitt's readiness to place his pen at the service of the new regime, and to become an active participant in its activities, that raised accusations of cynical betrayal. He became director of the University Teachers' Group of the National Socialist League of German Jurists, and in two significant tracts, one written in 1933, and the other shortly after the purge of 1934, he endorsed the 'leadership' principle, and the concept of the 'movement' as a dynamic third element linking 'state' and 'people'. His endorsement was mitigated by the fact that he indicated that the 'movement' should respect certain limits, and that the 'leader' held the responsibility for upholding 'right' and taking action against those who infringed it—Schmitt believed right had been infringed during the purge in which Schleicher died. It was, needless to say, a naïve expectation.

From 1934 onwards Schmitt became subject to increasing attacks from Nazi ideologists who believed his conversion to their cause was not genuine, and that his ideas were not in line with party doctrine. In 1936 he came under investigation by the SS. It was in his efforts to stave off these attacks, and to convince his opponents of the sincerity of his attachment to the Nazi regime that he compromised his intellectual and moral integrity most deeeply. Anti-Semitism now became a marked feature of his writings—something not present at all before 1933—and he began to use racial and biological terminology wholly at variance with his previous convictions. Even this was not enough to save him, and the pressure against him mounted. At the end of 1936 he retired abruptly from the public scene. 'To avoid further complication,' Bendersky writes, 'he never again dealt with domestic or party politics, but turned his attention to the study of international relations, and soon passed into obscurity.'[1]

Such, briefly, was Schmitt's association with National Socialism. It was an extraordinarily reckless alignment, guided in part at least during the early stages by the mistaken belief that the new regime was susceptible to traditional forms of containment, and it redounded humiliatingly on Schmitt's own head by being condemned as mere opportunism by the Nazis themselves. Schmitt's moral and intellectual integrity buckled in a grotesque situation of his own making. He expressed his shame later—during interrogation at the end of the Second World War—at what he had written at this time. 'It is definitely horrible. Nothing else can be said about it.'[2]

Does this three-and-a-half-year episode mean that Schmitt and all his writings should be permanently spurned? No: understandable as such a blanket revulsion may have been in the immediate aftermath of the war, it is far too crude a response, in the long term, to the man and his works. As Bendersky reminds us, Schmitt never became an ideological convert to Nazism, he did not pave the way for the Nazi regime, and he did not provide its legal foundations. He behaved ignominiously by publicly espousing false and brutish doctrines that he did not believe in, but other great writers have erred—Rousseau, the moralist, for example, when he abandoned all his children—without suffering a general proscription as a result. Schmitt's alignment with National Socialism occupied a short period in a long life that produced works of great insight and

---

[1] Joseph W. Bendersky, *Carl Schmitt: Theorist for the Reich* (Princeton, 1983), 242.
[2] Ibid. 269.

profundity that were not so aligned, a life which displayed, when the whole span is taken into account, an impressive intellectual coherence and consistency. The lurch towards National Socialism in 1933 will remain a disturbing puzzle. Is it to be ascribed to 'personality' weaknesses (ambition, vanity, and so on)? Or was there something in Schmitt's *Weltanschauung* (romanticism? adventurism?) that encouraged it? The puzzle will not be answered, however, and no good purpose will be served, by refusing to look at his works.

The Concept of the Political: Aim, Structure, Method

The Concept of the Political was first published in 1927. A longer version with a number of corollaries attached was published in 1932, and a further edition containing certain textual alterations to make it more palatable to the new National Socialist regime appeared in 1933. It is to the main text of the 1932 version, republished in 1963, that the present discussion refers.[3] In his foreword to the republication of 1963 Schmitt described the essay as a response to the challenge of an 'intermediate situation' in which the 'classic' European concepts of the state and of interstate relations had come under attack and were no longer understood. The essay is indeed an attempt to reaffirm, in a highly original way, these classic concepts. It seeks to rehabilitate the state by means of a dissection of the meaning of politics.

The more immediate challenges to which the essay was a response have already been touched upon. On the one hand, there was the growing instability of the Weimar Republic and the growth of ideological forces devoted to its overthrow. The Republic, constructed to embody the twin ideals of liberalism and democracy, had developed in practice into what Schmitt called a 'total' state, meaning by this, not a totalitarian or one-party state, but rather one in which the boundary line between 'state' and 'society' had been washed away and replaced by their wholesale interpenetration. The state, instead of standing over society, had become the 'self-organization of society'.

---

[3] Carl Schmitt, *Der Begriff des Politischen* (Berlin, 1963). References in the text are to this edition. All translations of the original are by the author of the chapter.

This interpenetration had come about chiefly through the development of the party system, itself encouraged by the strictly proportional 'list' system of elections adopted in 1919. The German parliament had become an arena in which a dozen or more parties, each representing a particular economic, cultural, religious, or ideological segment of society, fought for a share in government, or against the government, in order to further their segmental interests. The result was a perpetual forming and reforming of governmental coalitions, and a steady expansion of state activity into every area of society. To make matters worse, the ideological parties were themselves 'total' in the sense that they embraced the whole lives of their members and sought to instil them with the 'right doctrine' on everything. These 'closed' units acted as a spur to the other parties to follow suit and broke up the state yet further.

The second issue was the external one. The new international system established after the war, again in the name of liberalism and democracy, concealed beneath its sententious moral façade a lack of genuine order. The system had as its twin bases the Versailles Treaty and the League of Nations— the one criminalizing the defeated enemy in a way that broke with the long tradition of the European states-system, the other seeking in an extraordinarily optimistic, spatchcock, and unrealistic way to do what no other international system had ever tried to do—namely, to outlaw war.

Schmitt's essay is remarkable in that it simultaneously attacks both these issues, the internal and the external, by seeking to make plain the true nature of the political, and hence of the state, and by this process to indicate the right way out of the morass. Rooted in the problems of the day, the essay argues, like all great political theory, from 'the nature of things'.

The text of 1932 consists of fifty-eight pages divided into eight untitled sections. Does Schmitt have a method? In his 1963 preface he refers briefly to the two opposed approaches of 'system-building' and 'aphorism' (p. 17). He rejects both and says the only way out lies in 'fixing one's eye on the phenomenon' and in investigating the 'questions that are constantly thrown up by ever-changing, tumultuous situations in the light of its criteria'. In this way 'one perception grows out of another and a series of corollaries arises'. To get at the 'criteria' of a 'phenomenon' and to draw 'corollaries' from them—this is the heart of Schmitt's method, and it is perhaps best termed 'phenomenological', though, as we shall see, it has a close affinity with traditional modes of reasoning.

The Central Thesis of Schmitt's Essay

Despite his rejection of 'aphorism', Schmitt begins his essay in characteristically aphoristic way: 'The concept of the state', he writes, 'presupposes the concept of the political' (p. 20). He continues: 'State, according to current usage, means the political status of a people organized in a closed territorial space.' Then, a little later: 'All the distinguishing features of this conception—status and people—derive their meaning from the additional distinctive feature of the political and become incomprehensible when the essence of the political is misunderstood.'

There are three propositions here, of equal weight. The political is not synonymous with the state; the political is logically prior to the state; the state is inherently political. It is important to realize at the outset that, in 'divorcing' the political analytically from the state, Schmitt is not denying the political nature of the state. On the contrary, the central aim of his analytical distinction between the state and the political is to reveal as cogently and clearly as possible the political core of the state. His 'phenomenological' essay is, in fact, an excellent example of the process of 'analysis' and 'synthesis' used by earlier writers such as Hobbes. Schmitt analyses the political by identifying its logical presuppositions, and then, on the basis of these presuppositions, reconstructs the state as a political phenomenon.

The exposition that follows will first concentrate on tracing Schmitt's analytical investigation to its ultimate conclusion, and then examine the reconstructive process that develops out of it. In doing so it will not always follow exactly the sequence of the essay, and will ignore, in particular, certain polemical elements. The polemical side will be treated separately in the next section.

To grasp the significance of Schmitt's initial distinction between the state and the political, it should be recalled that perhaps the commonest shorthand definition of 'politics' is 'that which relates to the state', by which is meant usually 'the structure and processes of government'. For Schmitt this equation was legitimate when the state was clearly distinguished from the non-state arena of 'society', as it was for most of the nineteenth century. The state was then the monopolist of the political. However, the process of democratization—and Schmitt was clearly thinking here of the developments that had taken place in Germany since the establishment of the Weimar Republic to which reference has already been made—had led to a close interpenetration, if not an identification, of state and society. In a sense everything had become 'state', but equally in a sense everything had become 'non-state'. The monopoly had been broken. The old convenient touchstone of the 'political' had hence lost its usefulness. A fresh definition was needed.

The task, Schmitt argued, was to find the ultimate, underlying categories or criteria of the political, those that gave political activity its specific character and marked it off from economic, moral, aesthetic, or any other kind of human activity. Underlying moral activity was the differentiation between good and evil; underlying aesthetic activity was the differentiation between the beautiful and the ugly; underlying economics stood the antithesis between the useful and the harmful, or the profitable and the unprofitable. What was the political equivalent? Schmitt's reply was characteristically incisive: 'The specific political differentiation, to which political activities and motives can be led back, is the differentiation of *friend* and *enemy*' (p. 26).

It is crucial at the outset to grasp the status of this differentiation. Schmitt was careful to explain that it provided

a conceptual specification in the sense of a criterion, not of an exhaustive definition or statement of content. In so far as it cannot be derived from other criteria, it provides the political counterpart of the relatively independent criteria of other antitheses: good and evil in the moral world, beautiful and ugly in the aesthetic, and so forth. However, it is independent, not in the sense of a separate area of activity, but in the sense that it can neither be derived from one or more of the other antitheses, nor be led back to them. (pp. 26–7)

Schmitt's contention was thus that the friend–enemy antithesis does not describe a separate area or field of activity that lies, so to speak, *alongside* the economic field or the moral field.

This kind of spatial differentiation was misleading and erroneous. The differentiation was rather the ultimate, irreducible,
and hence essential *presupposition* of political activity. It was
that to which political activity, and only political activity, could
be 'led back'.

It also provided a criterion for determining when any activity took on a political character. The more a human activity,
whatever its ostensible content, crystallized into a friend–
enemy relationship, the more it became political. In Schmitt's
words:

> The political can draw its strength from the most diverse areas of human
> life, from religious, economic, moral and other antitheses; it does not
> refer to a particular area of human activity, but only to the *level of
> intensity* of an association or dissociation of human beings whose motives
> can be religious, national (in the ethnic or cultural sense), economic, or
> of some other kind, and can cause different unions and divisions at
> different times. The real friend–enemy grouping is by its nature so
> strong and decisive, that, in the very moment that a non-political anti-
> thesis causes this grouping, it replaces its hitherto 'purely' religious,
> 'purely' economic, 'purely' cultural criteria and motives, and becomes
> subject to the completely new, specific, and, from the 'purely' religious,
> 'purely' economic, and any other 'pure' standpoint, often highly incon-
> sistent and 'irrational' conditions and consequences of what is now a
> political situation. (pp. 38–9)

And again:

> The political antithesis is the most intense and extreme antithesis and the
> closer any concrete opposition approaches the most extreme point, the
> friend–enemy grouping, the more political it is. (p. 30)

What was the precise nature of the 'added factor' that made
an activity political? Schmitt concentrated throughout on the
negative pole, the pole of 'enmity'. He stressed in particular
three aspects of it. First, an enemy was not a norm or idea, and
still less a metaphor or a symbol; an enemy was a concrete
threat to one's very being and existence. Enmity was an existential relationship. Schmitt, in fact, continuously emphasizes,
throughout his essay, the primacy of the 'existential' in relation
to the 'normative'. To this extent his political theory can be
called an existentialist one.

Secondly, armed conflict with the intention of negating or

destroying the 'other'—in other words, war, another existential relation—is the extreme realization of enmity, and hence
the extreme realization of the political. Schmitt immediately
stressed that this did not imply any general advocacy or glo-
rification of war. 'The definition of the political given here is
neither bellicose, nor militaristic, nor imperialist, nor pacifist.
It is also not an attempt to present the victorious war or the
successful revolution as a "social ideal", for war or revolution
is neither something "social" nor something "ideal"' (p. 33).
Schmitt was not a Sorelian, however much he may have studied Sorel. He explains further: 'War is by no means the goal
or aim or ever the content of politics, none the less it is, as a
real possibility, the ever present *presupposition*, which determines human acting and thinking in a peculiar way and thus
gives rise to a specific political relationship' (pp. 34–5).

Schmitt differentiates his conception at this point from that
of Clausewitz, for whom war was an 'instrument' of politics.
War was indeed this, Schmitt observes, but it was also more
than this; it revealed the inner core of politics. Clausewitz himself seems to have recognized this in certain parts of his classic
work on the subject.

Finally, enmity was not necessarily related to any one of the
other antitheses of human activity—moral, economic, religious,
and so on.

The political enemy does not need to be morally wicked, nor to be
aesthetically ugly; he does not need to stand forth as an economic com-
petitor, and it can perhaps even appear advantageous to do business with
him. He is precisely the other, the alien, and it suffices for him to be, in
a particularly intensive way, existentially something other and alien, so
that in the extreme case conflicts with him are possible which cannot be
decided by previously established general norms, nor by the sentence of
a 'disinterested' and therefore 'impartial' third party. (p. 27)

It will be noted that Schmitt here referred to 'the political
enemy'. This reflects an important qualification which he makes
of his basic thesis in the course of his discussion. He distinguished the 'political enemy' from the 'private enemy'. He
wrote:

The enemy is . . . not the private opponent whom one hates out of
feelings of antipathy. The enemy is solely a totality of men who in the

last resort, i.e. as a real possibility, engage in *struggle*, and confront another totality of a like nature. The enemy is only the *public* enemy, because all that has relation to such a totality of men, and in particular to a whole people, becomes thereby *public*. The enemy is *hostis*, not *inimicus* in the broader sense. . . . (p. 29)

Does this qualification undermine his thesis? If the political is defined as resting on the friend–enemy distinction, can the term political also be used to define a certain type or kind of enemy? Does the political also signify 'public'? There would seem to be the germ of a contradiction here, but its significance can easily be exaggerated. The notion that the enemy presupposed by the political is not an individual but a totality can surely be deduced—though Schmitt curiously does not do this—from the fact that enmity is from the start linked by him to *friendship*. It is hence *ab initio* a question of people combining together against a common enemy, and not of solitary enmities.

It might be argued—it is perhaps the commonest kind of argument against this type of reasoning—that war is an exceptional occurrence and therefore it seems wrong to build a theory of politics on this 'abnormal' basis. Schmitt firmly rejected this kind of argument. Wars might have become less frequent but they had become more destructive. They still remained the ultimate test. The exceptional occurrence of war did not negate its quality as a determinant, but actually founded it.

One can say that here, as elsewhere, the exceptional case has a particularly decisive significance as the revealer of the kernel of things. For it is precisely in a real struggle that the most extreme consequence of the political friend–enemy grouping manifests itself. From this most extreme possibility the life of human beings derives its specifically *political* tension. (p. 35)

In other words, it is not the quantitative frequency of war that gives it its significance but its qualitative intensity. It reveals what is 'normally' modified, tempered, negated.

The final resting-point of Schmitt's analytical deduction of the political is provided by his reflections on the nature of man himself (sect. 7). All political theories, he wrote, can be classified on the basis of whether they assume man to be by nature good or bad. This, he added characteristically, should not be taken in a special moral or ethical sense. Nor was the question settled by psychological remarks about 'optimism' or 'pessimism'. 'The decisive thing is the problematic or unproblematic conception of man as the presupposition of any further political consideration, the answer to the question whether man is a "dangerous" or non-dangerous, a risky or a harmless non-risky being' (p. 59). Schmitt's own position on this issue follows on logically from his earlier deductions. He endorsed the views of another German political philosopher, Helmut Plessner, who defined man as primarily a 'distance-asserting' (*Abstandnehmend*) being, one who remains in essence indeterminate, unfathomable, and an 'open question' (p. 60).

Schmitt pressed his argument yet a stage further, and asserted that 'all genuine political theories' presuppose man as 'bad'—that is, 'as by no means unproblematic, but rather as a "dangerous" and dynamic being' (p. 61). He cited as examples of genuine political theorists Macchiavelli, Hobbes, Bossuet, Fichte—'as soon as he forgets his humanitarian idealism'—de Maistre, Donoso Cortes, H. Taine, and Hegel—'who admittedly also occasionally shows a double face here' (p. 61). Unfortunately writers such as these, because 'they always have the concrete existentiality of a possible enemy before their eyes', often manifest a kind of realism that terrifies others (p. 65). Human beings do not like to be reminded of the dark side of things; they cling to the illusion of undisturbed peace, particularly when they seem to be prospering.

The political opponents of a clear political theory therefore do not find it difficult to proscribe the clear understanding and description of political phenomena, in the name of some autonomous area of activity, as being immoral, uneconomic, unscientific, and above all—for this is where the political culminates—as being something devilish to be fought against. (p. 65)

The irony of this passage is not only that it describes a political assault on the political, but also that it describes what has largely happened to the author, Schmitt, himself, partly because of his activities in 1933–6, but partly too because of the 'realism' of his writings.

We have attempted here to trace the logic of Schmitt's

deduction of the political as accurately and as clearly as possible. It can perhaps best be summarized as the elaboration of a scale or hierarchy of presuppositions leading step by step from the state to man. The state presupposes the political, the political presupposes the friend–enemy distinction, the friend–enemy distinction presupposes the real possibility of war, and the possibility of war presupposes man as by nature a dangerous and distance-asserting being. Political theory, in so far as it is genuinely political theory, and not moral or economic theory masquerading as political theory, must base itself, in Schmitt's view, on presuppositions such as these. The affinity between Schmitt's theory and that of Hobbes—who is frequently mentioned and praised in the text and footnotes—is abundantly evident.

Implications and Corollaries

Now we can turn to the reconstructive side of Schmitt's argument. The deduction of the political was made, as emphasized earlier, in order to reveal the true character of the state as an essentially political body. It has a normative intent. Schmitt's objection to the dominance of the normative over the existential should not be allowed to obscure this fact. All arguments which take the form analysis–essence–synthesis are normative in character, they all combine 'is' and 'ought', and Schmitt's is no exception.

What then are the implications of Schmitt's definition of the political for an understanding of the state?

First and foremost the state, as a friend–enemy grouping, is not an 'association' or 'society', but a unity (p. 45). It is the highest, the most intense unity, the one that decides in the final instance. Here we catch a glimpse of Schmitt's definition of the sovereign, advanced in an earlier essay (*Politische Theologie*), as 'he who decides in the exceptional situation'. Here we can also grasp fully his profound rejection of the dissolution of the state into society that was taking place during the Weimar Republic. The state, by reason of its unity and intensity, is and must transcend society, and our allegiance to it is of a different kind to our allegiance to merely social groupings.

Secondly, the state, as an essentially political unity, 'possesses the *ius belli*, i.e. the real possibility, in a given case, through its own decision, to define the enemy and to struggle against him' (p. 46). The right of war, Schmitt explained a little later, signifies, on the one hand, the possibility of demanding from members of one's own people a readiness to kill and be killed, and, on the other, the possibility of killing those standing on the enemy side. 'Through this power over the physical life of men the political community raises itself above every other kind of community or society' (p. 48).

In the midst of this discussion of the *ius belli*, Schmitt makes a highly interesting reference to the 'normal state'. The achievement of a normal state, he wrote, consists above all

in introducing *within* the state and its territory a complete pacification, in producing 'peace, security and order', and thereby creating the *normal* situation, which is the presupposition for the general validity of legal norms, because each norm presupposes a normal situation and no norm can be valid in the face of a completely abnormal situation. (p. 46)

Schmitt had no time for those who spoke of the 'sovereignty of law'. Law only became valid after the decision that created the state.

The necessity for internal pacification makes it necessary in turn for the state, so long as it remains a political unity, to define for itself, not merely the external enemy, but also, in critical situations, the 'internal enemy'. Throughout history, Schmitt pointed out, states have claimed the right to proscribe or outlaw, in one form or another, those who pose an internal threat to their existence. Such an act, depending on the conduct of those who have been proscribed, is the signal of civil war— that is, 'the dissolution of the state as an organized political unity which is internally pacified, territorially closed, and impermeable to the alien' (p. 47). This right to proscribe the internal enemy is as indispensable to the constitutional state, Schmitt emphasized, as it is to any other state. In such a state the constitution is the expression of the existence of the body politic; when the constitution itself is attacked, the struggle must take place outside the constitution and by force of arms.

The relevance of this argument to the problems of the Weimar Republic again deserves notice. Schmitt is here combating the agnostic, positivist, legalistic standpoint—or liberalism in one of its guises—according to which any party that observed the law was as eligible to hold office as any other, and must be allowed an 'equal chance'. For Schmitt, a party whose aims were anti-constitutional, i.e. were expressly directed at the overthrow of the existing constituted order, could not be allowed to rule in a constitutional state, however legally it might behave. A state that did not take action—if necessary, action outside the constitution—to defend itself against its internal enemies was a state that was near its end.

From the internal implications of the political nature of the state, Schmitt turned to the external implications. He introduced them in a typically incisive manner:

From the defining characteristics of the political follows the pluralism of the world of states. A political unity presupposes the real possibility of an enemy and thereby another, coexisting, political unity. Hence so long as there is one state on earth there will always be several, and there cannot be a 'world state' embracing the whole world and all humanity. The political world is a pluriverse, not a universe. To this extent all state theory is pluralist, though in a different sense from the . . . theory of pluralism within the state. (p. 54)

In this superbly succinct formulation of the basic presuppositions of 'international relations', Schmitt is combating those who, in the name of the League of Nations, or of 'humanity', or of various well-meaning pacts and declarations, assumed either that the possibility of war had been ended, or that it could, with relative ease, be ended. 'Humanity', he emphasized, was not a political concept, and no political unity or community or status corresponded to it. '*Humanity* as such cannot wage war, because it has no enemy, at least not on this planet. Humanity excludes the concept of the enemy, because even the enemy does not cease to be a human being and no specific differentiation inheres in it' (pp. 54–5). This, of course, did not prevent combatants in real wars from identifying their own cause with that of 'humanity,' and denying 'humanity' to the other side—thereby driving warfare to the pitch of inhumanity.

This irony leads us once again to stress the normative content of Schmitt's reasoning. It might seem, at first sight, as if Schmitt's insistence on the real possibility of enmity between states carries only a negative message. It warns against pacifism, against utopianism, and so on. There is, however, a positive side to his doctrine. His determination to disentangle the political from the smothering embrace of other categories—and in particular from the categories of morality—carries with it a determination, not to remove the political from all forms of limitation or restraint, but rather to place it within *its own* inherent boundaries. Thus in the world of states the political enemy, properly so called, is, for Schmitt, not necessarily 'immoral' or 'inhuman'; he is simply an 'other' who threatens one's own existence. War, authentic war, can hence be fought only in order to remove or repel such a concrete threat; to fight and kill people, and to demand that one's own people sacrifice themselves, for the sake of abstract principles is absurd. Similarly, when the concrete threat has been removed, then war must cease. Political war, genuine war, is not a crusade; it has its own limitations.

Schmitt makes this plain when he discusses the paradox that pacifism, or the moral hatred of war, can intensify to the point where it becomes political—that is, when pacifists call for a war against the non-pacifists, or a 'war against war', justifying war in the process of condemning it. War then takes the form of an 'ultimate war of humanity'. Schmitt continues:

Such wars are necessarily particularly intensive and inhuman wars, because, *in going beyond the political*, they must simultaneously degrade the enemy in moral and other categories and make him into an inhuman monster, who must be not only warded off but definitively *annihilated*, and who is *hence no longer simply an enemy to be pushed back within his boundaries*. (p. 37)

The political for Schmitt contains its own normative demands, different from those of morality.

The Critique of Liberalism and Pluralism

Schmitt's analysis of the political is accompanied throughout by a vigorous polemic against liberalism. The great offence of liberalism, in his eyes, was precisely that it had 'changed and degraded' all authentically political concepts (p. 68). Liberalism, originally a counter-movement against absolutism and feudalism, had no genuine, positive political theory of its own.

It sought solely to restrain and subordinate the political. Certainly, it did not seek to abolish the state, it was not anarchism, but it eyed the state *a priori* with profound mistrust. Seeing everything from the point of view of the individual and his freedom, it tended to define the state as 'force' and thereby to stamp it as something inherently bad or wicked. The idea that the state could legitimately demand the sacrifice of the individual's life was not accessible to liberal theory.

Liberalism refused to confront the reality of the friend–enemy distinction. Instead of arguing from a political starting-point to a political conclusion, liberalism drew its intellectual resources from the ethical and the economic spheres, and from these twin vantage-points sought to stifle if not 'annihilate' the political. 'In a thoroughly systematic way', wrote Schmitt, 'liberal thought bypasses or ignores the state and politics and instead moves in a typical, constantly recurring polarity between two heterogeneous spheres, namely ethics and economy, spirit and business, education and property' (p. 69). As a result,

the political concept of *struggle* becomes in liberal thought, on the economic side, *competition*, and, on the other, 'spiritual' side, *discussion*; in place of a clear differentiation between the two distinct statuses of 'war' and 'peace' appears the dynamic of eternal competition and eternal discussion. The *state* becomes *society*, seen from the ethical–spiritual side as the ideological–humanitarian concept of '*humanity*', and from the other as the technical–economic unity of a uniform *production and exchange system*. . . . (pp. 70–1)

There is much that is valid in this attack. One has only to read some of the liberal writings of the post-war epoch—those by Berlin, Hayek, and Rawls, for example, which are discussed elsewhere in this volume—to recognize how strong is the tendency not to look directly at the state and its rationale, but to concentrate instead on how the state is to be limited, disciplined, and subordinated to liberal norms, either ethical or economic. Thus Berlin is preoccupied with the norm of negative liberty, Hayek with the norm of society as an exchange process, and Rawls with the norm of social justice. The state appears only incidentally in their discussions. It is an immense lacuna.

On the other hand, one must ask: is liberalism as a whole

to be identified with 'anti-politics'? Is a tough-minded liberalism, rooted in the realities of politics, which Schmitt identifies, impossible? Do not Hobbes, Hamilton, and Sieyes fit into this category? Schmitt's attack compels a re-examination of liberalism's pedigree and credentials.

The second doctrine that Schmitt attacks in his essay is the 'pluralist' theory of the state. By this Schmitt meant primarily the doctrines developed by the British writers G. D. H. Cole and Harold Laski during and after the First World War, though he saw these doctrines as being part of a more general movement of ideas that embraced the French syndicalists (influenced by Sorel) and Léon Duguit, and had roots in the ideas of Otto Gierke and J. N. Figgis. Schmitt attacked the ideas of Cole and Laski because they were the theoretical counterpart of the very real process of 'pluralization' that was taking place in the Weimar Republic, in other words the interpenetration of state and society whose features were outlined earlier.

For Schmitt it was possible to conceive of a genuine pluralist theory of the state; it would be a theory of state unity achieved through a 'federalism' of social groups. Otherwise pluralist theory could only be a theory of the dissolution or refutation of the state. Cole's and Laski's theory fell into the second category. It was characterized by an attack on the idea of the sovereignty and personality of the state, and by the assertion that the state did not differ in kind from other societies and associations or groupings to which individuals belonged—families, trade unions, religions, nations, and so on. It built up a picture of a world in which individuals were bound by a plurality of 'loyalties' and 'allegiances' of basically the same kind, the final and most inclusive concept being in Cole's case 'society' and in Laski's 'humanity'.

It is not necessary to elaborate Schmitt's objections to this doctrine, for his whole theory of the political is directed against it. For him there could be no question of the political association or group existing *alongside* other associations or groups from which it did not differ in kind. The pluralism of Cole and Laski was but an extension of individualist liberalism, playing off one association against another in the service of the free choice and decision of the individual.

In reality [Schmitt countered], there is no political 'society' or 'association', there is only a political unity, a political 'community'. The real possibility of the grouping of friend and enemy suffices to create an authoritative unity that goes beyond the purely social and associative, and is something specific and decisive in relation to all other associations. (p. 45)

Conclusion

Schmitt's argument is as relevant today as it was when it was written. Indeed, the weaknesses that it drew attention to, both in the liberal-democratic structure of Weimar and in the brave new world of the League of Nations, have been widely recognized as such. Today, however, as has been mentioned earlier, there is still a strong tendency not to confront directly, and not to ponder the full implications of, the political dimension of human existence. Confronted with the threat from totalitarian regimes, liberalism has, over the past half century, tended to eschew consideration of the necessities of politics and the state and to base itself—in line with Schmitt's critique—on the ethical and the economic. There are signs, too, that the 'pluralist' doctrines that Schmitt confronted are burgeoning once again. The huge vogue currently enjoyed by the doctrine of 'subsidiarity' is perhaps the best example.

It is in Schmitt's resistance to the persistent tendency to avert attention from the uncomfortable assumptions of man as a political animal, and in particular in his determination to cut his way beyond the moral or ethical to the distinctively political, without baulking at the consequences, that the lasting worth of his essay resides. Most would argue that there is surely more to the political than the concept expounded in the essay, but that is not really the point. Schmitt is essentially concerned with drawing a final line of distinction, not with making a complete map. The real question is whether the 'more' that is contained within the political is best or most logically and coherently approached and explained from the baseline defined in Schmitt's reasoning, or whether the fundamental relationships—the 'tension' and its precipitations—to which he draws attention can be adequately explained or deduced by reference to other, deeper presuppositions.

The originality of Schmitt's resolution of the political is that it culminates not in a single 'substance', such as 'freedom', but in two basic determinants of the human will—another being away from whom it moves (enemy) and another being towards whom it moves (friend), the two permanently implying one another. The negation or neutralization of enmity in certain areas, and the tempering of enmity in others, are possible and desirable, according to Schmitt's schema, but the complete eradication of enmity is not possible, and (the conclusion is inescapable) should not be sought for. What Schmitt calls the 'tension' of the political will be with us always, or at least for as long ahead as we can foresee, and we should act in clear-eyed understanding of this.

Bibliographical Note

There have been relatively few translations of Schmitt's works into English, but the number has increased recently. *The Concept of the Political* has been translated and edited by George Schwab (New Brunswick, NJ, 1976). This edition contains a useful translation of Leo Strauss's comments on the essay, which were originally published in 1932. Guy Oakes has translated Schmitt's *Political Romanticism* (Cambridge, Mass., 1985), Ellen Kennedy has translated Schmitt's *The Crisis of Parliamentary Democracy* (Cambridge, Mass., 1985), and George Schwab has translated Schmitt's *Political Theology: Four Chapters on the Concept of Sovereignty* (Cambridge, Mass., 1985, 1988).

Secondary works on Schmitt in English are also beginning to proliferate. Schwab's pioneering study *The Challenge of the Exception: An Introduction to the Political Ideas of Carl Schmitt between 1921 and 1936* (New York, 1970) was republished in 1989 with a new introduction. It contains extensive bibliographical information about works on and by Schmitt in German, English, and some other languages. Joseph W. Bendersky's biographical study *Carl Schmitt: Theorist for the Reich* (Princeton, 1983) provides an admirably thorough and balanced investigation of the 'Schmitt problem', though doubtless fresh historical evidence will surface as time passes.

In German, of course, there is a far richer literature, to which it is impossible to do justice here. A good introduction to the scope of contemporary discussion about Schmitt in Germany is provided by the volume edited by Helmut Quaritsch entitled *Complexio Oppositorum:*

Über Carl Schmitt (Berlin, 1988), which also contains a useful essay on 'The Concept of the Political' by Ernst-Wolfgang Böckenförde. An earlier two-volume collection of essays relating to Schmitt is entitled *Epirrhosis* and was edited by Hans Barion and others (Berlin, 1968). For those interested in intellectual affiliations, Helmut Rumpf's *Carl Schmitt und Thomas Hobbes* (Berlin, 1972) may be recommended.

5

Michael Oakeshott: *Rationalism in Politics*

BRUCE HADDOCK

OAKESHOTT has always been regarded as an arresting and original thinker. He has tended to chart his own course, in apparent disregard of, or opposition to, the theoretical concerns which have principally occupied his contemporaries. His first book, for example, *Experience and its Modes* (1933), was cast in an idealist philosophical idiom which had long been unfashionable.[1] To unsympathetic critics Oakeshott seemed simply to have restated Bradley's position, without troubling to respond to the criticisms levelled against idealism in the 1920s. His distinctive contribution to political philosophy began to emerge slowly and obliquely in the 1930s. A series of essays and reviews on Hobbes culminated in a definitive edition of *Leviathan* in 1946.[2] A studied rejection of the ideological style of modern politics was evident in his collection *The Social and Political Doctrines of Contemporary Europe* (1939), and in essays published in the 1940s and 1950s which would later be brought together in *Rationalism in Politics and Other Essays* (1962).[3] By then it was clear that Oakeshott could not be dismissed as an unfashionable eccentric. His rejection of the dominant trends in political thought was the product of a considered view of knowledge and practice. He had sought to understand political and moral conduct not in relation to contested preferences but in terms of a certain conception of action and its necessary limitations. This set him apart from both

---

[1] Michael Oakeshott, *Experience and its Modes* (Cambridge, 1933).

[2] See the items on Hobbes listed in John Liddington, 'Bibliography', in Jesse Norman (ed.), *The Achievement of Michael Oakeshott* (London, 1993), 107–43; and, in particular, Michael Oakeshott (ed.), *Hobbes's Leviathan* (Oxford, 1946).

[3] Michael Oakeshott (ed.), *The Social and Political Doctrines of Contemporary Europe* (Cambridge, 1939), and Michael Oakeshott, *Rationalism in Politics and Other Essays* (London, 1962). A considerably enlarged edition of *Rationalism in Politics and Other Essays* has recently been issued (Timothy Fuller, ed., Indianapolis, 1991). References in the text, however, are to the first edition of 1962.

ideologically committed political theory and the emotivism and utilitarianism which dominated academic discussions of political philosophy. It was a view based upon a close reading of the classic tradition in political philosophy. And, with the publication of *On Human Conduct* (1975) and *On History and Other Essays* (1983), it became clear that Oakeshott could be classed in the small band of twentieth-century political philosophers whose work could properly be accorded classic status.[4]

The choice of *Rationalism in Politics and Other Essays* as the focus for this essay requires some comment. The book is a collection of ten essays written between 1947 and 1961 which Oakeshott claims 'do not compose a settled doctrine' (preface). He sees them rather as displaying 'a consistent style or disposition of thought' with a common focus on 'understanding and explaining' (preface). They range in scope from discussions of the broad sweep of modern intellectual history, through considerations of forms of knowledge and experience, to (what appear to be) polemical contributions to debates regarding economic and educational policy. The book is far more, however, than a collection of occasional writings. The denial that the essays compose a 'settled doctrine' is itself a comment on the limits of philosophy. As philosophers we can gain an understanding of what it means to engage in various sorts of activity (politics, history, cooking, and so on) without having any ground for recommending that specific activities should be conducted in a particular way. Political philosophy, in other words, cannot be translated into political policy, any more than philosophy of history can tell us what actually happened, or linguistics can help us to write poetry. When we come across 'settled doctrines' in political philosophy, it is very often the mark of a failure to observe a proper distinction between philosophical reflection and specific practical activities. That there is something philosophically significant about the fact that human beings do things self-consciously is one thing; what they do is quite another.

Some of the conceptual problems which confront us as political philosophers might very well arise as a result of a

<hr>

[4] Michael Oakeshott, *On Human Conduct* (Oxford, 1975), and Michael Oakeshott, *On History and Other Essays* (Oxford, 1983).

failure to sustain certain distinctions in our practical affairs. If we are unclear about the nature of the state, for example, we might be tempted to see the activity of governing as similar in kind to managing a competitive enterprise. Our concern as philosophers, however, is not to resolve the practical dilemmas which bedevil us every day of our lives but rather to clarify the formal conceptual confusions which prevent us from thinking clearly about ourselves. We are concerned, in other words, with the nature of human activity, and the relation of various activities (including moral and political activity) to one another, rather than with specific engagements and skills.

What makes *Rationalism in Politics and Other Essays* a classic of political philosophy is its studied relation of moral and political experience to a wider conception of human experience as a whole. Apparent lack of systematic connection between the essays should be seen as an indication not of carelessness but of a sceptical view of practical experience. How we conceive of things at the most basic level, respond to circumstances, interact with one another, pursue ends, order our lives, and so on are seen by Oakeshott as related dimensions of practical experience. But it would not be appropriate to construe that experience in deductive or overly schematic form. Practical life takes many and varied forms, each a product of traditions of conduct, standards, and institutions which constitute a way of life. To focus on one practice as the ideal form for all others, or one society as the ideal model for all others, is thus to distort a necessarily variegated dimension of experience. The fact that a great many political philosophers of the first rank have made this mistake does not make it less of a mistake. But it should put us on our guard against treating 'system' and 'rigour' as synonyms.

Whether or not *Rationalism in Politics and Other Essays* should be regarded as Oakeshott's masterpiece is much disputed. *On Human Conduct*, for example, is often seen as the culmination of his life's work.[5] But this is not a formal treatise, but another series of connected essays in which Oakeshott's concern is to tie together a number of themes about understanding, practical

---

[5] See e.g. Paul Franco, *The Political Philosophy of Michael Oakeshott* (New Haven, 1990), 8.

judgement, and association that were largely implicit in *Rationalism in Politics and Other Essays*. It was nevertheless the earlier book which constituted an indispensable point of reference for a generation of political philosophers at a time when political philosophy in the classic style was treated with deep suspicion. The range of the essays, together with their accessibility, still makes the volume the best introduction to Oakeshott's political thought, though it would be wrong to regard any single statement of his view as definitive. What we gain from Oakeshott is not so much a definitive position as an invitation to conduct political philosophy in a certain fashion. As we read Oakeshott we find ourselves drawn into a philosophical conversation. It is surely the mark of a philosophical classic that this should be so.

Philosophy, Knowledge, and Practice

When Oakeshott distinguishes a philosophical from a practical view of politics, he is aware that he is insisting on a distinction which was not always observed in the classic texts of political philosophy. Order, liberty, equality, or whatever value would be variously stressed in the classic texts as the keys to human well-being and fulfilment. Philosophers advancing arguments in defence of these values were aware that they were contributing to practical political debates. It is often supposed, indeed, that the defence of particular values rather than others is what distinguishes normative political philosophy in the classic tradition from modern analytical political philosophy. In Oakeshott's view, however, it is not the normative stance which philosophers happened to adopt which interests us but the cogency of their arguments. A classic text will look at political life in relation to what human beings can possibly know or do, and not in relation to what they happen to know or do. It is the argument back to basic presuppositions rather than towards specific goals which properly distinguishes the work of the philosopher.

The initial interpretative problem confronting us in *Rationalism in Politics and Other Essays* is complicated because Oakeshott presupposes rather than defends the sophisticated view of knowledge and experience he had elaborated in *Experience and Its*

Modes. The crucial point to recall from his earlier statement is that he insists on treating knowledge as a *factum* rather than a *datum*. Our knowledge is an achievement based upon assumptions we make. These assumptions will differ in our various fields of enquiry. In *Experience and its Modes* Oakeshott distinguished, in particular, history, science, and practice from one another. In history we presuppose a world of discrete events which are alleged to have taken place in a past we can no longer directly examine; in science a world of mechanical quantitative relations between entities which we can neither see nor touch; in practice a world of given social relations which we are ceaselessly (but necessarily unsatisfactorily) trying to transform into something better. In none of these fields can it be claimed that what we are said to know corresponds with a world out there (in the past, in the natural environment, enshrined in tablets of stone). What we know, instead, must be seen as a product of the world of ideas in which we are working. The assumptions we make furnish us with more or less plausible (but contestable) judgements. Truth is a function of the coherence of a given world of ideas. A world of ideas will change, of course, as new arguments are advanced. But it is never possible to leap outside a world of ideas in order to assess its overall adequacy against an external standard. The reservations we have about a world of ideas are themselves a consequence of the contradictions and fissures within it. Our intellectual endeavours are bent on making a given world of ideas more coherent. Coherence is the only criterion of truth we have.

Knowledge in specialized fields is thus conditional upon specific constitutive assumptions. A crucial implication which Oakeshott insists upon in *Experience and its Modes* and further develops in *Rationalism in Politics and Other Essays* is that constructive dialogue between distinct modes of knowledge is impossible. A mode of discourse operates within designated conceptual parameters. To attempt to cross constitutive conceptual boundaries is to lapse into irrelevance or absurdity. The divisions between modes of discourse or experience are in fact sharper than the divisions between natural languages. For, while we can make reasonable translations from French into Italian, we cannot intelligibly 'translate' knowledge couched in one idiom into knowledge couched in another. The scientist cannot learn from the historian, nor the politician from either. The modes of science, history, and practice are categorially distinct. Only philosophy is exempt from these modal limitations because it is occupied not with a world of substantive facts, events, or desires but with the conditions of intelligibility which make any kind of discourse possible. All other modes of discourse are committed to a species of conceptual limitation in order to function.

Oakeshott refines his conception of modes of experience in important ways in *Rationalism in Politics and Other Essays*. In 'The Activity of Being an Historian' (pp. 137–67) he pays much closer attention to the actual practice of history than he had in *Experience and its Modes*. His principal concern is to show that it is not the object of historical enquiry (the past) but the manner in which that enquiry is conducted which constitutes the character of history as a discipline. In a literal sense the past itself cannot be an object of enquiry at all since all we have before us is a world of present evidence from which we can make various kinds of inference. We may be interested in the past in so far as it facilitates our practical interests, helps us to justify our political, moral, or religious points of view, or in a more general sense simply makes us more contented with ourselves. There is nothing intrinsically wrong with an interest in the past motivated by practical concerns; but it is not history.

Nor is the attempt to render the past in the idiom of science compatible with the specific criteria of historical discourse. The report of a scientific experiment purports to portray something that actually happened but it could not be mistaken for a historical narrative. It is equally misleading for a historian to treat types of event in terms of necessary and sufficient conditions or individual events as exemplifications of general laws. The 'facts' in scientific theory are not actual but hypothetical. They are meaningless outside specific theoretical parameters. And the historian is interested not in types but in individuals.

Nor (finally) is a 'contemplative' attitude to the past compatible with historical criteria, where more or less plausible situations and circumstances which might resemble actual occasions are conjured up as possible contexts for imaginary happenings. The Napoleon depicted by Tolstoy in *War and Peace* should not be checked for accuracy against the historical record, any more than Prospero should be seen as an actual Renaissance magus. Historians and 'historical' novelists ask different questions of their material and order their narratives in quite different ways, even if their work happens to be informed by the same reading and might (at least notionally) respect similar chronological conventions.

What, then, distinguishes a purely historical approach to the past? In the first place, the past must be seen not in relation to 'a subsequent or present condition of things' but as a whole in which 'everything that the evidence reveals or points to is recognized to have its place; nothing is excluded, nothing is regarded as non-contributory' (p. 154). The detached attitude of the historian might seem to resemble that of the scientist, but the affinity is deceptive and largely misleading. The historian is not interested in generalized statements but instead seeks to set 'before us the events (in so far as they can be ascertained) which mediate one circumstance to another' (p. 157). His goal is a complete account of change 'in which contingencies are intelligible, not because they have been resolved, but on account of the circumstantial relations which have been established between them' (pp. 166–7). The narrative structure of historical discourse is thus a constitutive feature of history as a mode of knowledge. The proper historical response to a puzzle within a narrative is always to search for further detail rather than to have recourse to the illusory security of generalized statements. Most important of all, however, the historical past is a construction of the historian. He is not discovering or 're-enacting the past' but literally creating it (p. 164). All we ever have at our disposal as historians is evidence which enables us to draw certain inferences. Not all statements about the past are historical. Oakeshott's concern is to highlight the special characteristics of specifically historical inferences.

Oakeshott's conception of philosophy should be clear from 'The Activity of being an Historian'. He had set himself the task of dispelling the confusions which flowed directly from failure to observe the proper criterial distinctions between the various modes of experience. Science and practice posed the principal threats to a clear designation of history as a discipline, though the contemplative or purely aesthetic portrayal of the past was presented as no less corruptive of a purely historical disposition.

The introduction of a separate 'contemplative' mode was itself an innovation in *Rationalism in Politics and Other Essays*. In the preface Oakeshott describes 'The Voice of Poetry in the Conversation of Mankind' (pp. 197–247) as 'a belated retraction of a foolish sentence in *Experience and its Modes*'. In *Experience and its Modes* he had described art, music, and poetry as 'wholly taken up with practical life'.[6] In 'The Voice of Poetry in the Conversation of Mankind', on the other hand, he maintains that the poetic or artistic idiom is typified in pure delight or contemplation of an object, image, or artefact, where all utilitarian considerations are set aside and we gain momentary release from the daily burden of wanting, doing, and thinking. The point to focus upon in this context is Oakeshott's insistence upon the manifold nature of the reality we create for ourselves. Here as elsewhere he rejects any view which would 'impose a single character upon significant human speech' (p. 197). What the world amounts to for us is a function not of the passive impression of its objective qualities but of our variously modulated intellectual, practical, and aesthetic endeavours. Nor is there any limit (in principle) to the guises we might devise in order to enrich our experience.

Politics and Experience

Where, then, does political conduct fit in this elaborate conception of experience? Most of the essays in *Rationalism in Politics and Other Essays* focus on this issue in one form or another. Characteristically, however, they are not principally first-order contributions to political debate but rather second-order discussions of how political conduct should properly be understood. It is true, of course, as many critics have pointed out, that second-order positions might appear to have controversial first-order implications. But the purpose of clarifying conceptual confusion at the second-order level is not to make a first-order point. Oakeshott's own position on this hotly contested

---

[6] Oakeshott, *Experience and its Modes*, 297.

issue is unambiguous. We all have political opinions and may well be disposed to persuade others of the rectitude of our views. Yet practical persuasion of this kind is not philosophy, no matter how sophisticated we might take ourselves to be at marshalling arguments. What we want as practical agents should not be confused with the wider philosophical problem of characterizing practical life.

Politics as an activity is thus an integral part of the practical realm. Yet political discourse always has a tendency to overreach itself. We are tempted to present what is good for ourselves as good for others. The need to secure the cooperation of others if we are to attain our own ends encourages us to present the things we happen to want as somehow objectively desirable. For the most part, we are entirely innocent when we deceive ourselves in these ways. Philosophers themselves have sometimes succumbed to the false allure of their own pet projects, defending their idiosyncratic conceptions of fulfilment as necessary conditions for human well-being. It may be, indeed, that the temptation to political and moral overstatement is irresistible to us. But it remains a philosophical error. The challenge of political philosophy for Oakeshott is precisely to disentangle the confusion of idioms which we have habitually employed in considering our practical affairs. If a principal task of philosophy is to establish appropriate criteria of intelligibility in the various modes of experience, the practical mode has consistently proved to be the most difficult to contain within its designated sphere. History, science, and the arts have often been misleadingly justified in practical terms. More fundamentally still, argues Oakeshott, the way we live and regard ourselves has been distorted by a failure to recognize the conceptual limits of practical life.

Oakeshott invites us to consider, for example, our understanding of 'rational conduct' (pp. 80–110). To act rationally, we might assume, would be to set aside habit, custom, or prejudice and to regulate our conduct solely in terms of the goals we had determined for ourselves. A basic presupposition of rationality, in this scheme of things, is that our goals can be separated analytically from the activities we happen to be engaged in. But when we begin to reflect intelligently on our various pursuits, it is with a mind already informed by the practices and procedures which constitute those pursuits. We know what we mean, as batsmen, when we say we have given away our wicket playing a foolish stroke. Selecting the appropriate stroke to play, however, is a matter not of 'rational' calculation but of fine judgement, taking into account the state of the game and the pitch, one's own form and that of the bowler, and a host of other factors. It is a judgement specifically informed by experience. So it is with all our practical activities. We cannot think 'rationally' about cricket, chess, cooking, carpentry, politics, and so on unless we already know something about them. We may be casually inducted into these pursuits in the first instance. Yet it would be unwise to ask our advice until we had gained some 'know-how'. To treat a condition of pure innocence, where all acquired knowledge is discounted, as a paradigm case of rational reflection is pure folly.

Lurking behind the error, in this case, is a widely held but wholly misleading conception of mind. The mind is not an entity which subsequently acquires 'beliefs, knowledge, prejudices' (p. 89). The mind is what it does. It is inseparable from the judgements we make in the course of thinking and doing. It is not 'an apparatus for thinking' but is thought itself (p. 90). It follows that we cannot step outside our thought in order to check its rationality. Whatever we think and do is informed by specific assumptions. These can be reviewed as we develop a more sophisticated awareness of what we are doing. But it makes no sense to seek an independent rational standard for conduct as such. We may be said to act rationally when our conduct 'exhibits the sort of intelligence appropriate to the idiom of activity concerned' (p. 110).

The implications of this position for our understanding of political and moral discourse are far-reaching and radically subversive. Oakeshott argues that, at least since the Renaissance, respect for practical judgement has tended to be undermined by an obsession with technique ('Rationalism in Politics', pp. 1–36). Practical judgement is refined in the course of our experience of various arts, crafts, and pursuits. It may be passed on in some measure by a master to his apprentice or by a supervisor to his research student. But it 'cannot be formulated in rules' or committed in preceptive form to a textbook (p. 8).

Technical knowledge, on the other hand, 'is susceptible of formulation in rules, principles, directions, maxims' (p. 10). It 'can be both taught and learned in the simplest meanings of these words' (p. 11). What cannot be taught and learned, however, is the judgement required in order to put our technical skills into practice. We cannot learn to cook from a cookery book nor to drive from close study of the Highway Code. Books of this kind may be extremely useful to us once we know something about cooking and driving. But we need to be shown how to do these things in the first instance and subsequently improve upon our initial incompetence only with practice.

Why should practical knowledge have been so undervalued in modern times? To answer this question properly would require an elaborate excursion into intellectual and cultural history. In 'Rationalism in Politics' Oakeshott offers no more than a tantalizing abridgement of a highly contentious position. He argues that Western culture in the last 400 years has become afflicted by a kind of collective impatience. We crave to better ourselves and to better ourselves in a hurry. We no longer have the time to devote to the acquisition of specialized skills and instead seek short cuts in technical manuals of one kind or another. Above all we need to be assured that forced instruction will fit us for our tasks once and for all. What cannot be learned quickly is dismissed as an irrelevance. If judgement is set aside, all we have left to rely upon is technical certainty.

The quest for certainty has a distinguished intellectual pedigree. Oakeshott focuses on Bacon and Descartes as 'the dominating figures in the early history' of the rationalist project (p. 14). Bacon argued that certain and demonstrable knowledge could be attained only if steps were taken to remedy the deficiencies of 'natural' reason. What was needed was a method of enquiry which could be specified in a set of rules and learned and applied mechanically. Received knowledge and scientific practice were to be ignored. Reliance was to be placed instead on method, applicable indifferently by anyone to anything.

In Oakeshott's interpretation, Bacon's *Novum organum* is a technical manual for the scientifically illiterate. The point to stress is that scientific illiteracy is regarded as an advantage rather than a hindrance to research and enquiry. In this rationalist scheme of things, sound method is the necessary corrective to our intellectual idiosyncrasies. Truth and certainty cannot be dependent upon individual caprice.

The argument was extended and elaborated in more systematic logical form in Descartes's *Discourse on Method*. Descartes contended that whatever could not be known with certainty should be dismissed as error. And since we know that the evidence of our senses can always deceive us, it followed that we should seek a foundation for truth elsewhere. Descartes's preferred method was to doubt systematically everything that could possibly be doubted. But we could not doubt the fact that we existed without lapsing into absurdity. From this simple and self-evident truth (*cogito ergo sum*) Descartes held that he could deduce other more complex truths in a chain of argument which would follow tight procedural rules. As with Bacon, it is strict adherence to method which guarantees truth, not experience or expertise.

Neither Bacon nor Descartes made a significant contribution to political thought in the narrow sense. Oakeshott argues, however, that the attitude of mind which is so clearly articulated in their works has informed political thought and practice with disastrous effect. Politics in the rationalist idiom is always 'a matter of solving problems', of applying 'reason' to politics in much the same way as an engineer would tackle the business of construction and repair (p. 4). Just as the technical skills of the engineer are held to be universal in scope and application, so too the 'politician' who knows his business will be able to apply his instrumental criteria in any circumstance or situation. He will rely not upon received political wisdom ('prejudice') but the most up-to-date technical manual ('science'). On closer inspection, however, it will be evident that the rationalist politician understands neither politics nor science. His basic conception of what it means to engage in any sort of practice is so wide of the mark that anything that has been accomplished is bound to appear unsatisfactory to him. He cannot accept accommodation and compromise because what he seeks is perfection. Yet even to envisage perfection in his terms is to conceive of human life completely other than it is.

The rationalist analysis of politics is thus untenable in theory and unrealizable in practice. Yet its hold on modern discourse and practice has been almost complete. It is manifested most obviously in the predilection for abstract formulations of political doctrines and programmes. A political party or movement without its ideology is now considered to be lamentably ill-equipped for the cut and thrust of argument and debate on a public stage. The 'politics of the book' has replaced the kind of practical understanding and discrimination which was once entrenched in an older (and narrower) political class (p. 22).

What the 'book' offers in a modern context is clear. New classes have risen to power and influence without the benefit of a traditional political education, addressing an enlarged citizenry whose ignorance is even more complete. In these circumstances both rulers and citizens desperately need 'a crib, a political doctrine, to take the place of a habit of political behaviour' (p. 25). Some of the best political 'cribs' have been written by thinkers of genuine distinction (Machiavelli, Locke, Mill, Marx) who have managed to abridge complex traditions of political conduct in pocket-size form. But the flexibility of a living tradition is lost in the very best abridgements; and in the worst, political argument gives place to the raucous exchange of slogans.

In Oakeshott's view, then, the intrusion of a rationalist frame of mind has seriously corrupted political thought and practice. Yet the damage wrought by rationalism extends far beyond the conduct of public affairs. What we are dealing with is 'an identifiable error, a misconception with regard to the nature of human knowledge, which amounts to a corruption of the mind' (p. 31). And because it is the mind itself which has been corrupted, it is difficult to see how we might best take stock of our situation and remedy our shortcomings. Following rationalist precepts in all walks of life ('living by the book') leads 'not only to specific mistakes, but . . . also dries up the mind itself', generating an 'intellectual dishonesty' which renders intellectual effort to improve affairs more dangerous than the malaise itself (p. 31). The rationalist is a liability not only because his projects are ill-advised but because he fails to recognize what he is doing. He cannot accept that all practices are rooted in traditional modes of conduct. If he sees a problem, he seeks always to wipe the slate clean and to start again. Yet

the supposition that we can simply 'start again' is the root of
our difficulties.

What makes rationalism so difficult to counter in practical
life is its insistence that premeditation and planning is always
to be preferred to habit and custom. We pride ourselves on
our self-consciousness, our restless pursuit of improvement or
even perfection. We regard it as a mark of intellectual sloth or
worse if we rest content with time-honoured patterns of conduct. Not to be aware of alternatives in our moral life, to
renounce choice and deliberation, is to lead a stunted existence, appropriate perhaps for children or primitive peoples but
quite out of place in the dynamic world we have fashioned for
ourselves.

All this, argues Oakeshott, is an error, a *folie de grandeur*, of
which we had been warned in one of the great foundational
myths of our civilization ('The Tower of Babel', pp. 59–79).
To pursue perfection, each in our own way, is to condemn
ourselves to 'a chaos of conflicting ideals, the disruption of a
common life' (p. 59). Moral life always involves choice of a
kind, for it only arises in situations where we are freed from
natural necessity. But it does not follow that alternative courses
of action should always be consciously before our minds or
that we should act in certain ways only if we can give ourselves good reasons. A preoccupation with moral justification
in fact casts us off from one possible form of the moral life,
where conduct is governed by 'a habit of affection and behaviour' rather than 'a habit of reflective thought' (p. 61). We
cannot accept a settled mode of life because we see moral
conduct as 'the reflective application of a moral criterion',
either in 'the self-conscious pursuit of moral ideals' or 'as the
reflective observance of moral rules' (p. 66). In this scheme of
things, the self-conscious formulation of abstract principles or
ideals is a prerequisite for conduct. Principles and ideals, however, have to be balanced against one another before they can
be put into practice. As sophisticated moral agents, we know
that principles and ideals can clash. Even if we are confident
that we can defend a particular moral stance in theoretical
terms, we are still left with the problem of responding to
infinitely variable circumstances. We end up in the lamentable
position of knowing what to think but not what to do.

It may be that the 'ideal' form of the moral life would

amount to a synthesis of habitual and reflective modes of conduct. For historical reasons, argues Oakeshott, the reflective mode has tended to predominate in the Western tradition. The pattern was set in the Graeco-Roman world, where 'old habits of moral behaviour had lost their vitality' and were replaced by an 'intense moral self-consciousness', in which 'intellectual energy' was 'directed towards the determination of an ideal' and 'moral energy towards the translation of that ideal into practice' (p. 76). The predominance of reflection was confirmed in the early history of Christianity, where the community of faith of the first Christians gave place by the third century to the more familiar Graeco-Roman form of 'the self-conscious pursuit of moral ideals', with an abstract catalogue of 'virtues and vices' and stress on the 'translation of ideals into actions' (p. 77). Oakeshott does not suggest that the rationalistic ethos of Graeco-Roman and Christian morality could necessarily have been avoided. But he insists that it remains a mistake. He describes it as 'an unhappy form of morality, prone to obsession and at war with itself' and, as such, 'a misfortune to be deplored' (p. 78). He is aware that we cannot return to a more 'habitual' style of moral conduct simply because we have grasped the implications of a particular moral philosophy. What philosophy can do, however, 'is to disclose the corrupt consciousness, the self-deception which reconciles us to our misfortune' (p. 79). Whether or not we make any practical sense of that philosophic awareness is quite another matter.

Oakeshott's view, then, is that all conduct is in an important sense tradition-bound. This does not mean that we must simply accept the patterns of conduct we happen to have inherited. Traditions are not static; and even a veneration for the past contains within it intimations of how we should respond to the vagaries of circumstance. A tradition 'is neither fixed nor finished; it has no changeless centre to which understanding can anchor itself; there is no sovereign purpose to be perceived or invariable direction to be detected; there is no model to be copied, idea to be realized, or rule to be followed' (p. 128). But there is 'a principle of continuity', with authority 'diffused between past, present, and future; between the old, the new, and what is to come' (p. 128). Even as we strive to chart new directions we are enmeshed in a complex web of practices and attitudes which both constrain and facilitate our dealings with one another.

Politics so conceived will clearly not be understood through exclusive focus on the abridgements ('ideologies') which have been devised to simplify the intricacies of affairs. But neither will we gain enlightenment through consideration only of the ends agents happen to pursue. Our passing desires may well be infinite and random. As soon as we start pursuing specific goals, however, we find ourselves involved in relationships with others. We are committed to doing things in particular ways. When we speak of politics we have in mind a more or less consistent style of conduct informed by identifiable assumptions. Our concern is to grasp the nuances of a style as it develops through time and the wider implications of the assumptions which inform it.

The Limits of Political Understanding

The study of politics thus involves a variety of academic skills. In 'Political Education' (pp. 111–36) and 'The Study of Politics in a University' (pp. 301–33) Oakeshott distinguishes history and philosophy as the disciplines best suited to make politics as an activity intelligible. Both disciplines must be understood, however, in the special senses Oakeshott develops throughout *Rationalism in Politics and Other Essays* and elsewhere. They must be seen as languages or idioms which confer specific sorts of intelligibility on an otherwise mysterious subject-matter. Neither is concerned to contribute directly to the resolution of practical political problems, though it may be that thinking clearly about ourselves and knowing something in detail about a tradition of conduct will save us from the grossest folly. Philosophical and historical acumen do not guarantee political success. What they provide is intellectual discipline (exemplified magisterially in Oakeshott's classic study of Hobbes, pp. 248–300). And intellectual discipline is to be valued not as a means towards a richer and more fulfilled life but as an integral part of that life.

Underpinning Oakeshott's conception of political thought and practice is a deep theoretical scepticism. We rely on traditions of conduct not because they are the best we can conceive of but because they serve our purposes. There can be no theoretical resolution of the many conflicting ends we happen to desire. In this respect Oakeshott's position might be described as Hobbesian. But whereas Hobbes, writing with the dire consequences of civil war before him, sought a practical remedy to our (inevitable) failure to agree in a *Leviathan* blessed with overbearing power, Oakeshott, with twentieth-century totalitarianism before him, stressed instead the maximum diffusion of power through the various institutions and practices of a society. Given that we cannot settle our moral and political differences theoretically, it follows that we should allow one another the greatest possible discretion compatible with security and order. Oakeshott sees government through the rule of law as the best means of guaranteeing freedom of choice.

It is the method of government most economical in the use of power; it involves a partnership between past and present and between governors and governed which leaves no room for arbitrariness; it encourages a tradition of resistance to the growth of dangerous concentrations of power which is far more effective than any promiscuous onslaught however crushing; it controls effectively, but without breaking the grand affirmative flow of things; and it gives a practical definition of the kind of limited but necessary service a society may expect from its government, restraining us from vain and dangerous expectations. (p. 43)

Above all, the rule of law embodies the philosophical truth that we cannot envisage definitive answers to certain questions. We may (or may not) want one thing or another. Moral choices, in particular, cannot be made for us because there are no clinching theoretical grounds for preferring one way of life to another. The best that we can hope for is that our way of life might enable us to make these choices for ourselves.[7]

The rule of law, certainly, is not a sufficient guarantee of our liberties. In 'The Political Economy of Freedom' (pp. 37–58)

---

[7] Oakeshott develops the point more systematically in *On Human Conduct*, 108–84. He distinguishes between 'civil association', where human relationship is viewed 'in terms of the (formal) considerations which compose a practice', and 'enterprise association', where relationship is 'concerned with the satisfaction of chosen wants and from which an agent may extricate himself by a choice of his own' (p. 121). See also Michael Oakeshott, 'The Rule of Law', in his *On History and Other Essays*, 119–64.

Oakeshott stresses, in addition, freedom of association and the right to own private property. These rights enable economic decision-making to be diffused throughout society. The only relevant consideration in establishing a set of economic arrangements is how people can best be provided with the things they happen to want. His point is not simply that a competitive economy is the most efficient means of satisfying needs but that it constitutes an effective bulwark against excessive concentrations of power. Like his mentor, Hobbes, his concern is to establish minimum conditions of civil association. Our freedom can only be maintained if our diverse dealings with one another are channelled through the rule of law, where there is 'one law for the lion and the ox' and both 'have known and adequate motives for obeying it' (p. 293). That 'ideal' arrangement will be threatened whenever concentrations of economic power (monopolies of either capital or labour) effectively deprive us of practical options. What we make of our freedom, however, is another matter entirely.

In the last resort, we cannot rely on the state to provide the good life for us. Groups of people whom chance or choice have brought together cannot be assumed to share a common vision or to be inspired by the same ideals. Reflecting on their predicament, however, they might be expected to subscribe to certain procedural rules and practices in their pursuit of public business. To expect more in the way of a public commitment to substantive goals would inevitably leave those with other priorities in a position of abject subordination. Full membership of the community would effectively be identified with certain values rather than others, undervaluing the loyalty of people whose commitment to procedural rules and practices was otherwise impeccable. Even the best intentioned of governments would in these circumstances come to resemble a gentle tyranny, extolling a particular and exclusive way of life as a necessary condition for the good life as such.

These difficulties are only resolved, in Oakeshott's view, if the office of government is restricted to the maintenance of minimum conditions of civil association. In the broadest sense it might be described as a 'conservative' conception of government ('On being Conservative', pp. 168–96), though it should not be identified with the substantive goals which conservatives themselves sometimes uphold. It is an acceptance that the politics of mutual accommodation is the best that can be hoped for in the diverse circumstances we happen to find ourselves in. While restraint and detachment are called for in respect of government, energy and initiative are allowed to flourish in other spheres. When we think about our politics in the widest sense, it should be in terms of the very many satisfactions we are able to attain in our various capacities. But politics in itself will not transform our satisfactions into something altogether more delightful. At best it will enable us to carry on more or less as we are; at worst it will be a distraction.

Conclusion

What makes Oakeshott's view compelling is not the practical stance he adopts but the idea of agency which underpins it. In common with the classic texts of the Western philosophical tradition, he focuses on a conception of practical knowledge and its implications for action and self-understanding. Whether or not we happen to be attached to particular traditions, he asks us to envisage what we might find ourselves committed to if we denied the proposition that all action is in some sense traditional. Conduct divorced from tradition turns out, on inspection, to be not simply undesirable but untenable. Traditions, however, do not compel us to pursue specific ends but to go about our business in a particular fashion. No amount of philosophical reflection will tell us what we should do in determinate circumstances. Yet it can forewarn us that some of the ideas we entertain are foolish and dangerous.

This certainly accords a more limited role to political philosophy than was once the fashion. It should not be confused, however, with the relativistic position which is endorsed by modern communitarians.[8] In arguing that conceptions of practice are implicit within traditions, Oakeshott is not committed to the view that acceptance of any tradition can confer authority upon a practice. We cannot understand our practical lives outside traditions of conduct; but it does not follow that all

---

[8] See Alasdair MacIntyre, *Whose Justice? Which Rationality?* (London, 1988), and Michael Sandel, *Liberalism and the Limits of Justice* (Cambridge, 1982).

traditions of conduct are equally valid. Oakeshott's starting-point is not necessarily the arbitrary traditions we happen to have grown up with. He recognizes (with modern anti-foundationalists) that our practical judgements cannot be supported by an abstract deontological criterion.[9] Traditions, however, are not incommensurable. They contain within themselves different possibilities for conduct and achievement.

In seeking to provide definitive answers to practical dilemmas, some traditions will irredeemably stunt prospects for human well-being and fulfilment. Oakeshott, like so many of his generation, was haunted by the impact of the different versions of collectivist politics which had dominated the twentieth century. Yet he could not rest content with a straightforward reassertion of the priority of the individual over the community. He saw individuality as a specifically social product. But it would not flourish in any and every community. In focusing on human beings as the creators of meanings and values, he is clear that he is validating certain sorts of communities and not others. This is precisely the function that the classic texts had always performed within the Western tradition. If Oakeshott holds a sceptical view of the role of political philosophy, it is nevertheless a view rooted within the classical canon.

Rationalism in Politics and Other Essays is a sustained polemic against some of the leading philosophical, political, and moral misconceptions of the twentieth century. It is a vigorous contribution to the perennial debate about how we should see ourselves. If it does not offer a practical panacea, it at least frees us from conceptual confusion. And in thinking clearly about ourselves, we are thereby enabled to lead the best possible life in the only conceivable world.

Bibliographical Note

Quotation in the text is to the original edition (London, 1962) of *Rationalism in Politics and Other Essays*. The recently issued enlarged edition (Timothy Fuller (ed.), Indianapolis, 1991) contains interesting additional material. It reflects the recent revival of interest in Oakeshott. In

[9] See Richard Rorty, *Contingency, Irony and Solidarity* (Cambridge, 1989).

the context of the development of political thought in recent times, however, the 1962 edition constitutes a distinctive philosophical landmark.

Oakeshott's other work should not be neglected by the serious student. *Experience and its Modes* (Cambridge, 1933) remains indispensable for the philosophical foundation which underpinned Oakeshott's position throughout his career. *On Human Conduct* (Oxford, 1975) is an important restatement and development of some of the political and philosophical implications of *Rationalism in Politics and Other Essays*. The view of history and the rule of law is further refined in *On History and Other Essays* (Oxford, 1983). Important earlier essays which bear directly on the themes of *Rationalism in Politics and Other Essays* are now available in Timothy Fuller (ed.), *Religion, Politics and the Moral Life* (New Haven, 1993). Oakeshott's 1958 Harvard lectures, now available in Shirley Letwin (ed.), *Morality and Politics in Modern Europe* (New Haven, 1993), give an insight into the thinking that led from *Rationalism in Politics and Other Essays* to *On Human Conduct*. Oakeshott's writings on education are available in Timothy Fuller (ed.), *The Voice of Liberal Learning: Michael Oakeshott on Education* (New Haven, 1989).

The most comprehensive study of Oakeshott is Paul Franco, *The Political Philosophy of Michael Oakeshott* (New Haven, 1990). The gamut of Oakeshott's thought is covered more briefly in Robert Grant, *Oakeshott* (London, 1990). W. H. Greenleaf, *Oakeshott's Philosophical Politics* (London, 1966), is especially good on *Rationalism in Politics and Other Essays*. A collection of commemorations of Oakeshott is available in Jesse Norman (ed.), *The Achievement of Michael Oakeshott* (London, 1993), which contains a comprehensive bibliography by John Liddington. See also David Boucher, 'Politics in a Different Mode: An Appreciation of Michael Oakeshott 1901–1990', *History of Political Thought*, 12 (1991), 717–28. John Gray, 'Oakeshott on Law, Liberty and Civil Association', in his *Liberalisms: Essays in Political Philosophy* (London, 1989), 199–216, and 'Oakeshott as a Liberal', in his *Post-liberalism: Studies in Political Thought* (London, 1993), 40–6, seeks to incorporate Oakeshott's thinking into contemporary debates in political theory. For Oakeshott's view of history, see David Boucher, 'The Creation of the Past: British Idealism and Michael Oakeshott's Philosophy of History', *History and Theory*, 23 (1984), 193–214, and W. H. Dray, 'Michael Oakeshott's Theory of History', in P. King and B. C. Parekh (eds.), *Politics and Experience* (Cambridge, 1968), 19–42. For Oakeshott's relationship with Collingwood, see David Boucher, 'Overlap and Autonomy: The Different Worlds of Collingwood and Oakeshott', *Storia*, 4 (1989), 69–89.

6

Isaiah Berlin: *Two Concepts of Liberty*

IAN HARRIS

TWO CONCEPTS OF LIBERTY, the inaugural lecture that Sir Isaiah Berlin gave as Chichele Professor of Social and Political Theory at Oxford in 1958, is a minor classic of contemporary thought. Its significance is that it encapsulates the liberal rejection of those doctrines, totalitarian or otherwise, which imply the oppression of the individual in the name of the communal good. It does so through its specific manner of interpreting how one concept of freedom in particular, including its metaphysical antecedents, has developed, and also through providing a contrary view of the nature of values.

It may be doubted whether a concise treatment of only one of Berlin's many essays provides quite the best way of approaching the intellectual virtuoso whom a distinguished, though not especially sympathetic, critic may have called 'the Paganini of Political Thought'.[1] A more expansive treatment, drawing freely from a wider range of materials, and treating them at length with a higher degree of reflective sophistication, would be more adequate to the author of *Two Concepts*. Yet if Bowra was wrong to suppose that Berlin 'like Our Lord and Socrates . . . does not publish much', he was right to add that 'he thinks and says a great deal and has had an enormous influence on our times',[2] and Berlin's significance provides an occasion for a brief statement of some of his key opinions.

---

[1] See George Feaver, 'The Enduring and Elusive Legacy of Michael Oakeshott', *Studies in Political Thought*, 1/1 (1992) 95–122, at 121 n. 51, for the differing versions of Oakeshott's remark.

[2] Quoted by Noel Annan, 'A Man I Loved', in Hugh Lloyd-Jones (ed.), *Maurice Bowra* (London, 1974), 53.

Some Origins of *Two Concepts of Liberty*

Berlin was young at a time when European history bore the impress of both nationalism and, perhaps more saliently, totalitarianism, and he enjoyed an intellectually productive middle age in the decades when the rejection of totalitarianism coloured the social and political thought of the West. He was born at Riga, then part of imperial Russia, on 6 June 1909, and lived in St Petersburg between 1915 and 1919. It is not surprising, born as he was into an educated family at a time when dramatic political change wore an ideological aspect, that he should develop a precocious sense of the place of ideas in political activity. For

> I sensed that there was some awareness among the older members of my family of political ideas as an important factor in human history . . . [so that] as a result of this sense of the circulation of political ideas, liberty, equality, liberalism, socialism had begun to mean something to me quite early in my life.[3]

This sense would be fed in his undergraduate years at Corpus Christi College, Oxford, reading Greats and PPE in an era before their syllabuses had become radically specialized.

It was a sense which Berlin's early experience did not fill out in a way favourable to the Soviet or Nazi regimes. During the Bolshevik Revolution Berlin encountered privation, and observed, though he did not experience, oppression: 'the terror was all round us but did not reach us,' he recollected.[4] He remembered also 'seeing a policeman being dragged off, pale and struggling, by a mob, obviously to his death', and noted that 'one or two people we had known were shot quite early in 1918. . . . There were a great many executions—there was a terror, nothing like what it grew to be in Stalin's reign, but still a good many people were shot.'[5] This experience seems not to have been contradicted by Berlin's time as an Oxford student, for he was a little too old—perhaps in maturity as well as years[6]—to have been overexposed to the left-wing

---

[3] Ramin Jahanbegloo, *Conversations with Isaiah Berlin* (London, 1992), 10.
[4] Ibid.   [5] Ibid. 4, 9.
[6] A. J. Ayer, *Part of my Life* (London, 1977), 126, commented that Berlin had 'greater intellectual maturity' than himself.

enthusiasms that characterized the 1930s. Election to All Souls as a prize fellow in 1932 translated him to a college which is not given to enthusiasm of any sort. He seemed to at least one contemporary, who was politically engaged, to be a detached figure, absorbed in musical appreciation.[7] Yet, if Berlin was not engaged in political activity, he did have a political disposition: for, as a Jew, and a Zionist from his days at St Paul's School,[8] he can have found no grounds for ease in contemplating either Hitler or Stalin. He did not oppose the war against Hitler, even before losing seven close relatives to Nazi persecution in 1941,[9] and spent most of the Second World War working for the British government in Washington and in Moscow. He returned to Oxford as a tutorial fellow in philosophy at New College, where he had been elected in 1938, before migrating to All Souls again in 1950, this time as a research fellow. In order to understand the atmosphere in which his disposition was mediated into the statement of *Two Concepts*, it will be as well to say a little more about totalitarianism and the liberal rejection of it.

The concept of totalitarianism presents a generalized view of the dictatorial polities that characterized parts of Europe during the inter-war years, and, whilst it may have a wider application, it refers in the first instance to the regimes of Mussolini, Stalin, and Hitler. (It should be added, perhaps, that the usefulness of the concept or its application to specifics has been questioned by a number of recent scholars: but these doubts were not received in the 1950s). It is characterized by a combination of three features. In the first place, totalitarianism assumes that the state is in every possible way the superior of the individual, and therefore that it is entitled to direct him or her in every aspect of life and thought. This total direction, secondly, implies a single scheme of values within society, deviation from which would be impermissible. The total character of the state's claims, thirdly, implies the non-recognition of those who dissent in their opinions or differ in their practices: and it need hardly be added that in practice this non-recognition means treating them as non-human.

[7] See Sheila Grant Duff's letter to Adam Von Trott, c.8 Nov. 1933, in Klemens von Klemperer (ed.), *A Noble Combat* (Oxford, 1988), 23 and nn. 6–7.
[8] Jahanbegloo, *Conversations*, 85.   [9] Ibid. 85, 203.

A theoretical idiom which explained these positions is especially apparent in Italian fascism. Fascism, Mussolini explained (with help from Gentile), regarded people in relation to a superior law which directed the whole of society. This direction was to be equated with the state. Mussolini used the idiom of objective will, a phrase that sounds more mysterious than it need do. For, if we understand the 'will' to be the decision-making apparatus of an individual or a group, and the 'objective' to be contrasted with the individual's will (the will of the subject, and so called the 'subjective will'), it becomes clear that the 'objective will' means the decision-making apparatus of the group rather than the individual. It is no great distance from this to identify the state as that decision-making apparatus (though this view is by no means a logical implication). So, if fascism conceived 'man . . . in his immanent relationship with a superior law and with an objective Will that transcends the particular individual', it is no surprise that 'the Fascist conception is for the State'.[10] The state's direction, moreover, was total, for, 'if the nineteenth was the century of the individual . . . it may be expected that this one may be the century of "collectivism" and therefore the century of the State'. More pointedly still, individuals were understood *in terms of the state*: 'for Fascism the State is an absolute before which individuals and groups are relative', and so the latter would be recognized to the degree that they corresponded to the state—'individuals and groups are "thinkable" in so far as they are within the State.'[11] Hence, as Gentile observed, the state was the explanation of values and rights, 'the basis of every value and every right possessed by the individuals who belong to it'. From here it was a small step to suggest that the state was the agent of producing values: 'in this sense Fascism is totalitarian, and the Fascist State, [is] the synthesis and unity of all values.'[12] It is easy to see that the claims of the state would be total and the recognition of the individual's very being would be a matter for the state in terms of this treatment

[10] Benito Mussolini (with Giovanni Gentile), *The Doctrine of Fascism*, in Adrian Lyttleton (ed.), *Italian Fascisms from Pareto to Gentile* (London, 1973), 41.

[11] Ibid. 53.

[12] Giovanni Gentile, *The Origins and Doctrine of Fascism* (1934), in Lyttleton (ed.), *Italian Fascisms*, 307; *Doctrine of Fascism*, 42.

of 'objective Will'. Everything tended to suppose that 'collectivism' made the state prior to the individual.

It should not be supposed that this doctrine rejected the idea of liberty *sans phrase*: rather it interpreted liberty in a way that suited fascist prepossessions. If the state was understood as 'an absolute', it might follow that *it* was the appropriate bearer of liberty, and individuals would be indulged in their propensities to the degree that these underwrote or were consistent with the state's well-being. Hence fascism was 'for the individual in so far as he coincides with the State', and explicitly emphasized 'the liberty of the State and of the individual within the State', and conceived that the 'State . . . educates citizens for civic virtue'.[13] Fascist doctrine concentrated on the state, and saw individuals as parts of the state: in Gentile's revealing phrase, 'it forms one single personality with the individual citizen'.[14] The obverse of this civic solidarity requires no labouring. Collective conceptions of this sort leave no place for individual dissent.

If fascism was explicit in its assertions, liberalism could recognize an alternative. The total collectivism of the former was opposed to the absolute character of the individual's claims: liberals would contrast the totalitarian prepossession for collective identity with an assertion of individual claims, and an insistence that the state should be conceived in a way that made room for them. Hayek, for instance, identified 'the common feature of all collectivist systems . . . as the deliberate organisation of the labours of society for a definite social goal', and went on to assert that

The various kinds of collectivism, communism, fascism, etc., differ between themselves in the nature of the goal towards which they want to direct the efforts of society. But they all differ from liberalism and individualism in wanting to organise the whole of society and all its resources for this unitary end, and in refusing to recognise autonomous spheres in which the ends of the individuals are supreme. In short they are totalitarian in the true sense of the new word which we have adopted to describe the unexpected but nevertheless inseparable manifestations of what in theory we call collectivism.[15]

---

[13] *Doctrine of Fascism*, 41, 42, 54.   [14] *Origins and Doctrine of Fascism*, 313.
[15] F. A. Hayek, *The Road to Serfdom* (London, 1944), 42.

This insistence that there should be spheres within which the individual should to be free from state interference and the concommitant rejection of the view that society was a collectivity answering a total purpose, made in 1944, would be echoed in later works by the same author. Hayek was not alone. One of the chief purposes of Karl Popper's *The Open Society and its Enemies* (1945), of Jacob Talmon's *Origins of Totalitarian Democracy* (1952), and of some of Hannah Arendt's writings was to construct a genealogy for totalitarian doctrine, blaming its character variously on Plato, Descartes, Rousseau, Hegel, and Marx. More generally, the assumption that the domestic function of the state is not to pattern the whole of society but rather to provide a basic structure of order consistent with many different types of life and thought has been found in much political philosophy since 1945, and may be seen in works otherwise as diverse as John Rawls's *A Theory of Justice* (1971) and Robert Nozick's *Anarchy, State and Utopia* (1974).

Whether in *Two Concepts of Liberty* or elsewhere, Berlin's position is not to be *identified* with any of these books, but like them *Two Concepts* offers a statement which is fundamentally inconsistent with the assumptions of totalitarianism. It is liberal in the sense that it recommends the protection of the individual's propensity to differ and treats other topics in a congruent way—thus, for instance, it defines negative and positive liberty, as we shall see, with a primarily *political* reference. It outlines a genealogy of an interpretation, or rather misinterpretation of the concept of positive liberty, which challenged the status of the individual and exalted the state. It identifies the metaphysical assumptions of this misinterpretation. It offers an account of the nature of values which is radically inconsistent with the monolithic character of the totalitarian account of ethics. Berlin's reading of the plurality of values suggests not merely that values are diverse but more especially that the content of each ethical scheme is internally inconsistent, and so implies that the totalitarian ambition of a monolithic scheme of values is impossible.[16] It should be understood, of course,

---

[16] That Berlin's attention seems to lie primarily here rather than on the inconsistencies amongst different schemes of values is significant. Cf. on this point Richard Wollheim's essay in Alan Ryan (ed.), *The Idea of Freedom* (Oxford, 1979). The former

that *Two Concepts* offers not a condemnation of the concept of positive liberty as such, but rather an explication of its misuses. Besides which, the lecture gives a *nuanced* account of the concept's appearances: for Berlin saw that it lay, too, behind a variety of other twentieth-century movements.

This chapter will give an exposition of the main steps of *Two Concepts*. Having first delineated the concepts of negative and positive liberty, it will examine Berlin's genealogy of abused positive liberty, and will go on to examine his sense of the place of positive liberty in other contexts. Lastly, it will outline Berlin's alternative view of values, not least his view that freedom must be an end in itself.

Liberty: Negative and Positive

It will be as well to define negative and positive liberty in general terms. That they, together or singly, are far from exhausting the possible meanings of the word 'liberty' would be warrant enough for this: but there is an additional ground for distinguishing them. Berlin set out to treat negative and positive liberty only in their reference to politics, and this intention, whilst perfectly reasonable in itself and certainly appropriate to the purpose of his lecture, does not offer the easiest avenue of approach to these concepts.[17]

Negative liberty may be understood as the absence of obstacles to the agent's activities, actual or projected. Its *negative* quality resides in the fact that there is *nothing* to stop the agent from executing his or her projects. For the same reason, it is sometimes described as freedom *from*, though this usage is perhaps less perspicuous than the idea of an absence of obstacles.

This idea may be applied in many ways. Perhaps the most fundamental of these, both in the sense of being a condition of at least some of the others and in that it provides an analogy

may be more important for excluding what Berlin conceived as the logical foundations of totalitarian doctrine. See below, esp. 'Pluralism and Freedom'.

[17] The treatment of negative and positive liberty, and their relations, which follows is partly common coin and partly the result of individual reflection. For the purpose in hand it does not matter much which is which. Those who wish to distinguish the two will be helped by the guidance to the literature about liberty that is to be found in Tim Gray, *Freedom* (London, 1991), esp. chs. 1 and 2, and David Miller (ed.), *Liberty* (Oxford, 1991).

used in some non-physical instances, is the illustration of there being an area within which the agent encounters or contemplates no physical obstacles. There are plenty of other illustrations: of movement unopposed by signs or signals, of practices free from legal penalty, or of political activity free from coercion. Some exemplifications take up the analogy between a physical and a non-physical area or domain. Thus, for instance, political freedom might be conceived in terms of an area or areas of life within which the agent is protected from coercion on the part of the state because he or she possesses relevant rights. Political liberty might be seen in other ways, too, but these and the other cases mentioned exemplify the negative sense of freedom: that there is a condition in which the agent is faced with no obstacle.

If negative liberty is a very transparent concept, the same is less obviously true of positive liberty. Or, to speak more candidly, it is less obviously true that the proponents of positive liberty have been at sufficient pains to explain the fundamental logical form which underlies the various uses to which the term has been put. Their case is not logically on all fours with negative liberty. If negative liberty is a condition, positive liberty more obviously suggests an activity or series of activities. Positive liberty may be understood to denote action calculated to addressing, and often removing, obstacles by applying a relevant capacity or capacities. Sometimes the capacity in question is reason, and some applications of reason, though by no means all, consist in recognizing the obstruction, whether merely to register that it is immovable and so to direct our energies to working with it rather than against it or, more usually, to appreciate it in order to overcome it. In the latter connection, the characteristic strategy for reason, if it reflects upon the agent's inability to overcome certain obstacles unaided, is to suggest that cooperation with others would enable people to deal with those obstacles. This may take the form of recommending human cooperation to deal with the threat posed by physical nature to the agent's survival, or of suggesting that the agent can ward off oppression from other people or groups within society by virtue of appealing to state action.

Such projects of liberating the agent from the restrictions imposed by other human beings or by physical nature are likely to be identified as good. If we find T. H. Green, for instance, declaring that man in isolation was 'the slave of nature' and that the first step to freedom was to submit to the restraints implied by cooperating with others, to 'restraint by society', it is no surprise to find him also writing of 'a positive power or capacity of doing or enjoying something worth doing or enjoying, and that, too, something that we do or enjoy in common with others'. This treatment of cooperation in relation to securing ends in concert with others is, as we see, extended without deliberation to the notion of enjoyment in common. Green, in fact, had in mind the notion that positive liberty involved establishing a condition from which all benefited. To this he added the further ethical supposition that people, once liberated from obstacles in nature or society, were to contribute to the common good—that, as he put it, 'freedom in the positive sense' was 'the liberation of the powers of all equally for contributions to a common good'. In short, Green found a sequel to the liberation implied by positive liberty in applying people's energies to 'a common good'.[18] No doubt further developments of the concept of positive liberty are possible, for the exemplifications, as with negative liberty, could be multiplied: but the logical core of such examples is the same—that action, especially such rational action as cooperation, is required to dispose of obstructions.

It will be seen that the fundamental logical forms of negative and positive liberty are complementary. This may be stated in two ways. First, positive liberty, in so far as it embodies a method of clearing obstacles, offers an account of how to obtain a condition of negative liberty, for such a condition is one void of obstacles. Secondly, by the same token, positive liberty presumes the understanding of liberty embodied in negative liberty. No matter how elaborate the constructions put upon positive liberty, it presumes that to be free is to face no obstacle. Thus, for instance, we find Berlin stating that the 'essence of the notion of liberty, both in the 'positive' and the 'negative' senses, is the fending off of something or someone—of others, who trespass on my field or assert their authority

---

[18] T. H. Green, 'Liberal legislation and Freedom of Contract', in Miller, *Liberty*, 21, 21, 23.

over me, or of obsessions, fears, neuroses, irrational forces—
intruders and despots of one kind or another' (p. 43).[19] For
both negative and positive readings, then, the agent left un-
hampered is free.

Berlin cast his definitions, like the example just given, in
terms of the political applications of these concepts. Although
he called his lecture *Two Concepts of Liberty*, and spoke of
examining 'two of these senses' (p. 6), it became apparent that
he understood both concepts in reference to 'political liberty'
(p. 7) and that he was prepared to exclude from consideration
senses of the word 'liberty' that were not political.[20] He located what 'I shall call the "negative" sense' in terms of an
interpersonal account of an area without obstacles: 'the "negative sense" is involved in the answer to the question "What is
the area within which the subject—a person or group of persons—is or should be left to do or to be what he wants to do
or be, without interference by other persons?"' (pp. 6–7). A
little later (p. 11) this view was stated in terms of 'absence of
interference beyond the . . . frontier', and an 'area of non-in-
terference' was mentioned. Positive freedom Berlin related to
the source of control which an agent or agents might enjoy
over others, an account which draws on the notion of a capacity to direct others. For Berlin, 'the positive sense, is involved in the answer to the question "What, or who, is the
source of control or interference, that can determine someone
to do, or be, one thing rather than another?"' (p. 7). Later in
the lecture, this presumption of control was referred directly to
'the wish on the part of the individual to be his own
master . . . to depend on myself, not on external forces of
whatever kind' (p. 16). This gloss, of course, is familiar enough
from the general meaning of positive liberty, as distinguished
from the more specific political application that Berlin had in
mind. His definitions, whilst cast with political reference, are
related to the fundamental logic of negative and positive liberty.

---

[19] *Two Concepts of Liberty* (Oxford, 1958). References in the text are to this
edition.

[20] e.g. *Two Concepts*, 9: 'Mere incapacity to attain your goal is not lack of political freedom.' For a revision in Berlin's definition of negative liberty subsequent
to the publication of *Two Concepts*, see his *Four Essays on Liberty* (Oxford, 1969),
pp. xxxviii–xxxix.

Berlin could write of that logic in terms suggesting little opposition between the two concepts. In the lecture itself he described them as seeming 'concepts at no great logical distance from each other—no more than negative and positive ways of saying the same thing' (p. 16). In a less formal context he has said that 'positive and negative liberty are both perfectly valid concepts', and has identified the concept of positive liberty as 'of course essential to a decent existence'.[21] More recently he stated that 'positive freedom or liberty is an unimpeachable human value',[22] a statement which, as no one ever thought that Berlin placed too little value on negative liberty, allows us to conclude that to his mind the two concepts are consistent (though that consistency does not extend necessarily to their working out in practice, of course).

The arguments of *Two Concepts*, however, involve a different emphasis. Berlin's official account of positive liberty adumbrates, though it in no wise implies, that there is likely to be interference, and so suggests that one agent's negative liberty may be under threat from another's direction. Such, in fact, is the sequel. *Two Concepts* lays its emphasis not primarily upon conceptual analysis but rather, though not exclusively, upon giving an account of how a certain usage or misuse of positive liberty had developed in ways that were, in every possible way, deeply unattractive. It was not the concept of negative liberty which was inconsistent with that of positive liberty, but rather it was the way in which the latter had been developed by some hands that was problematical. Berlin was at pains to state that such developments 'or sleight of hand . . . can no doubt be perpetrated just as easily with the "negative" concept of freedom' (p. 19), and subsequently he identified senses in which negative liberty 'is twisted'.[23] Yet, if both concepts admitted distortion, positive liberty did so more easily (p. 19), and so received Berlin's attentions. We may add that exploring the genealogy of a degenerate positive liberty will lead us to a view of metaphysics that Berlin rejected (and to manifestations of collective action that he wished to temper) as well as to his own assertion of a quite contrary view of values.

[21] Jahanbegloo, *Conversations*, 41.
[22] See I. Berlin, 'A Reply to David West', *Political Studies*, 41 (1993), 297–8 at 297.
[23] Jahanbegloo, *Conversations*, 41.

Positive Liberty Abused

The design of *Two Concepts of Liberty*, it will be seen, extends beyond the diagnosis of the ill-usage inflicted upon positive liberty to an account of the metaphysical assumptions behind these moves and to their attributed consequences for practice. Thence Berlin moved to delineate an alternative view of meta-physics or, more precisely, meta-ethics. It is worthwhile to delineate the steps he traversed in order to show both the char-acter of his rejections and how these form a preface to his con-structive views.

Berlin's first step is to outline a sequence of five stages by which the concept of positive liberty can be distorted into an instrument of collective oppression on the individual, 'at times no better than a specious disguise for brutal tyranny' (p. 16).

The first of his five stages was the notion of positive liberty as being beyond the control of 'external forces of whatever kind' (p. 16). This starting-point, we may assume, implies that the agent will not be be mastered by 'external forces' but on the contrary will be master of himself or herself. That assump-tion provokes enquiry into the source of mastery over the self. One way of answering this question—and this provides the approach to his second stage—is to suggest that a faculty or faculties within the self provides the means of controlling its other faculties. This notion, of course, is implied in the very idea of the will being free, which suggests that certain of our attributes are adequate to control the others. Berlin's second stage occurs when this control and that which it controls are identified respectively as two *separate* selves. 'Have not men', he asked, 'had the experience of liberating themselves from spiritual slavery, or slavery to nature, and do they not in the course of it become aware, on the one hand, of a self which dominates, and, on the other, of something in them which is brought to heel?' (p. 17). This distinction between the self that controls and the self which is controlled may sound innocent enough, but it provides a cue for more radical separations.

The first of these, Berlin's third stage, is itself transparent, if dubious enough. The controlling, dominant self is identified with the long-term concerns of the agent, whilst the other self is conceived as an obstacle to the realization of these, and so implicitly as something to be overcome. This dominant self, Berlin wrote,

is then variously identified with reason, with my 'higher nature', with the self which calculates and aims at what will satisfy it in the long run, with my 'real' or 'ideal', or 'autonomous' self, or with my self 'at its best', which is then contrasted with irrational impulse, uncontrolled desires, my 'lower' nature, the pursuit of immediate pleasures, my 'empirical' or 'heteronomous' self, swept by every gust of desire and passion, needing to be rigidly disciplined if it is ever to rise to the full height of its 'real' nature. (p. 17)

Whilst this is an austere and possibly schizoid conception of psychology, it is, at any rate, a distinction between the attributes of a single agent who is divided into two selves. It is when the two sets of attributes are identified with different agents that more sinister developments begin.

Here we reach the fourth stage. The higher self, Berlin suggested, may be conceived as 'something wider than the individual (as the term is normally understood), as a social "whole" of which the individual is an element or aspect: a tribe, a race, a church, a state, the great society of the living and the dead and the yet unborn' (p. 17). This *collective* identification is the prime assumption of the oppressor. It turns the social whole into the bearer of liberty and, by an obvious transition, finds the obstacles to that liberty in those individuals who kick against its designs. Such individuals, of course, are members of the whole in question.

We may think that when the 'whole' overrides the wishes of such individuals that the latter are being obstructed and so, obviously enough, suffer a loss of liberty. Liberty is a good, but it is not always the case that their being overriden thus compromises their good in other respects. Cannot it be the case, we may ask, that we can coerce such individuals for their own benefit and the coincident benefit of the community? Surely it is possible to envisage cases in which their good, and the good of the whole community also, would be found in a course that they had not acknowledged, which in fact they would resist, but which others might see (correctly) should be imposed upon them for their own good and at the same time the good of others? Obviously we can, and Berlin acknowledged as much, for 'we recognize that it is possible, and at times justifiable, to coerce men in the name of some goal (let us say, justice or public health) which they would, if they were more enlightened, themselves pursue, but do not, because they are blind or ignorant or corrupt' (p. 17). It is true, of course, that in such cases the individual's negative liberty is being abridged by coercion and that the collective capacity of the group is the source of this coercion. But no doubt it could be argued that this coercion answers to disposing of an obstacle to realizing some collective end.

Oppression, in fact, is manifested in its full extent when we come to the fifth stage. The group has been identified as a bearer of liberty and it has been seen that there is a type of case in which individuals can be coerced in order to bring about an end from which they and the rest of the community benefit. The additional stage needed to paint in a picture of oppression is to claim that each person has within him or her a higher self which does really prefer the good of the whole community to whatever position the manifested will of that person adheres. In other words, the notion of a higher self appears now not only as the collective will but also as the higher will of the individual. If this were so, whosoever take it upon themselves to guide the community could take it also that such people *really* want what the community as a whole wants: and this provides a licence to ignore the stated position of such people.

I may declare that they are actually aiming at what in their benighted state they consciously resist, because there exists within them an occult entity—their latent rational will, or their 'true' purpose—and that this entity, although it is belied by all that they overtly feel and do and say, is their 'real' self. (p. 18)

'This monstrous impersonation' (p. 18) thus lends itself to claiming that a person's 'real self' wants quite the opposite of his or her stated wishes.

Thus we have seen how Berlin conceived that positive liberty had been distorted into something quite unlike its initial character. Beginning with the notion of a source of control, behind which collective capacity may be presumed, we have moved through five stages, first, to the idea of control over the self and thence, secondly, to the identification as separate selves of what controls and what is controlled. Thirdly, there is a further identification, this time (*a*) of the controlling part as the group of which the individual is a member and (*b*) of the individual as what is to be controlled. This identification admits, fourthly, the claim that a society as a whole or its representatives may know better what the individual requires than he or she does. Lastly, this can admit the further supposition that what the individual truly wants is quite the opposite of what he or she is conscious of wanting. Berlin's trajectory could hardly be clearer.

Whither does it tend? Berlin's intention was not merely to describe the genesis of a bastardized form of positive liberty in which the collectivity comes first to direct and then to oppress the individual. It is, rather, to lead the reader to understand the larger presuppositions of such views in order to scout both.

Berlin's path to this end took him, first, to the notion of self-abnegation. This notion suggests that, in order to be free under circumstances that are unfavourable to free action, it behoves the agent to limit or to give up altogether certain desires: in Berlin's words, 'I eliminate the obstacles in my path by abandoning the path' (p. 21). This notion may seem quite innocent, but, like the earlier of the five stages, it opens a logical door through which less attractive ideas can enter. This doctrine, says Berlin, 'is no very great distance' from 'the conceptions of those who . . . identify freedom not indeed with the elimination of desires, but with resistance to them, and control over them' (p. 21). This, in its turn, leads me to identify myself with my reasoning faculty, which is to do the controlling: 'I identify myself with my critical and rational moments,' Berlin observed (p. 23). When we turn from self-abnegation to self-realization, we see the consequences of this identification made plain.

Or, rather, they are made plain in two stages. The first of these relates to self-realization and the second to instituting a rational society. Self-realization can be understood to mean that freedom depends upon the exercise of reason. The argument might run something like this: the world obtrudes all manner of statements, institutions, and rules upon the individual agent, which present themelves to him or her as impositions from outside and so as invasions of negative liberty. But as soon as the reason gets to work and discloses the rationale of these matters, then, assuming they have a rationale, the individual agent will accept them as necessary to certain goals. This being so, they figure no longer as impositions, and the individual agent is thus liberated from a sense of oppression. More ambitiously, he or she may distinguish which of these matters are genuinely necessary, in the sense of conducing to some beneficial end, and which are superfluous or ineffective, and so which can, and should, be discarded. One form of necessity that can be perceived lies in the way in which nature or society manifests or should manifest certain features that can be turned to human advantage.

So far, we may think, so good. But there is, Berlin supposes, a metaphysical assumption present here. That is to say, it is being assumed that reason is considering a world, both natural and social, which is an harmonious whole: one which, despite any appearance to the contrary, discloses to rational scrutiny the *compatibility* of its different parts. Hence, Berlin suggests, this view would demand that 'all true solutions to all genuine problems must be compatible: more than this, they must fit into a single whole: for this is what is meant by calling them all rational and the universe harmonious' (p. 31). The natural sciences give some this impression of physical nature (p. 30), and on these assumptions the same must be true of society. In fact this assumption, that the nature of things is harmonious, provides the licence for the 'impersonation' that Berlin had decried earlier in his lecture.

To suggest that the social sphere is not only amenable to examination by reason but also discloses an harmonious order is to indicate that the appropriate guidance for society is one that makes it correspond to that order. As the order is obvious to reason, then the order will command the assent of those who think rationally: so, Berlin inferred, 'a rational . . . state would be a state governed by such laws as all rational men would freely accept; that is to say, such laws as they would themselves have enacted had they been asked what, as rational beings, they demanded' (p. 30). It followed from this that those who lack the attainments to recognize such an order require to be educated into it (p. 34). It followed, too, that the presence of an objective order of this sort provides an intellectual authority for doing what people might be supposed to desire if only they thought clearly, and so, once again, for acting against their manifested wishes when they remain obstinately uncomprehending. In other words, we find in the assumption of an harmonious order the intellectual licence for the oppression we encountered earlier. If so, an agent might 'conceive the idea of imposing on my society—for its own betterment—a plan of my own, which in my rational wisdom I have elaborated; and which, unless I act on my own, perhaps against the permanent wishes of the vast majority of my fellow citizens, may never come to fruition at all' (p. 35). This supposition, if it were applied to practice, coincides with the fifth stage on the road to oppression we saw earlier.

Of course, there is a logical jump between self-direction and its rational suppositions, on the one hand, and, on the other, the further supposition that there is any question of directing one's fellows: but, said Berlin, 'those who believed in freedom as rational self-direction were bound, sooner or later, to consider how this was to be applied not merely to a man's inner life, but to his relations with other members of his society' (p. 29). This jump matched another, which lies in the manner of directing others. The rational model of directing others has connections with doctrines of organization and education that involve eliciting individual potential rather than suppressing it. A dramatic variation might be possible which would show the potential of one individual being exercised in an unexpected way, albeit one which eschewed reason as a guide. For

abandoning the concept of reason altogether, I may conceive myself as an inspired artist, who moulds men into patterns in the light of his unique vision, as painters combine colours or composers sounds; humanity is the raw material upon which I impose my creative will; even though men suffer and die in the process, they are lifted by it to a height to which they could never have risen without my coercive—but creative—violation of their lives. This is the argument used by every dictator, inquisitor, and bully, who seeks some moral, or even aesthetic, justification for his conduct. I must do for men (or with them) what they cannot do for themselves, and I cannot ask their permission or consent, because they are in no condition to know what is best for them . . . (pp. 35–6)

and whether or not this is 'something close to a pure totalitarian doctrine' (p. 37), it represents an extrapolation from the course Berlin has described.

The exigencies of space mean that this is not the place to assess the validity of Berlin's account of the degeneration of positive liberty and of the metaphysical presuppositions that accompany its decline. It is certainly true, as we saw earlier, that a totalitarian conception of liberty envisages the state or party as a bearer of liberty and sees its individual members as having liberty only if they conform to its collective design. It is apparent, too, that this could be understood in terms of collective thought and action, and that conformity to an allegedly rational plan might be required. Many questions, no doubt, could be asked about Berlin's account. Whether his genealogies of a perverted positive liberty and of a rational harmony are historically valid; whether, if valid, they help to explain totalitarian thought; whether that thought is of much help in explaining totalitarian practices; and whether totalitarianism is itself a useful concept, are only a few of these. At any rate, the practice of European dictatorships was a destination that Berlin had ample grounds for rejecting, and which there are good grounds for rejecting still.

Related Developments

If totalitarianism found a vehicle in some strange version of positive liberty, there were other doctrines, too, which looked to positive liberty rather than to the other of the *Two Concepts of Liberty* that Berlin described. The 'positive doctrine of liberation by reason' (p. 29) he found in 'many of the nationalist, Marxist, authoritarian, and totalitarian creeds of our day' (p. 29). Berlin's lecture was not uniformly hostile to all of these developments, for nationalism or something like it receives a less critical, if also a more puzzled, treatment in *Two Concepts*.

Whilst Berlin was utterly critical of the 'moral or intellectual perversity' that he saw in the misuse of the concept of positive liberty, he held also that 'the notion of freedom in its "positive" sense . . . is at the heart of the demands for national or social self-direction which animate the most powerful public movements of our time' (p. 54). Here, too, there was a confusion about liberty that 'leads to similarly illiberal conclusions' (p. 39).

The demands of 'oppressed classes or nationalities' he identified with a desire for 'recognition (of their class or nation, or colour or race) as an independent source of human activity, as an entity with a will of its own' (p. 41). This desire for recognition might be supposed to exemplify something of positive liberty, if we equate that concept with the sort of collective personality that arises when the concept is misunderstood. But whilst Berlin related this desire to some form of positive liberty, and related the desire also to fraternity and solidarity, yet the desire in the end eluded categorization to his mind. If it issued in 'an ideal which is perhaps more prominent than any other in the world today', it was also 'one which no existing term seems to fit' (45–6).

It may clarify the elusive character of the matter to emphasize independence rather than liberty. Certainly a nation or other body, to answer to this impulse, must be beyond interference from those outside it, and thus far must be free in the negative sense (p. 44). Achieving this condition may involve some action of a positive kind (though in some cases it may not). But the crucial points, surely, are (i) that liberty is valued in this connection in so far as it is obtained without depending upon other bodies, and (ii) that, if such independence is the crucial matter, then the nation is the natural focus of a concern for liberty. Following from (ii), it may be that the members of a group will be concerned less for their individual liberties than for the independence of the group and so will tolerate oppression within it (cf. p. 43). Again, as external dependence would admit direction from those outside, so correspondingly self-direction is valued as evidence of independence. If this is right (and, like Alice, one only says 'if'), then it is neither negative nor positive liberty that is the central matter but rather independence. This much, however, is by the way.

Berlin's tone, perhaps, was less unfavourable to the impulse for recognition than to the totalitarian misuse of positive liberty, though he was clear about the confusions they both embody. Their structure, indeed, seems similar in some ways. Both assume that the group is in some sense logically more significant than the individual. Both identify the individual in terms of membership of the group. Both place a higher value on the liberty of the group than on the liberty of the individual. If these are truly common points, it is time to turn to an alternative view.

Pluralism and Freedom

Berlin discerned behind the conclusions of a misused positive liberty a much deeper pattern of metaphysical assumptions. This pattern indicated that the order of existence, which, we may add, obviously includes values, is one in which there is, once rightly understood, a fundamental harmony. It is hardly surprising that Berlin should propose an alternative view which is radically inconsistent with this and so, if valid, would exclude at once all that flows from the harmonic assumption.

By contrast with 'the conviction that all positive values in which men have believed must, in the end, be compatible, and perhaps even entail one another' (p. 52), he suggested 'that not all good things are compatible, still less all the ideals of mankind' (p. 53). He stated, more strongly, that 'it seems to me that the belief that some single formula can in principle be found whereby all the diverse ends of men can be harmoniously realized is demonstrably false' (p. 54). The illustration offered for this position in *Two Concepts* is drawn from within a single scheme of values ('it is a commonplace that neither political equality nor efficient organisation is compatible with more than a modicum of individual liberty' (pp. 52–3)), and this reading of the plurality of values meets Berlin's requirement of being inconsistent with an harmonious scheme of values. So, too, of course, is the inconsistency between different schemes of values, to which Berlin presumably alluded by mentioning 'all the ideals of mankind'. Yet the former sort of incompatibility, excluding as it does the very possibility of any monolithic scheme of values, perhaps makes this point more dramatically.

It is sufficient to endow the individual's freedom to choose with inescapable significance. If there can be no scheme in which all values are consistent, it follows obviously enough that choice amongst them will be necessary. Therefore, the freedom to choose must be necessary also, and will always be necessary. 'The necessity of choosing between absolute claims is then an inescapable characteristic of the human condition,' Berlin inferred, and this plainly makes the relevant freedom a matter of permanent significance. 'This gives its value to freedom as ... an end in itself, and not as a temporary need,

founded on a wider hostility to communalism and
binations that compressed people so tightly into
holes that they ceased to be separate persons. Dur-
r years she married Heinrich Blücher, who was a
polymath of ruggedly independent views. A talker
a writer, Arendt acknowledged her husband's in-
ompanionship by dedicating her first book, The
Totalitarianism, to him.

d in 1951, The Origins of Totalitarianism established
ion in the USA and led to a series of academic
nts and awards. The preoccupations of the book
ly reveal some of her own experiences, but the
of the various elements that came to compose Na-
her account of how they became 'fused' into an
novel form of 'totalitarian' government, attracted
cism. She was, for example, taken to task for having
red Stalinism, for picking on terror and concentra-
as the signal feature of totalitarianism, and, perhaps
gly, for treating racism, nationalism, and imperialism
rrents in European civilization that somehow did
to its main traditions. Marxism could hardly be
aberration or as the outgrowth of barbarism, and it
to meet this criticism that Arendt began a study of
se influence and progress can be detected in many
publications. As we shall presently see, The Human
first published in 1958, is in part an argument about
ount of productive labour as humanly creative, and
a rejection of the kind of politics, or rather anti-
which it gave rise. Unlike The Origins of Totalitari-
also a rigorously organized and developed argument.
the themes of these two books complement one
oth explore how a civilization that first invented the
politics as a way of life and regarded it as among
achievements reduced itself to barbarism largely
wngrading politics and replacing it with less worthy

lt had once been drawn to the vita contemplativa, the
hich she lived persuaded her of the need for philo-
address their minds to the vita activa, the life of
gagement in worldly affairs. Her own most memorable

arising out of our confused notions and disordered lives, a
predicament which a panacea could one day put right' (p. 54).

Thus Berlin's ethical pluralism—that is to say, his sense of
the inconsistency of values at a fundamental level—is the pen-
dant to his rejection of a misunderstood positive liberty. Where
the latter presumed a specific view of metaphysics to Berlin's
way of thinking, a quite different view of the nature of things
both pre-empted that misreading and suggested the inescapable
necessity of choice, and therewith of freedom to choose. Thus
a recognition of the incompatibility of values provides a logical
warrant for excluding the misuses of positive liberty that Berlin
distinguished and, in so doing, that recognition rounded off
the project of Two Concepts of Liberty.

Bibliographical Note

The fullest listing of Berlin's own works is in the 1991 impression of his
collection of essays, Against the Current (Oxford), compiled by the edi-
tor, Henry Hardy. A slightly more up-to-date, albeit selective, listing
will be found in Claude J. Galipeau, Isaiah Berlin's Liberalism (Oxford,
1994). His later published work includes the revealing correspondence
with Conor Cruise O'Brien, printed as an appendix in O'Brien, The
Great Melody (London, 1992), 605–18; 'A Reply to David West', Political
Studies, 41 (1993), 297–8 (answering West's, 'Spinoza on Positive Freedom', ibid. 284–96); 'England's Mistaken Moralist', Times Higher Education Supplement, 1093 (15 Oct. 1993), 20; (with Bernard Williams),
'Pluralism and Liberalism: A Reply', Political Studies, 42 (1994), 306–9
(answering George Crowder, 'Pluralism and Liberalism', ibid. 293–305);
the introduction to Richard Lebrun's translation of de Maistre's Considerations on France (Cambridge, 1994); and 'Introduction', in James Tully
with the assistance of Daniel M. Weinstock (ed.), Philosophy in an Age
of Pluralism: The Philosophy of Charles Taylor (Cambridge, 1994), 1–3.
Galipeau also contains a list of pieces about Berlin, which is fairly full but
has at least two notable omissions (both included below).

Berlin's writings have usually appeared as essays or lectures, and his
Karl Marx (London, 1939; 4th edn., Oxford, 1978) is, strictly, the sole
volume he has written as a book, though he also edited an anthology
on The Age of Enlightenment (Boston, 1956; Oxford, 1979). He has
himself collected (and revised) several of his essays in Four Essays on
Liberty (Oxford, 1969) and Vico and Herder: Two Studies in the History of

Ideas (London, 1976). Henry Hardy had collected many of the others, though by no means all of those concerning Judaism and Zionism, as *Russian Thinkers* (London, 1978), *Concepts and Categories* (London, 1978), *Against the Current* (London, 1979), *Personal Impressions* (London, 1980), and *The Crooked Timber of Humanity* (London, 1990), as well as unearthing the lectures that form *The Magus of the North: J. G. Hamann and the Origins of Modern Irrationalism* (London, 1993).

Much of the writing about Berlin is stronger on appreciation than either philosophical criticism or historical insight. There are three full-length monographs, namely Galipeau's, which cites a very wide range of materials; Robert A. Kocis, *A Critical Appraisal of Isaiah Berlin's Political Philosophy* (Lampeter, 1989), which tries to be more incisive; and John Gray, *Isaiah Berlin* (London, 1995), which is the most enterprising of the three. Many of the best essays about Berlin and on themes raised by his work will be found in the two *Festschriften* presented to him, namely Alan Ryan (ed.), *The Idea of Freedom* (Oxford, 1979), especially the essays by Charles Taylor, Bernard Williams, and Richard Wollheim, and E. Margalit and M. Margalit (eds.), *Isaiah Berlin: A Celebration* (London, 1991), especially the essays by G. A. Cohen, Ronald Dworkin, Charles Taylor, and Richard Wollheim. Also important is Williams's introduction to *Concepts and Categories*. The most incisive criticism of *Two Concepts of Liberty* is L. J. Macfarlane, 'On Two Concepts of Liberty', *Political Studies*, 14 (1966), 293–305, and there is a decidedly sceptical treatment of Berlin's illustrations in Anthony Arblaster, 'Vision and Revision: A Note on the Text of Isaiah Berlin's *Four Essays on Liberty*', *Political Studies*, 19 (1971), 81–6. Some work relevant to *Two Concepts* is assembled in David Miller (ed.), *Liberty* (Oxford, 1991), including G. C. Maccallum Jr., 'Negative and Positive Freedom', which originally appeared in *Philosophical Review*, 76 (1967). G. C. Maccallum Jr., 'Berlin on the Compatibility of Ideals and "Ends"', *Ethics*, 77 (1967), 139–45, should be compared with G. A. Cohen, 'A Note on Values and Sacrifices' in the same journal, 79 (1969), 159–62. For the view that Berlin should have explored the consequences of pluralism more fully, see Perry Anderson, 'England's Isaiah', in his *Zones of Engagement* (London, 1992). For an independent development of the wider implications of pluralism, see Joseph Raz, *The Morality of Freedom* (Oxford, 1986). Berlin's historical work has yet to receive a full treatment, but there is a very important critical essay by Hans Aarsleff, 'Vico and Berlin', *London Review of Books*, 3/20 (5–18 Nov. 1981), with Berlin's response, and ensuing correspondence (3–16 June, 1982). There is as yet no biography of Berlin (though two are said to be in preparation), but there is biographical material (of variable worth) to be found in a variety of published memoirs, letters, and diaries, some of which are listed by Galipeau.

Hannah Arendt:

MAURIC[...]

HANNAH ARENDT was b[...] despite losing her father at t[...] the upheavals of 1914–18, s[...] class German education. He[...] ary socialist Rosa Luxemburg[...] her university studies, all the[...] what she later called the *vi*[...] learning. She studied philos[...] whom she had a brief affai[...] time Heidegger was prepar[...] *Time*, and the 18-year-old [...] teacher whose reputation alr[...] to his austere and unworldly [...] Jaspers was more of a father fi[...] looking view of existential e[...] perhaps had the more lasting [...] Arendt's own thinking.

It was, in any case, worldly [...] redirected her intellectual int[...] lated into German life but, wi[...] she was forced to see herself [...] Germany in 1933, she becam[...] homeland. Stateless, she foun[...] the USA, where in 1951 she [...] Jewish organizations and beg[...] enough she was anything but [...] not only that German was he[...] man culture remained her or[...] Arendt developed a principle[...]

[1] Elizabeth Young-Bruehl, *Hannal*[...]
[2] Ibid., p. xxii.

nationalism[...]
to all con[...]
uniform w[...]
ing the wa[...]
self-taught [...]
rather than [...]
tellectual [...]
Origins of [...]

Publishe[...]
her reputa[...]
appointme[...]
undoubted[...]
treatment [...]
zism, and [...]
altogether [...]
much criti[...]
all but ign[...]
tion camps[...]
most tellin[...]
as undercu[...]
not belon[...]
seen as an [...]
was partly [...]
Marx, wh[...]
of her late[...]
Condition, [...]
Marx's ac[...]
even more [...]
politics, to [...]
anism, it is[...]
Even so, [...]
another. [...]
practice o[...]
its highes[...]
through d[...]
activities. [...]

If Aren[...]
times in w[...]
sophers to[...]
human en[...]

opportunity came in 1961 with the trial in Jerusalem of Adolf Eichmann. She seized the chance to cover the proceedings for a newspaper. The centre of attention was the story of a man whose worldly activities had included treating the mass extermination of an entire class of human beings as a job. The result of her observations was published as *Eichmann in Jerusalem*, and, true to form, some of what she had to say caused a rumpus that spread her name to a much wider public. She saw in Eichmann not an outsize monster but a nondescript, embodying 'the banality of evil'. She was accused of lacking feeling for the victims of the Nazi policy of extermination and of implying that Jews could have done more to save themselves. The meaning of the phrase that occasioned so much bother was, however, plain and designed not to hurt but to illuminate. In Arendt's view, it is not evil but goodness that is inexplicably deep but also frail. In other writings of the same period she continued both to explore themes announced in her first two books and to comment critically on current events. Her writings mostly took the form of essays and many dealt with the public affairs of her adopted country during the troubled times of racial desegreation and the Vietnam War. She was always the radical and the critic, but her contributions to public debate reveal how difficult it was to pigeon-hole her within the familiar spectrum of left and right. For much of the time Arendt taught in American universities, while making annual trips to Europe. Until his death in 1969, these included regular visits to Jaspers. In her last years, and after her husband's death in 1970, Arendt returned to her first love of what Jaspers had called the 'free air' of philosophy. At the time of her death in 1975 she had written the gist of two volumes of what was published posthumously as *The Life of the Mind*. In them she explores what it is to think, to know, and to judge.

The *vita activa*

Arendt expressly omits 'the life of the mind' from the scope of *The Human Condition*.[3] Although it represents the pinnacle

---

[3] Hannah Arendt, *The Human Condition* (New York, 1959), References in the text are to this edition.

of human achievement she confines her purpose to exploring 'only the most elementary articulations of the human condition' (p. 6)—activities, that is, which are common and familiar to all. The book is organized around three chapters which deal in turn with labour, work, and action. These are said to be the activities or capacities which 'grow out of the human condition and are permanent' (p. 6). Each is seen as a 'response' to a particular feature of the human condition, and their permanence is conditional upon the human condition itself remaining unchanged. This crucial qualification is what lends urgency, and at times a sense of catastrophe, to the book. For, in Arendt's judgement, the very terms of human life are now becoming subject to man-made alteration. Hitherto, human life has been 'a free gift from nowhere (secularly speaking)' (p. 3), but, thanks principally to modern science and technology, we are modifying our relationship to the earth—to the place, that is, that has thus far been the essence of the human condition. The urge to use knowledge to leave the earth and physically to re-engineer ourselves is seen by Arendt, not as an example of progress, but, on the contrary, as a rebellion by creatures whose novel powers have produced increasing alienation from their earthly home. This is a public issue of large significance which calls for deliberation, and for that reason Arendt calls it political. The trouble is that most of us cannot talk about scientific knowledge, and science itself deals in the idiom not of speech but of impersonal symbols. Without speech there can be no politics, and nor, more widely, can there be meaning of any kind when people are unable to talk to one another. The importance of speech could hardly be put more forcefully. Science and technology may at long last have begun to free us from the 'burden of labouring and the bondage of necessity' (p. 5), but the increasing automation of economic life carries with it only the illusion of liberation. The same inventive powers that promise release from backbreaking sweat and toil have produced what Arendt calls a 'labouring society' (p. 5) in which only the products of labour are valued. As a result, the price of being readily fed is spiritual diminishment, because the worth of other activities such as work and action is downgraded to the single denominator of labour.

It is this kind of current anxiety about the world about her that leads Arendt to propose a 'reconsideration of the human condition from the vantage point of our newest experiences and our most recent fears' (p. 6). She defers tracing the historical genesis of these matters to the concluding chapter of the book, but it is as well to keep in mind that they provide its motive. It is for present-day reasons that the book concentrates on what is collectively called the *vita activa* and seeks to elucidate how, in its three components of labour, work, and action, men developed themselves under terms of existence that were until recently unchanging. But what is the 'human condition' to which labour, work, and action are 'fundamental' and 'elementary'? What is meant by saying that each part of the *vita activa* 'corresponds to one of the basic conditions under which life on earth has been given to man' (p. 9)?

The most general feature of the human condition is also the most evident. We are all mortal, and all human existence is governed by this presiding fact of life. Subject to birth and death, or, as Arendt puts it, to 'natality' and 'mortality', we have as a result to busy ourselves in certain ways. Most rudimentary is the business of sustaining life. This natural, biological necessity is an ever-turning cycle of keeping our bodies fed and in good fettle. Even though some of us may induce others to sweat and graft on our behalf, it is labour that supports life and keeps it going. Noticeably, we share this necessary condition of life with all its other forms, and for that reason labour is the least distinctive of human activities. 'The human condition of labour', Arendt writes, 'is life itself' (p. 9). In contrast to labour, work is said to be 'unnatural', in the sense that in work we make things and furnish the world with them. In manufacturing objects, we create an 'artificial' world of our own that gives a measure of familiarity and durability to our fleeting lives. Hence 'the human condition of work is worldliness' (p. 9). If *homo faber*, man the maker of things, peoples the world with objects, action is largely intangible. It is so because all that is needed for action is the presence together of several persons. Because no things are required as intermediaries, and because, unlike labour, it is not tied to necessity, action is the most intensely human and hence most valuable part of the *vita activa*. Action thus 'corresponds' to the 'condition of human plurality, to the fact that men, not Man, live on earth and inhabit the earth' (p. 9). While all aspects of the human condition are related to politics, it is this plurality of distinct and diverse persons who are never identical that constitutes '*the* condition . . . of all political life' (p. 10). Action can thus occur and politics arise only among members of a species each of whom is distinct and irreplaceable. In the human condition of endlessly diverse plurality, action is always interaction.

Labour, work, and action are each pitted against the impermanence of mortal life. It is action, however, and especially action that takes the form of founding and preserving political bodies, that most notably outwits the grave. States are made to last—to outlast their founders and to provide continuity between generations. In doing so they generate the 'condition for remembrance, that is, for history' (p. 10). All three members of the *vita activa* also address the fact of human natality, but again it is action which reveals most about the fact that we are born into the world. What comes to life with (only) human birth is the appearance of a being with 'the capacity of beginning something anew, that is, of acting' (p. 10). The power to initiate, to found, for example, a state, and thus to act, leads to one of Arendt's striking formulations. 'Since action is the political activity par excellence,' she writes, 'natality, and not mortality, may be the central category of political, as distinguished from metaphysical, thought' (p. 11). In a later book, *On Revolution*, Arendt returns to the theme of the fresh political beginnings at work in the revolutionary foundation of new states. The belief that birth and beginnings bring with them at least the possibility of something new provided Arendt with one of her few sources of optimism.

In order to appreciate what is ultimately at issue one needs to fathom why Arendt attaches signficance to portraying labour, work, and action as items of the *vita activa*. Why does she use this expression? Arendt was schooled in the classics, but her plentiful use of Greek and Latin sources is far from the mere garnish of a well-stocked mind. Her use rests upon a belief that vitiates all her thinking and which may perhaps be traced to the influence of Heidegger. Heidegger considered that, along with German, Greek embodied the most profound human experiences of which we have shown ourselves capable. Arendt too believed in the unrivalled authority of classical antiquity. The same body of men who founded Western civilization also plumbed the depths of what it was to be human. Unlike Heidegger, whose contempt for politics was notorious —and which may have had something to do with his flirtation with the Nazis in the 1930s—Arendt saw in the Greek *polis* and the accompanying *bios politikos* ('the political way of life') an unmatched example of civilized being. The ancient Greeks and Romans believed that to be human, to be, as it were, most fully human, was to act and take part in public affairs. What Arendt shared with Heidegger was the view that language does not so much describe experience as embody it. When studied, the etymology of words provides direct access to the very pulse of life.

The claim that the phenomena of experience come to us already encapsulated in self-proclaiming categories is, of course, highly contestable, but it is the central tenet of the philosophical method inaugurated by Husserl and to which Heidegger and Arendt subscribed. One merit of phenomenology is that it makes for arresting formulations of the sort used to shape *The Human Condition*. Experience may, however, not speak and present itself in unambiguously distinct compartments, and, if it does not, the attempt to pretend otherwise conceals crucial elements of unavoidable arbitrariness in the formulation of meaning. The *vita activa*, for example, is composed of three 'fundamental activities' whose separate character is said to be explicit. Perhaps they are less so than Arendt would have it. Similarly and perhaps yet more radically, the entire *vita activa* is placed in contrapuntal relationship to the *vita contemplativa*. Although, according to Arendt, the former is a medieval rendering of Aristotle's *bios politikos*, it had, by the time it became latinized, forfeited its original meaning. Among citizens of the *polis*, a political way of life was regarded as of great worth, but what had made it possible for citizens to devote their lives to the public business was their freedom from other necessary but servile activities such as labour and work. By the time the expression *vita activa* gained currency, the special sense of politics had gone. Action had been reduced to the menial level of labour and work. What explained a loss of esteem which applied to the entire *vita activa* was the higher standing of the rival claims of the *vita contemplativa*. Active engagement in the affairs of the world had come to be placed at a lower level of dignity than the claims of a contemplative life, whose principal virtues were stillness of soul and wordless unworldly inactivity. The contemplative aspired not to this-worldly reputation among fellow mortals but to eternal salvation. In one of the most breathtaking charges ever made, and perhaps following Nietzsche's cue, the instigator who is charged with announcing this seesaw revaluation is none other than Plato, usually treated, along with Aristotle, as the founder of the entire tradition of political philosophy! In this view of the matter, Plato's contempt for the messy illusoriness of human affairs is set out in *The Republic*, where the plan is to put an end to politics and place power in the hands of men who valued contemplation of the good far above any sort of *vita activa*. In siting ultimate human concerns in heaven, Christianity reinforced and gave enduring institutional effect to this Socratic legacy of otherworldliness.

Arendt's philosophical method allows for further drama when it comes to interpreting the advent of the modern world in the seventeenth century. The period roughly between Galileo and Marx saw a rehabilitation of active life and a consequent disregard of contemplation in an increasingly secular world. By the time this occurred, action had spent so long in the company of labour and work that, instead of recovering the standing it had once enjoyed among the Greeks, it found itself upstaged by both, and especially by the new creative worth with which the industrial revolution endowed labour. If one remembers that in Arendt's scheme of reckoning labouring belongs to the world of necessity, and that in human terms its worth is negligible, one gets some idea of how she regards the achievements of industrial civilization. Her argument is wider and perhaps deeper than the claim that, since the industrial revolution, politics has functioned as the handmaiden of economics. The loss she minds about is not functional but spiritual. Deprived of the opportunities to act, men are fated to being less human than they might otherwise be. They also become exposed to the power and allurements of totalitarian government which thrives on servility and disdain for politics. For Arendt, then, action is of ontological significance and quite different from the power to get one's way.

The Public and the Private Realm

A measure of our current confusion which reveals how much we have lost of the Greek understanding of politics is present in the widespread use of 'social' and 'political' as synonyms. What distinguishes men is not their social gregariousness, which they have in common with other creatures, but their craving for distinction. Only men thirst after glory, and what made its realization possible was the existence of a *res publica*, a public realm in which men were present before one another and could thereby confer praise and recognition. As we have already noticed, if action is to 'shine', nothing that has to do with the mundane necessities of life can be allowed to obscure its way. The proper place for things that have to be done, that is, for labour, is the private world of the household. The political importance of this private realm is that it establishes the preconditions for the public realm where politics occurs. It is also noteworthy that households are ruled by their heads. This hierarchical setting stands in contrast to the public realm, whose principal feature is one of equality. Politics is the activity of persuasive deliberation that takes place among equals and it neither derives from nor serves any end other than itself. To the Greeks the very idea of 'political economy' would have been meaningless, because it closely associates distinct activities that belong in separate realms.

Arendt identifies what she calls a 'social realm' and considers its emergence and rise to prominence as among the most important features of the modern world. This social realm is composed of the activities of labour and work, and is her own formulation of what other thinkers refer to as civil society. With its 'rise', labour and work emerged from being of household importance to a position where they came to dominate and define the public realm. Arendt does not dwell on the exact historical forces at work, but it is plain that she is referring to the religious and scientific precursors of the industrial revolution and to the latter's embodiment in capitalism. Her portrayal is reminiscent of Weber's, and in her view the advent of industrial society produced uniformity of opinion and conformity of behaviour. Both are defining features of the social realm. One important result has therefore been not the flowering of individualism but the erosion of the very possibility of action. The public realm has been socialized so that what is valued is labour and work. Action becomes functional and loses its expressive character. A contrast is implied between behaviour, which is predictable because sociologically shaped, and action, which displays individual initiative, often in an assertive and surprising manner. After three centuries of accelerating economic growth, we now value not what is exceptional but what attaches us most closely to the rudimentary business of life. Since the 'life process' is common to all animate life, we should not be surprised that a society that values the common fact of life produces behavioural sameness.

Arendt does not for a moment underestimate the powerful energies released into the world once labour and work have escaped from the privacy of households. They are, however, not distinctively human. 'Society', she writes, 'constitutes the public organization of the life process' (p. 42), and the politics it produces is a misnomer because it is no more than administration. Household management on a large scale carries with it its despotic distinction between master and subject, ruler and ruled. In modern conditions of mass society there is no identifiable master; rule is by nobody—that is, by bureaucracy.

Socialization of the public realm has other effects. The existence of a true public realm is said to be indispensable to human identity because our very sense of reality turns on the presence of others. 'For us,' we read, 'appearance—something that is being seen and heard by others as well as by ourselves—constitutes reality' (p. 45). The sense that allows us to be at home in the world, to delight in its familiarity, depends on an exchange of recognitions that can only be conveyed in the light of publicity. The 'light' of the public realm which exposes and fixes is repeatedly contrasted with the 'shadowy' unfathomable reaches of a person's intimate sense of himself. Whatever the attractions of self-absorption in one's private affairs, they can provide no assured sense of the reality of the world. Seeking reality inside oneself is a blind alley. Private life is one of deprivation. The stability of the public world of mutual recognition is powerfully aided by the wealth of tangible objects we make and use. They provide a settled and familiar lay-out to the world: 'To live together in the world means essentially that a world of things is between those who have it in common, as a table is located between those who sit around it; the world, like every in-between, relates and separates men at the same time' (p. 48). This is perhaps an example of where the categorical separation of work and action is replaced by the assertion of mutual dependence. In any case, the things we make, the products of *homo faber* who works rather than labours, tend to outlast their makers. The durability of, say, cathedrals adds a sense of permanence, something that transcends individual lives. Denied this sense of continuity, we would be unable to act, because to try and do so would lack meaning. Hence the open presence of others and a common world of things both serve as bulwarks against the transience of life and the wider depredations of time. The public realm is 'the space protected against this futility' (p. 50). When Arendt explores how vital a plurality of viewpoints is to the credibility of the public realm, we are immediately moved close to the politics—or perhaps, the anti-politics—of our times. A true public realm is sustained by the diversity of standpoints from which what is held in common is seen and heard. It is typical of tyrannies that they prevent this interplay by keeping people isolated, but the barb in her argument is that the party politics of democracies also favours conformity of public opinion.

The Romans, here unlike the Greeks, did value the private world of 'home and hearth'. Private and public were seen as coexisting. The connecting link was private property, which served as a sort of entrance ticket to public life. Property, and especially land, gave a fixed sense of place in the world and was given the full protection of law. Property was not the same as wealth, and the pursuit of the latter in the modern world has, Arendt argues, been no respecter of private property. Wealth is socially dependent and is, therefore, less reliable as a means of underpinning the independence without which human diversity cannot show itself in the open. The 'rise of the social' in which the accumulation of wealth figures so prominently has redefined what we mean by politics. Where once property was the condition of entry to the public realm, politics is now largely occupied with protecting wealth and its further growth. Unlike private property, which gives a visible, tangible, and durable sense of place and belonging, modern wealth is unworldly because it is impersonal and fluid. Its lack of definition thus undermines both private and public realms, which in different ways private property supports. Private life has the value of keeping us in touch with the spurs of necessity, and without this energizing urge life would become inhumanly indolent. 'For the elimination of necessity,' she writes, 'far from resulting automatically in the establishment of freedom, only blurs the line between freedom and necessity' (p. 63). Inactivity is as servile as ceaseless labouring. Beyond that, the private realm is a refuge and respite, a protection for some entirely human qualities, such as goodness, which become harmfully distorted when forced to appear in public. Christ-like goodness is essentially shy and mute and it is no accident that attempts to erect public realms to embody unworldly virtues habitually result in dogmatic tyrannies. Machiavelli is cited with approval, not because he preferred badness to goodness but because he grasped what many philosphers have not— that neither the one nor the other can 'shine' in public or figure in political action.

Labour and Work

The distinction between labour and work is largely Arendt's and the reason for taking together what she is at pains to separate is to place both in their proper setting. Her discussion is part of a lifetime's argument with Marx, for whose grasp of the formative influences at work in the modern world she had the highest respect. Her standpoint is, of course, quite different. She claims that the distinction between labour and work, though largely ignored by philosophers, including Marx, is present in the major European languages and thus true to experience. Labour is the necessary activity that sustains life, while work produces man-made objects. According to Arendt, Marx's error was to glorify labour as the source of all value. In doing so he voiced the industrializing world's awe at the sheer productivity of labour, at what it could produce in excess of what is needed to keep the 'processes' of life going. In seeing labour as work he none the less confused the issue.

Productivity of labour under capitalism has indeed the power to terminate the reign of necessity to which the painful and scarce conditions of existence have hitherto condemned the bulk of mankind. But, in welcoming this, Marx celebrates what is least human, the very opposite of freedom. Like the fertility of life to which it is related, the fecundity of labour issues in new servitude to the never-ending appetites of consumption. In consumption, labour reduces all other aspects of the *vita activa* to itself—that is, to what denominates man as part of nature. Labour has twin aspects; producing what will support life and then consuming it. Productive labour has merely shifted the balance in favour of the latter. With automation, labour ceases to be laborious while leaving men still tied to the treadmill of generation and decay. This is the world of the *animal laborans*. A throwaway consumer's society remains a society wedded to the values of labour, to the 'unnatural growth of the natural' (p. 43). Instead of eating in order to labour and vice versa, we now consume and dispose in order to make room for more of the same. This triumph of the *animal laborans* is at the same time the defeat of *homo faber*, because modern consumption is incapable of producing a durable world. A waste economy destroys the 'objectivity' of the world because it produces what is designed to be replaced. It also undermines the public realm because the private activities of labour-based consumption may be as conspicuously displayed in the open as the munching of cows, without thereby constituting a public realm. The lowings of a herd are not the unified expression of opinion concerning a common world of public affairs, but only the multiplied sounds of identical private or social interests.

If the *animal laborans* reiterates nature, *homo faber* erects a world against it. Artefacts stand between, and thus connect, man and nature. Manufacturing a common and visibly tangible world from materials found in nature contains an element of violence. Tables are fabricated from felled trees. Similarly there is an element of consumption, of wearing out, in the regular use of even the most well-made object. As with seacliffs, cathedrals erode. Neither violence nor consumption is, for that matter, more than incidental to *homo faber*. In work the crucial element is the existence of a design or model which governs what is made. Hence means–ends thinking is the hallmark of work. Instrumentality and the tools it relies upon were, of course, invented in part to ease the pains of labouring, but they, and later on machines, were also devised not merely to perpetuate life, but to make things to outlast their makers and thereby provide continuity between generations. Men can dwell and not merely live in a world of their own creation. With the domination of labour, mechanization has come to subvert the world created by work. Rather than providing a measure of permanence and stability to creatures who naturally lack both, the automation of work now serves nothing so much as the cyclical roundabout of life itself.

Even at their most successfully worldly, *homo faber*'s utilitarian habits of thinking create dilemmas they cannot resolve. Every end for which something is made or done is inescapably a means for something or somebody else. In such a train of connections there is no way that meaning—lasting meaning, of independent value—can be established in the world. To raise 'Man' as the 'measure of everything' is to do more than license use and consumption, but still fails to subsume them in value. All of this notwithstanding, *homo faber* is a more valuable being than the *animal laborans*. The worldliness of man the maker goes a long way to redeem life devoted to nothing more human than its existence. The world of things operates through markets, and the place where they are exchanged is a public space, where values, albeit relative, are ascribed and inserted into the world. Art objects represent *homo faber* at his highest. The very uselessness of, say, a painting or sculpture illustrates how artifice supplies a vital element to stability and meaning in a world otherwise riven by the natural cycle of birth and death. This is how she makes the point:

It is as though worldly stability had become transparent in the permanence of art, so that a premonition of immortality, not the immortality of the soul or of life but of something immortal achieved by mortal hands, has become tangibly present, to shine and to be seen, to sound and to be heard, to speak and to be read. (p. 147)

What labour and action have in common is their impermanence. If *homo faber* erects a world of durable things as the public setting in which action can take place, it is the special task of artists to build 'monuments' to the words and deeds of men of action, whose otherwise useless and unworldly conduct would have no powers of remembrance and thus no lasting meaning.

Action

Human being is conceivable without either labour or work. Without evidence of action it would be unrecognizable. If *The Human Condition* has a centre to which it drives, it lies in Arendt's account of action. At first sight the 'plurality' of the human condition to which action is a 'response' seems more like a natural fact than something uniquely human. That it is 'men not Man . . . [who] inhabit the earth' (p. 9) may also appear so evident as not to bear mention. That does not, of course, dispose of its significance, and Arendt claims that philosophers have persistently failed to digest the consequences of human plurality. Plurality has little to do with demographics. According to Arendt, it has two aspects: equality and distinction. We are all alike enough to allow understanding and cooperation to occur, but also different enough to make action and speech necessary. Were we undifferentiated, grunts might be enough to transmit our needs and wants. As it is, human being is a 'plurality of unique beings' (p. 156) whose diversity is revealed by action and speech. Action is the commencement of something new and this ability to initiate is, we have already noted, related to 'natality'. The relation is, however, at one remove, a 'second birth' because what comes into the world with each arrival is the birth of a beginner. And this, Arendt considers, is the nub of freedom.

Because men are not replicas, what they set in motion, what they can begin, is in part something unexpected. The especial character of each new 'actor' appears in what they do and say. Speech in particular brings out distinctness. 'Speechless action' would be robotic behaviour because 'the actor, the doer of deeds, is possible only if he is at the same time the speaker of words' (p. 158). Actions do not speak without words. As action discloses the person of the actor, so words reveal the action. Behaviour does neither. Without denying the importance of speech as a means of communication and purveyor of information, Arendt's viewpoint is radically non-utilitarian. Were speech wholly functional, it could be replaced with other means—signs and images, for example—but deprived of speech we would be unable to determine who rather than what someone was.

Just as crucial is 'the surrounding presence of others' (p. 167). It is from other people that we learn about ourselves; who we are is shown to us in the responses we evoke in others, who in turn frame their estimations of us largely by reference to what we say and do. To believe that we can best know ourselves through introspection is a fallacy of Romanticism. The constant presence of others may be pleasurable or tiresome, but for human beings it is an ontological necessity. It is our 'appearance' before others that establishes a sense—a common sense—of reality and a sense of identity within it. The setting or 'space' in which we 'appear' before others is another description of the public realm. Only in the light of public glare can our actions acquire meaning. Unlike the fabrications of *homo faber*, whose works stand out anonymously, action is not akin to a piece of sculpture. Without the designation of an agent, of a 'who', action is worthless.

Frustration is inseparable from the ephemeral character of action. There are thus plausible reasons for shunning its transience for the surer grounds of labour and work, cognition and contemplation. Indeed, action often relies on the more solid dependability of things that stabilize the world and the interests that arise through their manufacture and exchange. None the less, the 'webs' of human actions, reactions, and countless further ramifications are not to be interpreted as forming part of some Marxist 'superstructure'. There is no *geist*-like puppet master calling the tunes to which we dance. Action is one of the greatest powers on earth and when men combine their powers of action and cooperate they can do more than move mountains. They can create a human world replete with meaning. To overcome the unstable combination of frailty and power inherent in action takes courage, and Arendt notes that philosophers' oft-expressed contempt for the fleeting nature of human affairs may have much to do with a lack of worldly nerve. Even so, all action, and not just political action, is caught up in what is called its 'boundlessness'. Action cannot help but generate consequences without limit. It may be the work of agents, but actions are usually without identifiable authors.

The new initiatives we fondly think our actions have begun as often as not are reactions to beginnings so distant that they lie beyond detection. The generative powers of action are, of course, both curse and blessing. In all cases action raises issues about how to contain its tendency to spread out in all directions. Politics is thoroughly familiar with the tasks of trying to 'house' the disruptive fertility of action. That is what a *res publica* is. The very idea of a 'body politic' is of something that can give harness and substance to the energies that animate it.

The *chef d'œuvre* of politics considered as action is this foundation of bodies politic. Arendt sees laws and institutions in this light. Just as boundaries are necessary to property and territory, so the state is to be viewed as a man-made bulwark raised to allow, contain, and set limits to action. This cooperative keeping of action within bounds thus figures as the prime political virtue of moderation. It was the achievement of the Greek *polis* to have invented a public space, the *polis*, resilient enough to modify the intensity of action yet dependent for its success on the virtue of self-limitation. For a while the modern European state offered something comparable, but, with the 'rise of the social', the state and politics replaced action first with work and then with labour.

The boundlessness of action is rivalled by its unpredictability. We are seldom in a position to know or determine the outcome of our actions. Most of the things we do and say carry unintended consequences. The meaning of action is only available after the event and from the outside, by somebody uninvolved. According to Arendt, the remedy for this practised in the Greek *polis* was to multiply the opportunities for citizens so to shine in public that their words and deeds carried beyond the grave. 'Immortal fame' salvaged the uncertain outcome of action from the meaninglessness of oblivion. As a public space composed of citizens acting and reacting in one another's presence, the *polis* was also an establishment of 'organized remembrance' (p. 176). Although only citizens could hope to glorify their lives in deeds and words, Arendt is quick to repeat that the capacity for action is rooted not in privilege but in human birth. To be cut off from this uniquely human experience is thus to suffer a loss of human being.

This estimate of action is often couched as a rebuke to the

drift of political philosophy since Plato inaugurated it. Faced with the assorted frustrations, frailties, and anarchic tendencies of action, Plato and his followers sought refuge in a view of politics that takes its cue from the more stable world of *homo faber*. The upshot has been a preference for rule at the expense of action. Rulership is related to the fabricator's mastery of his material in accordance with his governing idea or model. Translated from objects to human affairs, this readily becomes the idea of a ruler or master crafting a body politic from passive human material. In a notable phrase, Arendt charges Plato with treating 'the perplexities of action as though they were solvable problems of cognition' (p. 197). The organizational idiom of *The Republic*, whose ultimate purpose is to make the world safe for contemplation, is that of the craftsman. *Homo faber*'s distinction between knowing (his model) and doing (making an object) produces a view of public affairs in which the means used are less important than the end in view. The end result of means–ends thinking is, so Arendt claims, the totalitarianisms of the twentieth century, in which all means are justified as necessary to the end of exterminating classes of human beings or serving the progressive logic of history. What this entire cast of thinking omits is the understanding of action, and the fact that action has no determinate end and therefore no separable means. Representative democracy is also implicated, because action cannot be represented without ceasing to be. Only direct participatory democracy does justice to the necessary connection between agent and action.

It is plain that Arendt considers we have paid too high a price for our undervaluation and fear of action. She acknowledges that the freedom of action is burdensome, that men suffer from as well as delight in the webs of their interactions. Respite is needed from continuous exposure to public scrutiny. Some writers have, of course, denied that freedom can figure at all in the circumstances she describes, where 'The actor never remains the master of his acts' (p. 211). Freedom is not, however, the same as omnipotence, and the words and deeds that constitute action contain their own internal remedies to some at least of its most disturbing features. Although words cannot be unsaid or deeds undone, in the ability to forgive we find an antidote to action's irreversibility. Arendt claims that, in forgiving men 'who know not what they do', Jesus uniquely revealed the power of forgiveness. In the reciprocal release of forgiving we regain the freedom to begin afresh. This, in turn, allows men to trust their powers of action because all is not lost when we go astray. Punishment also puts a stop in the way of action, but operates unlike forgiveness. With the 'radical evil' of totalitarianism perhaps in mind, Arendt notes that 'men are unable to forgive what they cannot punish and that they are unable to punish what has turned out to be unforgivable'. (p. 217).

If forgiveness mitigates the irreversibility of action, the uncertainty of the future is redeemed in the capacity to promise. The giving and receiving of promises allow that binding together in respect of future action which sets up 'islands of security' (p. 213) in the face of unpredictable events. Forgiveness and promising exhibit powers that counter an otherwise implacable 'automatic necessity' (p. 221) where the course of history appears as determined as the movements of nature. Action interrupts necessity, and, because this becomes possible with each new birth, faith and hope in human affairs have a footing here on earth.

The achievement of *The Human Condition* is to have elucidated a number of categories designed to urge the value of the public realm and specify the character of action. These, in turn, are said to be the settings in which the activity of politics is located. In this sense, the book is less an exercise in exploring the domain of politics than in offering an outline of its prepolitical suppositions. The final lengthy chapter of *The Human Condition* is somewhat different. It develops into a more generalized account of the genesis and development of the modern world. As we have seen, Arendt has both a philosophical and historical purpose, but, whereas in earlier portions of the argument history is used to argue a philosophical theme that is ultimately ontological in purpose, the concluding part of the book is discursive. It seeks to establish the general character of the modern age within which the 'double reversal' suffered by action, first *vis-à-vis* contemplation and thereafter at the hands of work and labour, actually occurred. At times the argument is so general as to be dangerously permissive. What does emerge from a discussion that is not perhaps on the same level as what precedes it is how politically dangerous she considers the misconceived belief in historical progress. Whereas many who believe in progress centre their convictions in modern science and its applications, Arendt finds Galileo and his successors responsible for the estrangement of men from their worldly habitat. The advent of space travel, which is mentioned in the first line of the book, gives dramatic expression to an alienation that reaches back to the origins of modern science. What the cognitive powers of science have bequeathed is the capacity to subvert the given and once durable terms of the human condition and replace them with man-made conditions. The effect of this is to redefine what we mean by 'the human condition', because, if it becomes something we are continuously making, it ceases to be a given. Our position thus becomes indeterminate and as boundless as the inventiveness of science. To make matters worse, science increasingly dispenses with speech and so we risk losing what makes meaning possible. In Arendt's view, this development is a perversion of action; on the one hand, the accelerating 'new beginnings' of science represent a form of 'acting into nature', while, on the other, its impulse refuses to accept the discipline of limitations, without which action is dangerous. This line of argument may appear remote from politics until one recalls the potency of scientific knowledge and the historical fact that hubris—confidence in the unboundedness of human powers—was part of totalitarian belief that everything possible was thereby permissible. Arendt makes clear her opinion that capitalism also suffers from a refusal to submit to limits, and that its appetite for growth is thus another source of alienation.

Criticism

As with all powerfully framed and highly charged arguments, *The Human Condition* invites criticism. Some are prompted by the sweeping generality of the views expressed. How, for example, is one to assess the claim that Western civilization, *tout court*, is a 'field of ruins' that has been in crisis since the scientific and industrial revolutions? Arendt is not the first German or European intellectual to scourge the bourgeoisie as philistines largely responsible for the 'decline of the West'. She is, however, more unusual in detecting a common fund of experience linking the pursuit of wealth with twentieth-century barbarism. Perhaps she was able to see the former only through the prism of totalitarianism. Where, in that case, one wonders, does that leave her judgement of the USA, at once the champion of economic growth and the country whose attachment to political freedom allowed it to salvage European civilization from its twentieth-century attempts to eradicate politics? One might equally question whether the public life of classical antiquity can serve as a fruitful measure with which to gauge the twentieth century. It is not so much that she indulges in nostalgia for a past sufficiently removed from the present to shine without blemish, but that she herself provides ample reasons why the recovery of public life which she favours is unlikely to come about. And to criticize the public life of democracies for not being the setting for the performance of exceptional and memorable actions may lead to the false conclusion that they possess no public realms. It may be that the public good, in providing welfare, for example, establishing justice, or holding government accountable to mass electorates, is largely an unheroic business which none the less inspires public-spiritedness. It is hard not to conclude that, for all her belief in the virtues of action and the importance of public life, Arendt finds distasteful the actual politics that makes up 'a political way of life'. In any case, one wonders whether the active citizens of Athens and Rome were as Homeric in pursuit of renown as one is led to believe. This is, however, to repeat a comment mentioned at the outset of this discussion; Arendt's method of enquiry produces categories that at one and the same time are indelible and watertight but which repeatedly fall victim to the passage of time.

Without much doubt *The Human Condition* succeeds in focusing attention on the public realm and action. By avoiding direct discussion of 'the modern state', room is left for the argument that public life is of spiritual significance. Here, too, questions abound. If action is indispensable to a sense of being at home in the world, what are we to make of the view that action is largely a matter of words and deeds performed in public on a single stage? Even if this is true of political action, is all action to be thus confined? It might, for example, be persuasively argued that there exist not only private, social, and public realms but varieties of each, and that the public realm in particular affords opportunities for action in a rich diversity of settings. Citizens move in and between a plurality of settings, some formal and others less dependent on publicity. On some, of course, the aim may well be to leave a mark, but even here it remains unclear what is to qualify action as remarkable. Is the hallmark the resonance actions succeed in generating at the time, or is what matters their later distillation at the hands of story-tellers and historians? How can we trust remembrance to cast our actions in the light they deserve? History may not be hagiography, but our own times warn against allowing reputations to become the playthings of propaganda and public relations. Monuments that until recently immortalized Lenin now provide rubble for the potholes of St Petersburg. Not all reputations are deserved or lasting, and nor do they always need publicity in order to become memorable. Mother Theresa is a household name, not a public figure.

Even agreement that action is, *par excellence*, public activity does not dispose of all the difficulties. Because of the prominence enjoyed in the public realm by force, one needs to know how it is to figure in an account of action. The 'great men' of the twentieth century whose names, if not reputations, stand out, include Hitler, Stalin, and Mao, all three celebrated mass murderers. Alert to the argument that Greek and Roman warriors had a better chance of joining the immortals than plain citizens, Arendt denies that glory can be won on the battlefield. Her reasoning is somewhat weak and amounts to saying that violence is excluded because it is crude, prone to excess, and wordless. Napoleon made his political mark, however, not in parliamentary debate but as the victor in great battles that raised the reputation of the French state to unparalleled heights. Although Arendt acknowledged the competitive and assertive element in action, she did not share Carl Schmitt's sense that, like it or not, 'the concept of the political' turns as much on the recognition of enmity towards outsiders as upon amity among fellow citizens or compatriots.

Criticisms that question the locus of action and what is to pass as action do not necessarily dispute Arendt's fundamental claim that it is of ontological importance, that it confirms the reality of the human world and our individual place in it. Nor do they impair the argument that connects action and freedom. One of Arendt's most striking themes is to deny that civil society is the domain of freedom. This, of course, has been a staple of liberalism from Locke via Hegel to Hayek. She does not deny the use and value of the civil liberties that arise in civil society and serve the interests of the *animal laborans* and *homo faber*. What is rejected is the view that civil liberties constitute political freedom. Civil liberties may be valued as much to protect the private realm as to gain access to public affairs, to avoid politics rather than engage in it. Arendt's philosophy of action may be grounded in belief in a 'plurality of unique individuals', but her austere regard for individuality is directed against liberalism and representative democracy, both of which serve material interests and private comforts. The contrast here with Isaiah Berlin's advocacy of 'negative liberty' comes readily to mind. What kind of political order is envisaged in *The Human Condition* is also unclear. Arendt is no more of a communitarian than she is a liberal individualist. Any kind of communalism, nationalist or otherwise, is distasteful to her because it integrates people so closely as to stifle the 'spaces' necessary to action. Denied access to reality, the masses easily fall prey to ideologists promising a fictive sense of belonging. On the other hand, and as we have seen, Arendt regards the existence of a public realm as indispensable to freedom. A common world or body politic has to be sustained by the spiritedness of citizens. Her reasoning suggests the need for no further or more primary underpinnings of attachment, with the result that ethnic, religious, or even cultural ties remain irrelevant. Perhaps they are also undesirable. With modern authority of all kinds in tatters, the task of politics appears to Arendt as the existential creation of states resting on neither absolutist principles, religious sanctions, Sorelian myths, or the prescriptions of tradition. The republicanism favoured is none the less hostile to the 'willing' of Rousseau, whose 'general will' imposes such integral unity that the plurality essential to freedom is compromised. How far it is tenable to envisage the creation of states from which the integuments of collective identity have been excluded is not a topic which figures in *The Human*

Condition. Arendt's personal aversion to the excesses of nationalism did not blunt her belief in collective self-government, including the claim of Jews to their own homeland.

In one respect *The Human Condition* is conceptually conservative. In keeping with the originators of political philosophy, the standpoint around which argument revolves is that of a single body politic conveniently detached from other similar entities. There is scant awareness that the external setting of states is a conditioning element in their formation. When they figure at all, foreign affairs do so as considerations circumscribing the actions of states rather than determining their internal composition. This is perhaps odd in the case of Arendt, because, just as action is understood to imply plurality, so one might expect her political theorizing to emphasize a multiplicity of states and the interactions of international politics. Whatever the omissions of political philosophy, this has usually been the 'field of action' in which public events have enjoyed their widest resonance. As Thucydides describes them in *The Peloponnesian War,* the character of Athens and Sparta and not merely their fate was determined by the force of their conflict. The same might be said of the principal actors in the Cold War and its aftermath.

When all is said, however, what has most disturbed Arendt's admirers is the account of action as its own end. As we have noticed, what matters is neither what motivates action nor what aims it pursues. She deplores the transcription of instrumental, means–ends thinking, from the world of *homo faber* to the public realm. To conceive of action as subserving some useful purpose, that aims beyond itself to some portion of the world it seeks to preserve or modify, is said by Arendt to rest on a misunderstanding. Although Arendt shared none of Oakeshott's confidence in the indicativeness of tradition in the modern world, on this theme they appear to have much in common. For both the error lies in seeking to reduce to a means what cannot be made instrumental without being lost, and what is at stake for Arendt is nothing less than the freedom of political action. The difficulty with this formulation is in fathoming what it can mean, and, although it helps to see the matter as linked to Arendt's methodological abruptness, this only shifts the difficulty to a different level. To many who share Arendt's worldly preoccupations and the need to make explicit the assumptions on which they rest, the point of action is that it has a point, that it is pointed and purposeful. When Dante is quoted to the effect that 'in action the being of the doer is somehow intensified', so that 'delight necessarily follows' (p. 156), this cannot evoke a full response until one learns what is being done. Action may disclose who a person is, but it surely makes a difference to a person's identity whether he has been busy berating his neighbours or acting on their behalf. This determination to keep her chosen categories untainted and unrelated also sits awkwardly with other aspects of Arendt's thought. In treating the human world as the sole place where men can—by their actions—make themselves at home, Arendt is urging a philosophy of freedom wedded to responsibility. Space travel and journeys of inward pilgrimage are frowned upon, because they are evasions of reality which alienate us from treating the world as a secure place with meaning—that is, a home. Her summons is surely one demanding purposeful and courageous action rather than the public displays of men with only reputation on their minds.

Coriolanus scorned public reaction, and gestured instead towards 'a world elsewhere' that might better reward his abilities and desire to stand out. If men presently set out from earth to discover new places in space, this may not be the evidence of alienation Arendt took it to imply. It may, on the contrary, be a revealingly human call to action, to initiate dramatic new beginnings. The 'space of appearance' in which men would then appear would be in space. In that event, we should have to revise a view that takes the earth as the only home for men. The constitution of a politics where men were at home 'elsewhere', or had concluded that they could do without a *heimat*, would be a radical break with the human condition. Arendt's formulation of its once secure features prepares us to think beyond them.

Bibliographical Note

The Human Condition was first published in 1958 by the University of Chicago. Anchor Doubleday of New York issued a paperback edition in 1959. The most complete bibliography of Arendt's publications is in Elizabeth Young-Bruehl, *Hannah Arendt* (New Haven, 1982), 437–77. This is also a full-length biography, which provides the most through account to date. By far the most scholarly study of Arend's entire *corpus* is Margaret Canovan, *Hannah Arendt: A Reinterpretation* (Cambridge, 1992). This was issued in a paperback edition in 1994. Canovan emphazises how far her subject's entire thought is prefigured in *The Origins of Totalitarianism*. Arendt amended this work as it progressed from one edition to another. Her lastest modifications and additions are to be found in the paperback edition published by Andre Deutsch (London, 1986).

Among the gathering list of book-length studies of Arendt's thought, several deserve particular mention. B. Parekh, *Hannah Arendt and the Search for a New Political Philosophy* (London, 1981), and George Kateb, *Hannah Arendt: Politics, Conscience, Evil* (Oxford, 1984), are both learned and stimulating. The first explains Arendt's indebtedness to the phenomenological school of philosophy associated with Husserl, while the second seeks to rehabilitate American democracy within the scheme of Arendt's thinking. The more recent Philip Hanson, *Hannah Arendt: Politics, History, and Citizenship* (Oxford, 1993), and M. P. d'Entreves, *The Political Philosophy of Hannah Arendt* (Routledge, 1993), may also be recommended.

There are three noteworthy collections of essays which between them cover many aspects of Arendt's writings. Melvyn Hill (ed.), *Hannah Arendt: The Recovery of the Public World* (New York, 1979), the whole volume of *Social Research*, 44/1 (1977), and *Salmagundi* (Fall 1969–Winter 1970).

Among articles and essays, the following are especially useful for the reader of *The Human Condition*: N. O'Sullivan, 'Hellenic Nostalgia and Industrial Society', in A. de Crespigny and K. Minogue (eds.), *Contemporary Political Philosophy* (London, 1976), 228–52; L. P. Hinchman and S. K. Hinchman, 'In Heidegger's Shadow: Hannah Arendt's Phenomenological Humanism, *Review of Politics*, 46 (Apr. 1984), 183–211; L. P. Hinchman and S. K. Hinchman, 'Existentialism Politicized: Arendt's debt to Jaspers', *Review of Politics*, 52/3 (Summer 1991), 435–68.

The bibliography in Margaret Canovan's book mentioned above contains references to a wealth of recent scholarship which illustrates how Arendt's fertile mind continues to occasion interest.

8

Friedrich August von Hayek:
The Constitution of Liberty

ANDREW GAMBLE

FRIEDRICH VON HAYEK was born in Austria in 1899 into a well-established family of academics and civil servants. (Wittgenstein was a cousin.) He studied law and political science at Vienna before concentrating his energies on economics. He abandoned his early Fabian views through attendance at the seminar of Ludwig von Mises, one of the leading figures in the Austrian school of economics. At the invitation of Lionel Robbins, Hayek came to London and was appointed to the Tooke Professorship of Economics at the London School of Economics in 1932. During the 1930s he published a number of theoretical books on economics, became a strong critic of Keynes, and participated in the debate initiated by Mises on the possibility of rational calculation in a socialist economy.

In 1944 Hayek published his single most famous work, *The Road to Serfdom*. Following its success, he moved in 1950 to a Chair in Social and Moral Sciences at the University of Chicago. *The Constitution of Liberty* appeared in 1960. He moved to Freiburg in 1962 and during the 1970s published the three volumes of *Law, Legislation, and Liberty*. He was awarded the Nobel Prize for Economics in 1974. His last work was *The Fatal Conceit* (1988). He died in 1992.

Having spent the first half of his academic career as an economist, Hayek at first resented the diversion of his energies away from economics towards social and political theory. But he became convinced that there was no more urgent task than to restate the basic principles of a liberal society. His aim in *The Constitution of Liberty*, he wrote, was 'to picture an ideal, to show how it can be achieved, and to explain what its realization would mean in practice' (p. vii).[1]

---

[1] F. A. Hayek, *The Constitution of Liberty* (London, 1960). References in the text are to this edition.

Hayek published several important books which explored the foundations of a liberal society, including *Individualism and Economic Order* (1948) and the later three-volume *Law, Legislation, and Liberty* (1973, 1976, 1979), but *The Constitution of Liberty* is widely regarded as his most important and complete work. When it first appeared it was received respectfully but critically. Many saw it as an erudite but misguided attempt to return to the lost world of nineteenth-century liberalism.

Hayek in 1960 was seen as rather an isolated figure, out of touch with the main intellectual and policy developments of the time. He had founded the Mont Pèlerin Society after the war, an association composed mainly of liberal academics from a variety of disciplines who met regularly to debate their principles and to discuss how the liberal cause could be promoted. But most liberals had accepted the political compromises that created the welfare state and managed capitalism of the post-war decades.

The ideological and policy changes of the 1970s and 1980s gave Hayek a new status and created a new interest in his ideas, and brought a reassessment of *The Constitution of Liberty*. Hayek enjoyed the rare privilege for a public intellectual of apparently being proved right in his own lifetime. He had remained loyal to a set of beliefs and principles when they were unfashionable and often derided, but lived to see them rehabilitated. He was particularly known in the 1970s and 1980s for the attention paid to his writings by a number of prominent politicians, including, in England, Margaret Thatcher and Sir Keith Joseph. *The Constitution of Liberty* became one of the most influential books for the New Right, and Hayek was celebrated as one of its main inspirations. Many of his ideas were disseminated through the right-wing think-tanks of this period, particularly the Institute of Economic Affairs, the Centre for Policy Studies, and the Adam Smith Institute.

Structure

The Constitution of Liberty is Hayek's most complete statement of the principles of a free society. He was later to regret the title, realizing that he should have reserved it for his later three-volume work, *Law, Legislation, and Liberty*:

If I had known when I published *The Constitution of Liberty* that I should proceed to the task attempted in the present work, I should have reserved that title for it. I then used the term 'constitution' in the wide sense in which we use it also to describe the state of fitness of a person. It is only in the present book that I address myself to the question of what constitutional arrangements, in the legal sense, might be most conducive to the preservation of individual freedom.[2]

Hayek later described his purpose in *The Constitution of Liberty* as 'the restatement of the traditional doctrines of classical liberalism in a form suited to contemporary problems and thinking'.[3] The book sets out the basic principles of liberty in philosophy, law, and politics, and shows how the classical principles can be applied to the particular circumstances of the welfare state. The book is divided into three parts—The Value of Freedom; Freedom and the Law; Freedom in the Welfare State—and concludes with a famous postscript, 'Why I am not a Conservative'.

The Constitution of Liberty is a much less polemical work than *The Road to Serfdom*, but it is animated by the same concern. Hayek believed that Western civilization was imperilled both by the malice of its enemies, and by the ignorance of many of its friends, who adopted policies which were incompatible with it and paved the way for totalitarianism. Hayek's motive in writing *The Constitution of Liberty* was to provide a principled foundation from which Western civilization could be defended and criteria developed to evaluate proposals for changes in institutions and policies.

Writing in 1960, Hayek thought that the worst of the totalitarian danger had passed. In particular, socialism was in decline. In one of the key chapters of *The Constitution of Liberty*, chapter 17, 'The Decline of Socialism and the Rise of the Welfare State', which opens part 3, Hayek explains why this is so. Socialism, he argues, had been the dominant idea in Western civilization for over a century. It had captured a large part of the intellectual leaders and had been accepted as the goal to which society was proceeding, even by those like Joseph Schumpeter who were opposed to it.[4] In 1944 Hayek

---

[2] F. A. Hayek, *Law, Legislation, and Liberty*, i. *Rules and Order* (London, 1982), 3.
[3] Hayek, *Law, Legislation, and Liberty*, p. xix.
[4] J. A. Schumpeter, *Capitalism, Socialism, and Democracy* (London, 1943).

had been full of gloomy prognostications about how far social-ism had still to go. But by 1960 he had concluded that social-ism had passed its peak. Its high-water mark had been the Labour Government in Britain between 1945 and 1951. 'Fu-ture historians will probably regard the period from the revo-lution of 1848 to about 1948 as the century of European socialism' (p. 253).

What had changed the prospects for socialism was the ex-perience of socialism in practice. During the socialist century socialism had a precise meaning and a definite programme. Methods might differ as between Marxists and Fabians, but the basic conception of the society they wanted to create was the same. This was a society in which all resources would be em-ployed for use rather than for profit, which would be achieved through the nationalization of the means of production, dis-tribution, and exchange, so that 'all activity might be directed according to a comprehensive plan toward some ideal of social justice' (p. 254).

This great socialist idea was now defunct. Marxism had been discredited by the Russian experience. Although former sup-porters of communism were at first slow to face the truth, Hayek argued that they would eventually be forced to accept that what had happened in Russia was the necessary outcome of the systematic application of the traditional socialist pro-gramme. This intellectual sea-change was due to the recogni-tion of three key aspects of the soviet experience; first, that a socialist organization of production would be not more but much less productive than private enterprise; secondly, that instead of leading to greater social justice it would mean a new arbitrary and more inescapable order of rank; and, thirdly, that instead of the promised greater freedom it would establish a new despotism (p. 256).

These three themes are central to Hayek's work, and pro-vide the rationale for *The Constitution of Liberty*. It was not conceived solely as an intellectual exercise, an abstract enquiry into the formal properties of liberal principles. Its aim was rather to combat socialism by exposing its intellectual errors and its practical consequences, and to improve understanding and increase support for the only principles which could en-sure the survival of a free civilization. Hayek was concerned that Western civilization could perish because a generation had grown up which was unaware of its basic principles, and could therefore support policies which could establish socialism unintentionally: 'We are in danger unless we succeed in distinguishing those of the new ambitions which can be achieved in a free society from those which require for their realization the methods of totalitarian collectivism' (p. 257).

In this mood Hayek appears as a strong rationalist, who accords certain values supreme importance, and uses them as a criterion to assess all other beliefs, doctrines, and policies. Oakeshott noted this strain in Hayek: 'A plan to resist all planning may be better than its opposite but it belongs to the same style of politics.'[5] But Hayek is more complex than this. There is a tension in his thought between rationalism and evolutionism. The latter is responsible for many of his most important insights—on the decentralized nature of knowledge and the unintended consequences of social action—and makes him at times appear more conservative than liberal. In the Introduction to *The Constitution of Liberty* he writes:

My aim will not be to provide a detailed programme of policy but rather to state the criteria by which particular measures must be judged if they are to fit into a regime of freedom. It would be contrary to the whole spirit of this book if I were to consider myself competent to design a comprehensive programme of policy. Such a programme, after all, must grow out of the application of a common philosophy to the problems of the day. (p. 5)

The problem for Hayek is where the common philosophy comes from and how it is to be justified. Hayek seeks to show in *The Constitution of Liberty* that Western civilization arose through an unplanned, evolutionary process, but also that it expresses a particular ideal. If the ideal should be discarded or forgotten, the evolutionary process is not robust enough to preserve Western civilization. The existence of Western civilization is a precious inheritance which modern rationalism threatens to destroy. Yet only through an alternative rationalism can this threat be averted. Hayek believes strongly in the power of ideas. Only the reconversion of Western intellectuals to the ideal of a free society can save Western civilization.

[5] M. Oakeshott, *Rationalism in Politics and other Essays* (London, 1962), 21.

Hayek had no doubts as to what this ideal should be. He quotes Frederick Watkins approvingly:

the object of most Western thinkers has been to establish a society in which every individual, with a minimum of dependence on discretionary authority of his rulers, would enjoy the privileges and responsibility of determining his own conduct within a previously defined framework of rights and duties. (p. 3)

But he also notes that most Western intellectuals have become defensive, and that there has been little attempt to offer an ultimate justification for this ideal or to apply it to contemporary problems. This is what Hayek seeks to remedy.

Liberty

The fragility of civilization is a key theme of *The Constitution of Liberty*, and reflects Hayek's pessimistic view of human nature and the role of reason in human affairs. His general outlook is derived from some of the key thinkers of the Scottish Enlightenment, particularly David Hume and Adam Smith. Like them he does not believe in the natural goodness of human beings. The Scottish theorists he argues regarded human beings as 'lazy, indolent, improvident, and wasteful'. Only by force of circumstances could human beings be made to behave in a rational economic manner. The *homo economicus* of later economic theory Hayek derided as a fiction, a product of Bentham's rationalistic utilitarianism. The concept of *homo economicus* implied that human beings were naturally rational, in the sense that their behaviour was driven by calculations of the costs and benefits of alternative courses of action. Hayek argues that only institutions make human beings rational. The artifices of institutions and traditions are necessary to channel the drives of human nature in benign directions, by allowing the pursuit of private interests to serve indirectly the public interest. For this to be possible a framework of law and institutions is necessary.

Hayek sees civilization as something which has arisen despite human nature not because of it. Even Adam Smith's natural propensity to truck and barter is absent in Hayek. What he describes is a painful historical progress lasting eight thousand years during which human societies have gradually built modern civilization. The passage from hunting to agriculture to industry and urban life has taken only three thousand years, one hundred generations. Hayek's pessimism for the human species is rooted in his judgement that human beings have run ahead of their biological capability. Many human instincts and emotions are 'more adapted to the life of a hunter than to life in civilization' (p. 40). As a result human beings are not really at home in civilization, one sign of which is that in modern culture civilization is constantly depicted as unhealthy, unnatural, and artificial.

For Hayek civilization is an accident, an outcome which no one intended, and which partly for that reason is in danger of being heedlessly destroyed. Central to his conception of human nature are the limited powers of human reason and the extent of human ignorance. Human beings did not deliberately set out to build their civilization, and what has been created does not reflect a pre-existing plan. Human reason is not something outside nature; human beings do not possess knowledge and reasoning capacity independently of experience. Rather it is an integral part of experience and is most effective when the limits within which it has to work are properly understood.

These limits are set by institutions such as the market and law which have spontaneously evolved over many generations to solve particular problems of coordinating myriad individual plans and actions and make them compatible with one another. To disregard the knowledge that is contained in these institutions and to believe that they can be dismantled and new institutions imposed without serious social dislocation is for Hayek the heart of the modern intellectual conceit which has caused the disasters of the twentieth century.

The most important outcome of the way that civilization has developed is freedom. Hayek treats freedom not as a natural right, nor as something which is inherent in human nature, but as a value which the development of civilization has made possible. Through the development of institutions such as law and the market, conditions have been created in which coercion can be minimized. Hayek defines liberty therefore as 'that condition of men in which coercion of some by others is reduced as much as is possible in society' (p. 11).

Liberty here refers solely to the relation of one human being to another. Hayek is interested only in defining freedom as personal freedom, the condition in which a person is not subject to coercion by the arbitrary will of another or others (p. 12). He wants to distance the concept from political freedom, inner freedom, or positive freedom. Personal liberty he argues is quite compatible with political authoritarianism. Conversely, 'to choose one's government is not necessarily to secure freedom' (p. 14). Similarly the absence of wealth and power does not mean that an individual is not free; gaining them does not guarantee liberty.

Hayek wants to restrict the concept of liberty to personal freedom, which he regards as the most important outcome of modern civilization. He defines the essentials of personal liberty as follows:

if he is subject only to the same laws as all his fellow citizens, if he is immune from arbitrary confinement and free to choose his work, and if he is able to own and acquire property, no other men or group of men can coerce him to do their bidding. (p. 20)

Hayek offers two justifications for the importance of personal liberty. First is a Kantian argument that coercion is evil because it eliminates an individual as a thinking and valuing person, making him 'a bare tool' in the achievements of the ends of another. The second, and more characteristically Hayekian, is a utilitarian argument, derived from John Stuart Mill about the progress of civilization: 'The case for individual freedom rests chiefly on the recognition of the inevitable ignorance of all of us concerning a great many of the factors on which the achievement of our ends and welfare depends' (p. 29). Tolerating different choices is important because no one has sufficient information available to evaluate alternatives and prescribe the best solution. Trial and error are essential if civilization is to continue to progress.

One implication of Hayek's view of personal freedom is that, if coercion of one individual by another is to be reduced to a minimum, a significant role exists for the state, since, as Hayek explains, coercion can only be eliminated altogether by the threat of coercion. The justification for the existence of the state is that, if such a body can establish a monopoly of coercion throughout society, all individuals will then enjoy personal freedom to choose their activities and pursue their purposes. The problem, however, is how to limit the state's role to preventing coercion by private individuals. Once the state has a monopoly of coercive power, who is to stop the state using it to coerce its citizens in untold other respects?

The need for a constitution of liberty arises from this classic liberal dilemma. Ways must be found of restraining the state from abusing the powers it needs. Having once created Leviathan in order to ensure that all citizens can be free from most forms of private coercion, controlling Leviathan is a much harder task. This is partly because Hayek does not see the state as one of the core institutions which has evolved to make possible the spontaneous order which makes the exercise of personal freedom possible. The state is necessary to protect and police the market order, but it is a contrivance which is always in danger of exceeding its proper limits.

Hayek makes a sharp distinction between coercion and compulsion. Coercion refers to actions which individuals do to other individuals. The effects of physical circumstances involve compulsion but not coercion. Circumstances can compel, but only people can coerce. A problem arises as to whether coerced individuals still make choices. Hayek states that the coerced individual does choose, but the coercer determines the alternatives. The coerced can choose only what the coercer wants, and therefore are deprived of the possibility of using the knowledge they possess to pursue their own aims.

This criterion is not very clear, because there are very few situations in which the alternatives confronting individuals are not influenced by others. Since individuals are not equal, and there are wide disparities in wealth, power, and talent, the possibilities for influencing the choices people make are enormous. At what point does influence constitute coercion? Is the power of large organizations in respect of their members and employees an instance of coercion or not?

Hayek has a reverence for organization. He reserves his hostility for particular types of organization, mainly trade unions and governments. The presence of power in itself he argues is not enough to indicate the presence of coercion: 'there is no evil in the power wielded by the director of some great enterprise in which men have willingly united of their own will and for their own purposes' (p. 135). Hayek gives as examples Henry Ford, the Atomic Energy Commission, and the Salvation Army. He does not include the state, because he regards the state as a monopolist, while the others are subject to competition. Only monopolists can exercise coercion.

If an owner of a resource imposes conditions on its use, no coercion is involved provided the would-be purchasers of the resource have alternative sources of supply. If, however, there is only one spring in an oasis, and people have settled there 'on the assumption that water would always be available at a reasonable price' (p. 136), the setting of conditions for the use of that spring would be monopolistic. The individuals who want to use the spring are coerced to accept the conditions which the owner dictates.

Hayek intends his example as an extreme case to illustrate his general argument that private monopoly is extremely rare and therefore coercion itself is extremely rare between individuals in a market economy. But his example has been much criticized, because the basis on which the owner of the spring is deemed a monopolist seems inadequate. Libertarians deny that any coercion is involved. If the owner of the spring has a legitimate property right, only the owner can judge whether or not and under what conditions to make the spring available to others. Either the settlers should not have settled there in the first place or they are free to move away. They still have choices.

In talking of the settlers' assumption that water would always be available, Hayek introduces quite different criteria, of need and entitlement, concepts which he has sought to exclude in discussing allocation problems. The owner of the spring faces the settlers with unpleasant choices, but so does the owner of a factory who makes his workers redundant unless they accept new working practices and lower wages. Hayek agrees that in 'periods of acute unemployment the threat of dismissal may be used to enforce actions other than those originally contracted for' (pp. 136–7). But he asserts that these are rare exceptions in a prosperous, competitive society. In admitting that there are some circumstances in which private power in a market economy can be coercive, he opens the door for a very different discourse about coercion and liberty.

Hayek elaborates his position by considering other cases where coercion is said to exist, such as the withholding of benefits, or a refusal of employment. These are not true cases of coercion, he argues. The threat of starvation may compel me to accept a distasteful job at a very low wage, but the person willing to employ me does not coerce me because I have the choice of not accepting his offer. For Hayek coercion can arise only when one individual forces another to do specific things that would not otherwise have been done.

An obvious gap in Hayek's account is the sphere of personal relationships, domestic labour, and the family. Hayek agrees that all close relationships provide opportunities for coercion, but argues that this sphere falls outside the competence of the state. 'The coercion that arises from voluntary association cannot be the concern of government' (p. 138). Hayek's refusal to engage at all with the private sphere is a characteristic omission. Such issues are a distraction from his main theme—the problem of state coercion and whether it can be limited.

His solution to coercion in the private sphere, whether in the family or in civil society, is the same—allowing individuals to create for themselves their own private sphere where they can be protected from interference by others. Pushed to its extreme this might suggest that the only ultimate protection against coercion is to abolish families, companies, and organizations, and to allow all individuals to become independent property owners. Hayek resists such extreme measures. His pessimism about human nature is tempered by some faith in the ability of individuals to choose freely to stay within associations like families and firms, without suffering coercion. But he has no doubt that limiting coercion through the state is only part of the answer. The way of limiting the power of the monopolist whether in the public or the private sphere is to oblige the monopolist to be non-discriminatory and treat all customers alike. But even better is the provision of each individual with independence, which for Hayek means property.

Property is another key feature of Hayek's view of human nature. Human beings will coerce one another if they are given the chance. The only way of building a civilization in which coercion is reduced to a minimum and personal freedom is maximized is to promote property ownership: 'The recognition of private or several (i.e. individually separate) property is an essential condition for the prevention of coercion' (p. 140).

At this point, however, Hayek's argument encounters a difficulty. If private property is so important to personal freedom, does this mean that the majority of people in modern societies who have no such property are not free. Hayek provides ambivalent replies to this problem in *The Constitution of Liberty*. In places he vigorously denies it; in others he concedes that it may be so, or at least that it is a restriction of the development of personal freedom as he understands it.

His denial that propertylessness means an absence of freedom is based on the argument that all that is required for human beings to be free is that the material means necessary to pursue any plan of action are not controlled by a monopolist. Freedom, he insists, can be enjoyed by a person with practically no property: 'The important point is that the property should be sufficiently dispersed so that the individual is not dependent on particular persons who alone can provide him with what he needs or who alone can employ him' (p. 141).

Hayek then extends this argument by stating that the individual in a modern market economy need never be coerced. Even state impositions like compulsory military service or taxation do not have 'the evil nature of coercion' because they are predictable. The coercive power of government is apparently only truly coercive when it is neither avoidable nor predictable. Hayek's argument assumes a particular conception of the minimal state. Provided the state accepts the existence of a private sphere which is delineated in law by general rules which the state enforces, and provided the state confines its coercive actions to enforcing those rules, then the coercive power of the state, even when it involves such gross interference with personal freedom as compulsory military service, is legitimate.

But in other places Hayek is more critical of trends in modern society, and the obstacles in the way of individuals exercising personal freedom. The reason is that he sees liberty and responsibility as inseparable. Responsibility for Hayek presupposes that individuals are capable of learning from experience and of guiding their actions by knowledge thus acquired (p. 77). Individuals form plans of action and pursue their aims, and take responsibility for the outcomes. On their ability to do this much depends, including moral esteem. Freedom makes this possible, but it also carries risks: 'The necessity of finding a sphere of usefulness, an appropriate job . . . is the hardest discipline that a free society imposes on us' (p. 80). Unlike in an aristocratic society where individuals are assigned tasks and duties, in the market society individuals are obliged to be resourceful and to discover themselves, not wait to be discovered by others.

Hayek is well aware, however, that in the last hundred years the trend has been for most individuals to become employees rather than independent property owners. Employees enjoy personal freedom as Hayek has defined it, but because they do not own property they form a different conception of the market economy from those that do. The consequences are potentially serious once the franchise is extended beyond the ranks of the property owners. The opinions of the employees now constitute the majority and govern policy: inevitably politicians begin offering policies which favour the special interests of the employed. What the employed want is an assured fixed income which is available for current expenditure; they want automatic wage increases; and social security, including provision for old age; and much more.

The employed therefore gravitate naturally to supporting programmes which promise to relieve them of some of the uncertainties of economic life, and which talk the language of social justice, and the paternalistic state. The rise of this mentality makes the preservation of a class of owners of small businesses and independent wealthy individuals all the more important, both to maintain the dynamism of the economy, and to maintain support for a whole range of activities—arts, sports, as well as independent intellectual activity—which tend to get stifled according to Hayek if the dependent culture of the employee society takes hold.

Hayek writes elegantly and at length about the dangers to the kind of society he favours. But he has no serious proposals as to how the situation might be remedied. Writing in 1960 he could identify no trends that might move society towards self-employment again, and was not prepared to advocate any measure that might lead to the break-up of large companies and organizations. On the contrary, his theory of personal freedom indicated that freedom could still exist even if everyone was employed by vast conglomerates. But, as he admitted, there was no reason why these employees would support political programmes which protected the market order.

Democracy

Hayek's theory of the importance of both responsibility and property for freedom might have led him to advocate radical reforms to roll back the corporate economy. One reason why he did not is his deep suspicion of politics and the state. He sees nothing positive in politics; it is a means to guarantee the market order and the sphere of individual freedom. But it is also the main threat to it. If a politics-free world were possible, Hayek would no doubt favour it. He was, however, always aware that politics, although distasteful, was necessary if liberal civilization were to be preserved.

In *The Constitution of Liberty* he discusses two main dangers posed by the nature of contemporary politics. The first is the struggle within the Western tradition between two conceptions of rationality; the second is the doctrine of popular sovereignty.

Hayek argues that there are two traditions of liberty in the Western tradition, roughly divided between the British and the French, although there are important representatives of both nationalities in the other camp. The British tradition of Hume, Smith, Ferguson, Tucker, Burke, and Paley, supported by Montesquieu, Constant, and Tocqueville, understood liberty as the product of spontaneity, the absence of coercion, evolutionary growth, and trial-and-error procedures. The French tradition of the Enlightenment and Cartesian rationalism, as developed by the *encyclopédistes*, Rousseau, the Physiocrats, and Condorcet, with its English and American sympathizers, who included Godwin, Price, Paine, Priestley, and Jefferson, understood liberty as the product of planning and rational design, and the achievement of collective purposes through organization.

The British tradition as Hayek pictures it was an anti-rationalist tradition. Institutions and morals, language and law, had evolved by a process of cumulative growth. Only within this framework of unselfconscious historical understanding could the human race successfully operate. The task of reason was to understand this process and draw appropriate lessons from it. The French tradition believed that modern society was qualitatively different from what had gone before, and justified the use of human reason to remodel institutions and behaviour.

The conflict between the two traditions was at its sharpest over democracy. Hayek argues that the British tradition produced liberal democracy, and the French tradition, totalitarian democracy. For Hayek, democracy was not an end in itself but only a means to an end. Liberalism he defined as a doctrine about the scope and methods of government, while democracy was a method for reaching decisions, not an authority for what the decision ought to be.

Hayek argues that democracies can be totalitarian, while authoritarian governments may be liberal and may preserve personal freedom, the value he most cares about. He would prefer to have democratic arrangements, but only so long as liberal ideas shape policy-making. Democracy is dangerous because under it the principle of majority rule and the doctrine of popular sovereignty may be used to legitimate illiberal programmes and sweeping invasions of the private sphere. The doctrine of popular sovereignty makes majority rule unlimited and unlimitable. In this way, instead of being a check on arbitrary power, democracy can become the basis for a new arbitrary power. In the name of the sovereign people governments can expropriate property and impose taxation and controls without any regard for the preservation of personal freedom and the intricate workings of the market economy.

Hayek notes some of the arguments for democracy—that it is the only known method of peaceful political change; that in some circumstances it can safeguard individual liberty; and that it is the only effective method of educating the majority in liberal principles. But he remains unconvinced. The dangers loom larger than the benefits. The number of people who truly understand how the market order works are very few, and their views are likely to be drowned in the clamour of popular democracy. Intellectuals have a key role to play so long as they are genuinely independent and do not feel themselves bound by majority opinion. Their task is to warn ceaselessly that if democracies attempt too much and fail to impose limits on the power of the majority they threaten to destroy not only peace and prosperity but also democracy itself (p. 114).

The various devices developed to control government are given a substantial review by Hayek. He analyses the nature of law, and the growth of various legal doctrines which have attempted to prescribe limits to state power. He makes a sharp distinction between commands and law. Law, like language and the market, was invented by no one, and at its simplest is the delimitation of individual spheres by abstract rules. In order for a system of law to guarantee personal freedom, Hayek states that two key conditions must be fulfilled: lawgivers must not know the particular cases to which their rules will apply, and judges who apply the rules must have no choice in drawing the conclusions that follow from the existing body of rules and the particular facts of the case.

Hayek strongly opposes the development of positive systems of law, influenced by rationalism, in which general rules were discarded, and instead the law was equated with administrative decrees. The blurring of the distinction between law and administration he regarded as one of the greatest dangers to maintaining a liberal society. Once the border was crossed there was nothing to stop governments constantly invading the private sphere.

Underlying this conception of law is a notion of spontaneous order developed by Michael Polanyi among others, and which in turn goes back to the Scottish political economists and to Mandeville. A spontaneous order is achieved by allowing individuals to interact on their own initiative within a framework of rules which apply to all. It is the framework of rules which creates the conditions under which coordination of individual plans and actions can take place.

Hayek traces the development of ideas of the rule of law from the Greeks through the English revolutionary period to the American idea of constitutionalism and the German concept of *Rechtsstaat*. His main interest is in discerning the various practical means by which attempts were made to place limits on the coercive powers of the state. He saw the significance of constitutionalism as the attempt to ensure that long-term aims were not invariably sacrificed to immediate objectives. Although each solution was different, the important principle was that law was considered separate from government, so that it provided a means by which governments could be held accountable, and their actions restrained. The ideal was a government of laws not of men.

Hayek regarded the merging of law and government as one of the most disturbing developments of the twentieth century and the prelude to totalitarianism. He attacked those like Kelsen who rejected natural law and those who like Pashukanis proclaimed that all law is transformed into administration, or like Robson that the distinction between policy and law had become meaningless. But he was critical also of the Anglo-Saxon lack of interest and sometimes misunderstanding of the German *Rechtsstaat* tradition. The doctrine of parliamentary sovereignty in England which under the Whigs had been used to protect liberty had become a device under twentieth-century conservatives and socialists by which the protections formerly afforded by the Common Law were being brushed aside. Dicey and other constitutional lawyers, he argued, had failed to appreciate the value of having separate administrative courts to help restrain the power of an assertive executive.

Policy

Hayek devotes Part 3 of *The Constitution of Liberty* to freedom in the welfare state. He seeks to apply his broad principles to contemporary policy problems. There are chapters on the labour unions and employment; social security; taxation and redistribution; the monetary framework; housing and town planning; agriculture and natural resources; and education and research.

Many of the proposals may appear rather mild to the contemporary reader. But at the time, given the weight of opinion in favour of an expanding welfare state, they did offer a very different agenda. There is nothing, however, to compare with

Hayek's subsequent advocacy of the abolition of the government's monopoly of money, or his advice to the Thatcher Government in 1980 that there should be an immediate repeal of the 1906 Trade Disputes Act.

In 1960 Hayek finds much in contemporary welfare policies that is compatible with freedom. Some of his sharpest criticism is reserved for trade unions, which he sees as the only real example of monopoly and therefore of private coercion left in market economies: 'The present coercive powers of the unions rest chiefly on the use of methods which would not be tolerated for any other purpose and which are opposed to the protection of the individual's private sphere' (p. 274). But Hayek admits that legal prohibition of unions would not be justifiable. This is because in a free society much that is undesirable has to be tolerated if it cannot be prevented without discriminatory legislation (p. 275).

On social security he concedes the case for a public minimum of provision and compulsory insurance. What he opposes is any attempt to use social welfare as a device to promote redistribution of income. Such a programme carries grave risks of invading the sphere of personal liberty: 'while in a free society it is possible to provide a minimum level of welfare for all, such a society is not compatible with sharing out income according to some preconceived notion of justice' (p. 303). He also opposes the principles underlying the National Health Service, on the grounds that the demands that will be placed on any universal service will be unlimited, and ultimately incapable of being satisfied.

On taxation he accepts that those who earn more should pay more, but argues strongly that taxes should not be progressive but proportional. Everyone should pay the same proportion of their total income in direct taxation. The proportion should be low (no higher than 25 per cent) in order not to remove incentives. On inflation he reiterated the line which made him notorious in the 1930s, backing sound money, a strong central bank, and looking back nostalgically to the gold standard. The difficulty of preventing inflation he declared is political and not economic.

On education he accepted the case for the state providing minimum education, partly because of the benefits if all citizens share certain beliefs, and partly because democracy is unlikely to work with an illiterate people. He saw no reason for schools or universities to be run by the government, however. All advanced education should be left in private hands. He asserts the importance of intellectual freedom, but also argues that communists should not be given tenure in universities, on the ground that they oppose the principle of tolerance.

Hayek's liberal philosophy meant that he always accepted that the state had important functions, and was quite ready to see the state take on new responsibilities if a good practical case could be made. What he opposed was any attempt to drive policy in the name of social justice or any other over-arching idea, because this could mean the thoughtless dismantling of the institutions and safeguards of the market order. The conquest of old social evils could create new problems for the future. Hayek prophesied inflation, paralysing taxation, coercive labour unions, increasing dominance of government in education, and a social-service bureaucracy with far-reaching arbitrary powers.

Conservatism and Liberalism

The Constitution of Liberty ends with a notorious and intriguing postscript, 'Why I am not a Conservative'. It attracted a great deal of attention in the 1970s, when Hayek appeared to make common cause with Conservative politicians. Hayek agrees that the position he defends throughout the book is often described as conservative, but he argues that this is because the defenders of liberty and true conservatives have come together in opposition to developments which equally threaten their different ideals (p. 397). But he insists that the ideals are different, and that, although there are conservative insights from which liberals can benefit, there remains a wide gulf between a liberal and a conservative disposition.

The two key differences lie in the attitude to change, and the attitude to authority. Conservatives are willing to use the powers of government to arrest change or slow it down. Liberals are more optimistic that change will be beneficial, and have no wish to preserve things as they are: 'What is most urgently needed in most parts of the world is a thorough sweeping-away of the obstacles to free growth' (p. 399).

Secondly, Conservatives are more ready to trust authority. They are hostile to basing policies on abstract theories and general principles. As a result their understanding of how modern societies work is imperfect. Conservatives are temperamentally inclined to reinforce established authority. If an authority is one of which Conservatives approve, they are generally happy to see its powers strengthened. Liberals are much more suspicious of all power, and seek to place curbs upon it. Liberals are also prepared to be much more tolerant than Conservatives to ways of life and individual choices of which they personally may disapprove. Hayek argues that moral and religious ideals are not proper objects of coercion.

The basic problem with Conservatism for Hayek, however, is that it is rudderless. It is preoccupied with power. It defends privilege, it is frequently obscurantist, it is nationalistic, but, above all,

it cannot offer an alternative to the direction in which we are moving. It may succeed by its resistance to current tendencies in slowing down undesirable developments, but, since it does not indicate another direction, it cannot prevent their continuance. It has, for this reason, invariably been the fate of conservatism to be dragged along a path not of its own choosing . . . What the liberal must ask, first of all, is not how fast or how far we should move, but where we should move. (p. 398)

Providing the criteria for that alternative direction was the underlying purpose of *The Constitution of Liberty*. It remains a cautious, scholarly book, one of the least polemical of Hayek's social and political writings. But it is driven throughout by a very practical purpose, the restating of the basic principles of one strand of classical liberalism, not as an exercise in antiquarianism, but in an attempt to provide a programme for those liberals anxious to fight back against collectivism. Even Hayek may have been surprised retrospectively by the extent of his success.

Bibliographical Note

The main edition of the *Constitution of Liberty* remains that first published by Routledge in 1960 and subsequently reprinted. An edition will in due course appear in the *Collected Works*, which is also being published by Routledge. Other Hayek works which should be consulted to gain a full understanding of *The Constitution of Liberty* are *The Road to Serfdom* (1944), *Individualism and Economic Order* (1948), and *Law Legislation, and Liberty* (1973, 1976, 1979). The last was explicitly written to develop the argument and fill in some of the gaps in the earlier work.

There is a growing secondary literature on Hayek. Most useful on his general political and social theory are Norman Barry, *Hayek's Social and Economic Philosophy* (London, 1979), John Gray, *Hayek on Liberty* (Oxford, 1984), and Roland Kley, *Hayek's Social and Political Thought* (Oxford, 1994). See also Andrew Gamble, *Hayek: The Iron Cage of Liberty* (Cambridge, 1996), and the extensive discussion of Hayek by Raymond Plant in *Modern Political Thought* (Oxford, 1991). A more specialist monograph on the philosophical tensions in Hayek's thought is Chandran Kukathas, *Hayek and Modern Liberalism* (Oxford, 1989).

There is a very extensive collection of articles and reviews of Hayek's work in J. C. Woods and R. N. Woods (eds.), *Friedrich A. Hayek: Critical Assessments*, 4 vols. (London, 1991). A useful recent collection of articles on various aspects of Hayek's thought is J. Birner and R. Van Zip (eds.), *Hayek, Co-ordination, and Evolution* (London, 1994). Hayek as an ideological entrepeneur is covered in Richard Cockett, *Thinking the Unthinkable: Think-Tanks and the Economic Counter-Revolution* (London, 1995). Critical articles on aspects of Hayek's thought include Murray Forsyth, 'Hayek's Bizarre Liberalism: A Critique', *Political Studies*, 36/2 (June 1988), 235–50; Richard Bellamy, '"Dethroning Politics": Liberalism, Constitutionalism, and Democracy in the Thought of F. A. Hayek', *British Journal of Political Science*, 24 (1994), 419–41; and Norman Barry, 'Hayek on Liberty', in J. Gray and Z. Pelzcynski, *Conceptions of Liberty* (Oxford, 1990), 263–86. A critical assessment of his theories of evolution is provided by Geoff Hodgson, *Economics and Evolution* (Cambridge, 1993).

9

Herbert Hart: *The Concept of Law*

NORMAN BARRY

HERBERT HART'S *The Concept of Law* is both a profound contribution to analytical jurisprudence and a classic of social and political theory. Although it is rigorously analytic, and is scarcely tainted by ideology, it consists partly of a searching enquiry into the concepts typically used in contemporary political theory. No discussion of such phenomena as sovereignty, constitutionalism, the rule of law, justice, power, and authority would be complete without a careful consideration of Hart's views. In his other writings Hart engaged in some quite vigorous debates with political thinkers over law and liberty, rights, equality, and political obligation. Indeed, he espoused a sophisticated liberal utilitarianism in his controversy with Lord Devlin over the proper relationship between law and morality[1] —a dispute that revealed Hart to be clearly on the side of J. S. Mill in his claim that there is no justification for coercive law to be used for the enforcement of a public morality in purely private actions. Yet even these overtly normative arguments were reinforced with concepts carefully analysed in the earlier jurisprudence.

This disjuncture between analysis and recommendation provides us with the starting-point for the study of *The Concept of Law*,[2] for one of the book's main achievements is its persuasive argument for the logical separation of law and morality—that statements about the validity of law are conceptually independent of questions of its moral value. An account of law, and the features that differentiate it from other social institutions, must be more or less independent of its content, or its purposes in some teleological sense. This legal positivism, which

---

[1] H. L. A. Hart, *Law, Liberty and Morality* (Oxford, 1963).
[2] H. L. A. Hart, *The Concept of Law* (Oxford, 1961). References in the text are to this edition.

was a major feature of the jurisprudence of Jeremy Bentham and John Austin (although it probably originates with Thomas Hobbes), differentiates Hart clearly from the natural-law tradition which analytically ties the *meaning* of law to certain, presumed universal, moral standards. As we shall see, Hart slightly modifies this allegedly 'contentless' account of the validity of law with his claim that legality will ultimately depend on a purported system meeting certain conditions necessary for a society's survival. These conditions, however, although conceptually necessary for law, fall some way short of even the most modest claims for the connection between law and morality found in traditional natural-law theory.

Hart's major achievement has been to place law in the context of a general social theory. Law is a form of control and its rules have to be understood as contributing to the stability and continuity of a social order. In some respects legal rules have much in common with moral rules (where these are interpreted in a positivist sense as conventions and practices that may be different from particular ideals or values) in that both prescribe forms of conduct deemed to be essential for the preservation of social regularity and the maintenance of a certain kind of predictability. However, the exploration of the differences between moral rules and legal rules is one of the most important tasks that Hart sets himself in *The Concept of Law*. Although the book is analytic in style, it asks significantly different questions from traditional jurisprudence. For example, there is less concern with the dry, technical question of the necessary and sufficient conditions for the existence of a legal order and a much greater emphasis on the circumstances which generate typical legal institutions such as rules, constitutions, legislatures, and courts. Hart's claim, in the preface to *The Concept of Law*, to have written an essay in 'descriptive sociology' is partially justified, even though some critics argue that the book does not contain much concrete information on the sociology of law.

Hart's Method

The Concept of Law must be placed firmly in the tradition of linguistic philosophy, which was dominant in the English-

speaking world from about the early 1950s to the late 1970s.
It is an approach that may justifiably be said to be rather sterile
in some areas. Its obsession with meaning and conceptual analysis
in isolation from particular social forms distracted attention
away from real issues, and its deliberate downgrading of philosophy to a second-order discipline which can contribute nothing of substance to human knowledge seemed to render the
subject irrelevant to human affairs. However, these charges are
less sustainable in relation to law because the language that
we use to describe legal phenomena is richly informative of
social phenomena. Terms like 'obligation', 'rules', and 'rule-
following' are complex and have to be unravelled before the
(perhaps) more interesting task of critical appraisal of legal
orders can begin.

Above all, there is the question: what is law? Many people
are perfectly familiar with the word in its day-to-day sense but
very perplexed if asked to account for the connection between
law and morality, to explain its validity, or to answer the
question whether international law really is law. Conceptual
analysis that is rooted in given social forms can be informative
as to the structure and order of those forms.

Hart begins by arguing that the understanding of law cannot
be advanced by a definition. From logical positivism onwards
there has been a view that words have a straightforward counterpart in the empirical world and that to define a word simply
involved translating it into terms that described the phenomenon, so that one term could be substituted for another without loss in meaning. The definition of 'bachelor' as an unmarried
man is an example. The difficulty with law, however, is that
the phenomena it describes are too complex for so quick a
resolution: for such a definition to work there would have to
be a range of phenomena which displayed clear and uncontroversial characteristics. There are too many borderline cases,
where the use of the word law is genuinely questioned, for
that to be possible. Instead, Hart's enterprise is 'to advance
legal theory by an improved analysis of the distinctive structure
of a municipal legal system and a better understanding of the
resemblances and differences between law, coercion, and
morality, as types of social phenomena' (p. 17). He concedes
that the word law can be used to describe phenomena that do
not contain *all* of the features of law that he identifies.

There is still, though, a degree of generality about this enterprise. Law may be a 'cluster' concept in that the rules for its use vary and the phenomena it describes are not uniform and immutable, but Hart believes that it is important to identify certain common features of legal systems which, although they do not constitute the elements in a definition, are normally found whenever the word law is used. This claim to generality distinguishes Hart's approach from that of writers concerned with *conceptions* of law. They tend to eschew the search for more or less enduring features of law and instead concentrate on the problems that arise in particular legal systems. An influential contemporary conception of law emphasizes the adjudicative aspect and hence understands law almost entirely in terms of the principles and arguments which judges use to decide difficult cases. Such analyses are often evaluative and therefore reject the distinction between law and morality that Hart makes. Conceptions of law are less concerned with elucidating the connection between legal institutions and related phenomena, which is the type of analysis that Hart was specifically concerned with. It is an approach that implies very little for the solution of hard cases. Hart's work may be said to be in the 'grand tradition' of jurisprudence which from Hobbes onwards (if not before) has tried to specify the unique features of law as a social institution. His concept of law, therefore, has a much wider application than the various, and often competing, conceptions of law that feature in much of contemporary jurisprudence.

The Problem of Law

Hart writes that 'the most prominent general feature of law . . . is that its existence means that certain kinds of human conduct are no longer optional, but in *some sense* obligatory' (p. 6; emphasis in the original). This perhaps does not by itself distinguish law from other social phenomena—morality or religion, for example—but it does indicate that there is an element of compulsion about law. Its presence in any society often means that we have to act against our interests and inclinations. It is this feature that has led many legal theorists to define law in terms of sanctions and to claim that the elements of continuity and stability in society are brought about entirely by sanctions or the threat of sanctions.

In fact, Hart uses the ideas of the nineteenth-century writer John Austin as the starting-point for his own analysis. This theory was an attempted definition of law which tried to capture all its main features in a simple proposition. Austin wrote that law 'is a rule laid down for the guidance of an intelligent being by an intelligent being having power over him'.[3] Despite the use of the word 'rule' here, law is simply the *command* of a determinate sovereign, backed by sanctions and addressed to the bulk of the population, which in turn has a habit of obedience to the commander or sovereign. The structure of a legal system consists entirely of duty-imposing norms, and the legal community is, in effect, segmented into that part of the population which has this habit of obedience and the sovereign who owes no duty to anyone. This is not exactly a behaviouralist model of law. There is a notion of authority within it and the illimitability of sovereignty is described in legal rather than political or factual terms. However, it does attempt to describe certain *necessary* features of law in terms of easily observable phenomena. Systems that lacked these features —for example, custom, international law, and constitutional law—would not be legal in the proper sense.

Hart begins his analysis by pointing to certain obvious deficiencies in the picture presented. As a description of law the duty-imposing model captures only a part of a legal system: criminal (and possibly tort) law. Here people can be said to be compelled to obey through fear of sanction. Again, Hart does not deny that a large part of social regulation and control is brought about by the existence of a range of duties. But a municipal legal system consists also of *power-conferring* or enabling rules—rules that make it possible for individuals to make contracts and wills, convey property, conduct marriages, and so on. It is odd to describe citizens as being under a duty to obey these rules, since failure to comply with their provisions does not result in the imposition of a sanction but in the disappointment of expectations (a nullity). A society could not

---

[3] John Austin, *The Province of Jurisprudence Determined* (1832), ed. H. L. A. Hart (London, 1954), p. 14.

be properly understood if these legal arrangements were described as duties. Although the existence of power-conferring rules allows individuals to be, in effect, 'private' legislators in that they create duties by way, for example, of contracts, these cannot be plausibly interpreted as a species of command. Furthermore, in typical municipal legal systems other authorities, or legislatures subordinate to the sovereign, may also have powers conferred on them. But these do not normally involve duties. The conditions attached to them are disabilities, limitations on the exercise of power-conferring rules rather than commands to do certain things, because such restrictions are not backed by physical sanctions. In fact, we would not be able to explain a whole range of social phenomena, or the various ways in which otherwise disparate activities are coordinated, if we thought of law only in terms of commands.

Behind these more or less empirical observations lies a complex philosophical theory of society, a theory that explains order and continuity not in terms of habits of obedience but by references to rules and rule-following (pp. 27–32).[4] There is a crucial difference between a habit and a rule. A habit is convergent behaviour. People may do various things, such as going regularly to the cinema, without these activities involving normative considerations, the claim that certain things *ought* to be done. Now it may appear as if people's behaviour in society is passive, that they follow certain modes of conduct unthinkingly, but this conceals important features of social life. Rules set standards of appropriate conduct the breach of which is a cause of concern. Serious social pressure is brought to bear on those who flout the rules. Indeed in primitive, perhaps 'pre-legal', communities pressure for conformity might be a form of moral persuasion; law there might be little more than positive morality. However, in whatever form it takes, rule-following involves the use of key normative words such as 'should', 'must', and 'ought'. These normative terms prescribe certain forms of behaviour as obligatory, not because of their conformity to a *critical* morality, a value system that transcends current practice, but because the social rules set standards.

---

[4] There is some similarity between Hart's methodology and that of Peter Winch in his *The Idea of a Social Science* (London, 1958).

According to Hart, rules involve both an *external* and an *internal* aspect. Rules are viewed from an external point of view when an observer merely records that certain patterns of behaviour are followed, and regularities occur. It is not necessary that the observer accepts their obligatory force; he or she merely records that others do. Indeed, much of traditional jurisprudence is concerned with just this, as when it is said, for example, that '*x* is a law which is always followed in community *a*'. In this sense the rule is not seen as a guide to conduct for the observer but is merely a fact to be noticed. However, it is necessary for participants in a social process to take rather a different view; they must understand what the rule means for them (indeed, in advanced legal communities there may sometimes be doubt about what the rule means). As Hart says: 'What is necessary is that there should be a critical reflective attitude to certain patterns of behaviour as a common standard, and that this should display itself in criticism (including self-criticism), demands for conformity, and in acknowledgements that such criticism and demands are justified' (p. 56). For a rule to be internalized it has to be accepted by the participants in a legal system.

The familiar example of road-traffic behaviour illustrates the difference between the external and the internal points of view. When the lights change to red, from an external perspective this is a command to drivers to stop, followed by a prediction that a sanction will be imposed on those who fail to do so. But, from the internal point of view, the light changing to red *means* stop; it is a signal to drivers to conform to accepted standards of behaviour on the road. A mere external observer would have no further interest in the phenomenon (beyond collecting road-traffic statistics and making predictions) because it has no other meaning than that revealed by empirical facts. Moreover, even though an external observer could no doubt demonstrate that conformity to basic rules may be brought about by the imposition of sanctions, he or she could not understand that there is a *reason* or *justification* for such sanctions; they would appear as just facts, detached from the meaning and purpose of the rule.

It is important to note that, even though in modern societies it appears that uniform conduct is brought about by sanctions, they themselves cannot be a satisfactory explanation of order.

If, in a crude Austinian sense, fear were the only motivation for obedience, a society would need a rather large police force to guarantee security, and that would pose a further problem: how could the loyalty of the police be guaranteed? As Hume pointed out long ago, even the most blatant exercises of power depend on the acceptance of authority by some. Indeed, a good sign of the breakdown of order is the increased reliance on coercion: it is an indication that rules are no longer adequately internalized and appear as external obstacles to the participants.

Hart's explanation of the difference between the internal and external point of view is perhaps a little misleading. He suggests that it is a requisite for the understanding of rules that people actually accept them as appropriate guides to conduct. Someone taking an external point of view could not know what they really meant, or, equally important, could not know what they implied for future occasions when their application, and implications, might be uncertain. But it is not obvious that an understanding of the meaning of rules implies their acceptance.[5] From a 'hermeneutical' perspective it is perfectly possible to understand all aspects of rules; indeed one could put oneself in the position of a participant without necessarily accepting them oneself. This 'moderate' external perspective is presumably taken by anyone who studies legal systems.

Still, Hart's analysis is a necessary corrective to those Austinians who explain continuity and stability by reference to coercive commands, or those who define rules as disguised predictions of what courts may say in particular cases (the American 'realists'). Hart's explanation becomes particularly acute in relation to the conduct of the officials of a legal system who have to interpret the fundamental constitutional rules of an order, about which there is often much dispute. It may be true, as Austin very inadequately explained, that citizens are more or less passive in their attitudes to authority in stable orders, but such passivity cannot be a feature of the judiciary; it is constantly engaged in interpretive activity and must internalize rules of which citizens may have only slight acquaintance.

In his discussion of legal obligation, Hart shows that there

---

[5] For a discussion of this point, see Neil MacCormick, *H. L. A. Hart* (London, 1981).

is a confusion in Austin's theory between *being obliged* and *being under an obligation* (pp. 79–88). To be obliged is to be compelled to act in a certain way and this obedience is normally brought about by fear. The appeal here is to motives rather than any idea of rightfulness. But we would hardly say that a person was under an obligation merely because he or she had no alternative but to comply with the demand. When applied to an existing legal system, it would have the odd consequence that, if somebody could escape the penalties imposed by law, his or her obligation would cease. But being under an obligation means that in a system of rules—for example, the criminal law—not only is there a liability to punishment for their breach but that it is reasonable or justifiable for it to be imposed. It may be the case in certain aspects of the law that obedience by some is secured only by the threat of sanctions, but this cannot be descriptive of the behaviour of a whole society. After all, law does not exist solely in the act of enforcement but it functions as a guide to conduct for people unlikely ever to be in court. Thus while it is true that for a legal system to exist there must be a generalized obedience to its rules, this phenomenon is better explained by the internalization of these rules than by the notions of command and prediction.

The point becomes acute with regard to officials who are under a duty to enforce and interpret its rules independently of sanctions. It may be true (in an example not used by Hart) that under particularly illiberal regimes judges may be motivated by fear rather than by a full acceptance of the legitimacy of its rules, and here a distinction between legal and moral obligation is appropriate. Hart himself stresses the fact that because something is valid by the rules of a system this does not make it morally right and judges may sometimes be faced with a conflict between their legal and moral duties.

Primary and Secondary Rules

Austin's description of law reduces all rules to the single category of the duty-imposing type. Yet advanced legal systems are composed of a variety of rules. It is also the case that Austin failed to explain *authority* adequately. For him, a person is in authority when his commands are obeyed habitually and when his agents (including the judiciary, which lacks autonomy) enforce them. There is no explanation of who is entitled or authorized to make laws. The sovereign is somehow a 'given', a logical necessity for a legal system whose existence is not explained. The notion of authority is almost irrelevant to an understanding of the fundamentals of law, since the activity of the sovereign creates authority-relationships while not being subject to any authority itself. At most, the existence of sovereignty seems to be a consequence of a build-up of power in a Hobbesian manner. This poses intractable problems for the Austinian theory, for how can it explain the transition of one legal authority to another? And how can we explain the persistence of law long after the disappearance of the sovereign who originally commanded it? It is a feature of the command model that all law must have an author, yet in practice legal systems contain many rules that do not have a determinate author (as the common law does not) and that other rules, for example, constitutional rules, 'bind' putative authors of law and limit their authority.

To deal with these issues, Hart makes a very important distinction between primary and secondary rules. Primary rules consist of the basic prohibitions that any legal system must have if regularity is to be assured. In primitive societies legal systems consist of simple primary rules which set appropriate standards of behaviour. But they lack procedures for altering rules in the light of changing circumstances; they have no formal methods for enforcing obedience, which is thus brought about by diffuse social pressure. As a consequence, they often leave dispute-settling to decentralized individual agents and there exists no means for determining ultimate validity in law. These issues can only be dealt with by the discovery or, more likely, evolution of secondary rules. Unlike primary rules, those secondary rules are not concerned with setting standards of behaviour, for they have no substantive content: they are rules about rules and have as their focus such things as legislatures and courts.

The static nature of basic primary rules is overcome by the development of legislatures which have the authority to repeal rules and introduce new ones, and the inefficiency of decentralized rule adjudication and enforcement is remedied by centralized agencies (pp. 89–96). The latter are simple 'public goods', the monopoly supply of which reduces the cost of private law enforcement as well as ending the more or less permanent feuds and vendettas that characterize primitive society. Uncertainty about the rules as well as the determination of the authority of rule-makers is remedied by the emergence of a 'rule of recognition.' In advanced legal systems this will consist of basic constitutional principles (either written or unwritten). The development of these secondary rules is described by Hart as the movement from a pre-legal to a legal society, although this is a little misleading since he does not normally want to restrict the concept of law to the familiar modern legal order. Indeed, his final account of law as 'the union of primary and secondary rules' looks suspiciously like those essentialist definitions he was so anxious to avoid. The point here is that a system consisting of primary rules resembles positive morality rather than fully-fledged legality: it does control human behaviour but in significantly different ways from methods normally characterized as legal.

The emergence of secondary rules is, of course, accompanied by that of officials: specialist agents whose responsibilities extend beyond exacting the obedience of people charged with the duty of obeying primary rules. The behaviour of officials cannot normally be described in terms of their fear of sanctions. The existence of secondary rules implies that the demands of internalization are more onerous in the case of officials. The rules of adjudication imply that *de jure* authority exists and that judicial personnel have a formalized authority to settle disputes. A society characterized by primary rules only, or the rules of positive morality, might be more accurately described as one of *de facto* authority: obedience exists as a matter of fact rather than being a species of legal obligation proper.

The methods for bringing about change similarly implies the existence of a secondary rule, a rule that determines *who* has the authority to alter the primary rules. As Hart points out, even in the simplest command model of a society, where a sovereign exists to whom obedience is ensured through fear of sanctions, there is still the question of the authority of the lawgiver in a period of transition, i.e. from one lawgiver to another. When sovereignty exists, habits of obedience constitute the grounding of legal obligation or, rather, the condition of being obliged, but, as Hart says, 'mere habits of obedience to orders given by legislators cannot confer on the new legislator any *right* to succeed the old and give orders in his place' (pp. 53–4; emphasis in original). The need for authority is revealed by the fact that there is not sufficient time for the build-up of power from one legislator to another for continuity to be achieved. To use Hart's example of a very simple primitive monarchy, if Rex I were successful in establishing legal authority, that alone is insufficient to guarantee the efficacy of his successor. If his son Rex II, under a simple rule of hereditary succession, is to have legislative authority, this cannot be a function of his power but derives from his rights, as prescribed by the rule. Otherwise, there would be a legal hiatus every time the legislator died. Yet what has to be explained is 'the uninterrupted continuity of law-making power by rules which bridge the transition from one lawgiver to another' (p. 53). Any uncertainty about legal authority is then resolved by the invocation of the rule of recognition. The relationship between this rule and the logically different concept of sovereignty constitutes a crucial element in Hart's jurisprudence.

Sovereignty and the Rule of Recognition

It is the major claim of Austin's account of law that it is a logical necessity of a legal system that there be one determinate body to whom the bulk of the population owes habitual obedience while it owes obedience to no other institution or person. Its form does not matter; it could be a monarch or a parliament, or indeed any other institutional arrangement that has the prescribed features. These include not only superiority in a legal hierarchy but also illimitability and indivisibility. It is for these reasons that Austinians would claim that constitutional law is not really law, since it presupposes that law exists independently of the sovereign. The sovereign is not merely the originator of legislation but is also the author of the rules that determine legality. This doctrine ultimately emanates from Hobbes and derives some superficial plausibility from the British 'constitution'. Hobbes was aware of the aforementioned problem of the transmission of legal authority in the pure sovereignty theory but could not solve it.[6]

Apart from the obvious fact that primitive legal orders have no place for the concept of sovereignty in the modern legal world, there are numerous examples of limited and divided sovereignties. The US federal system is perhaps the best example of divided legislative authority *not* producing irresolvable doubt and uncertainty about the nature of law. It also shows that the judiciary has considerable autonomy, provided by a secondary rule, and in no sense can it be viewed as a mere agent of the sovereign. Austin himself appeared to be aware of the difficulty of identifying the sovereign with his claim that even in Britain parliament is not the ultimate sovereign, since it is itself the product of the will of the electorate: the latter must then be considered sovereign, because it is the final determinant of the composition of parliament. He said a similar thing about the US Constitution: the final sovereign authority consists of the citizens of the several states who determine the amending process. But, as Hart perceptively points out, this subverts the original picture of a bifurcated society, with one subsection commanding the bulk of the population. We now have the citizens in a kind of dual capacity, as both subjects of the sovereign and the sovereign itself. The difficulty emanates from the refusal to concede that rules must precede sovereignty. After all, we can only know what parliament is by reference to a rule. Parliament cannot create (by command) its own sovereignty without the question being raised as to the source of that authority; self-created sovereign authority is subject to infinite regress of explanation.

Even the supremacy of parliament does not make it the sovereign author of all law. The common law has been created spontaneously by the courts as a body of rules to govern social life, and, although it is subordinate to statute, it is still an independent source of obligation until overturned by parliament. To say that it exists by the 'tacit' consent of the sovereign is not to say that it is somehow commanded by it. No sovereign could have the knowledge of the infinite complexity

---

[6] Hobbes (*Leviathan*, Part Two, chapter XIX) thought that a sovereign would merely point to his successor. But this cannot create an obligation, for this can only be owed to the person who does the indicating.

of a legal system for it to be plausibly said that he is even its implicit author. By the same reasoning, laws passed by an earlier sovereign remain, until repealed, law. This is so because the rule of recognition which authorized them is not time-bound but is the source both of the persistence of law and of the continuity of legislative authority. It is also a feature of sovereign legislatures that they are bound by their own laws. Yet this is logically excluded by the simple command theory of law.

These contingent features of British parliamentary sovereignty reveal that the notion of sovereignty can take different forms. It is possible that within a legal system a legislature could be supreme yet limited by the terms of the rule of recognition (if, for example, the system had a bill or rights which could not be changed by normal legislative procedures). Certain clauses of a constitution can be entrenched, as in the US Constitution, where Article V, guaranteeing that no state shall be deprived of equal representation in the Senate without its consent, seems to be beyond the power of amendment. For all this, Hart's reasoning remains within the confines of positive law. The rule of recognition is a standard of legality not morality, and is not be to be confused with the doctrine of the 'rule of law'. Indeed, many critics of the rule of parliamentary supremacy, who claim that it permits arbitrary power, would clearly not be mollified by the argument that it is technically a feature of law in Britain.

The important question for jurisprudence is the explanation of this rule. Hart's argument is that its existence 'will be manifest in the general practice, on the part of officials or private persons, of identifying the rules by this criterion' and in a modern legal system 'where there are a variety of "sources" of law . . . the criteria for identifying the law are multiple and commonly include a written constitution, enactment by a legislature, and judicial precedents' (p. 98). Wherever we have law we will find a hierarchy of rules through which validity can be traced. In a parliamentary system the search for the rule of recognition is relatively simple and culminates in the declaration of the legislature which will normally take precedence over treaty law, common law, or the rules of subordinate bodies. In a federal system it is more complex, since the constitution reserves some legislative autonomy for the component units and grants the judiciary considerable power of review. Here the appellation *rules* of recognition is singularly apposite and it may be doubted whether such a legal order resembles a neat hierarchy. US constitutional history suggests that the determination of legality is not easily settled by the invocation of uncontroversial criteria of the type suggested by Hart. Only rarely are matters of identity and validity settled conclusively by the amending process. Short of this, questions of law are answered by the Supreme Court, which draws on a whole range of standards, including principles, morality, and quasi-legal practices.

Yet Hart insists that a rule of recognition exists 'as a matter of fact' (p. 107); evidence for it is available to an external observer. Of course, it is internalized by officials, who either explicitly or implicitly refer to it whenever the identity of law is in question. Indeed, Hart seems to imply that they are under a moral duty to apply it—although it is not like the duties of primary rules, which are normally backed by sanctions. It is true that sanctions are not *logically* necessary for the existence of a legal obligation, but Hart is a little unclear as to why the officials are under a duty to invoke it. That might not matter too much in tranquil times, but it is of importance when there is serious doubt about what the rule(s) means. For clarity about the identity of law may not always be available. Legal standards, which lack the precision of a rule of recognition as originally envisaged, may have to be invoked to determine validity.

However, Hart is clear about the distinction between his and similar sounding theories that locate validity by reference to some 'norm' or postulate of the system from which the validity of subordinate norms is deduced. In Hans Kelsen's[7] theory, the *Grundnorm*, or fundamental presupposition of a legal system, is understood to be a logical requirement for law. This is not an identifiable fact. In contrast, the rule of recognition is not a presupposition of a legal system but is a kind of instrument which is used by the judiciary in its daily activity. Thus the rule of recognition can subtly change without the whole structure of law being affected. For there to be a change in the *Grundnorm* there would have to be a revolutionary

---

[7] Hans Kelsen, *General Theory of Law and State* (Cambridge, Mass, 1959).

act, which would throw the integrity of the whole system in doubt.

In both European and US jurisdictions it seems that the identity and validity of law are a product of standards not easily reducible to even a complex rule of recognition. Nor do these standards have the rather precise hierarchical form that Hart's jurisprudence would seem to demand. The vagueness of legal standards, yet their undoubted applicability to legal processes, casts doubt on Hart's claim that law can be exhaustively accounted for in terms of rules. The problem is one of determining the legal *identity* of these standards.

The real issue centres on the role of the officials in a legal system, the judiciary. It is apparent from the history of stable legal communities that judges do more than accept, and internalize, the rule of recognition. They help to create it. It is supposed to be a 'a common public standard of correct judicial decision', yet on occasions its main features are actually determined by those who are supposed to be under a legal obligation to apply it. Of course, Hart rightly insists that the rule of recognition cannot itself be tested as right or wrong because it is the test of other claims to legal validity, but this does not solve the problem raised by the judiciary's role in, to some extent, determining that rule.

The American realists (and other judicial behaviourists) had a short answer to the question: legal validity is simply what the courts say it is. No doubt this is a crude characterization of the legal process; indeed it gets close to attributing 'sovereignty' to the judges, but it does have a resonance in times when, in an otherwise stable legal order, there is doubt about the ultimate foundations of legality. Hart, in a reluctant concession to realism, suggests that judges in cases at the edges of a legal system '*get* their authority to decide them accepted after the questions have arisen and the decision has been given. Here all that succeeds is success' (p. 149; emphasis in the original). It is at moments like this that politics becomes important and the distinction between it and law may be hard to sustain.

Still, despite such problems, we should not despair for the integrity of law. Hart himself makes a clear distinction between the validity and the efficacy of law. There may be occasions when a society becomes so divided that primary rules are simply not internalized, even though they fulfil the requirements of legality. In such circumstances, which Hart calls the 'pathology of law', obviously political sociology is more important than jurisprudence. But in cases short of revolution, ordinary civil and criminal law can go on, despite serious doubt about the 'superstructure' of constitutional rules and practices. Legal standards can be maintained in the absence of a clear delineation of rules of recognition.

Rule-Scepticism

The role of the judiciary in determining the rule of recognition is just one aspect of problems that were of great concern to Hart. Another is to what extent does a legal system consist of formal rules, from which deductive inferences are made to fit particular cases, and how far does it depend upon imaginative actions of the judiciary in the absence of a clear guidance from rules (ch. VIII)? These questions have both descriptive and normative implications. With regard to the former, a school of jurisprudence (realism) grew up in the USA that denied that law is a system of rules. The argument depended upon the fact of indeterminacy in law: because of this judges have a great deal of discretion. There is, in difficult cases, a gap between the legal materials (statutes, precedents, and so on) and the decision itself. The realists, or rule-sceptics, hoped to fill this gap by predictive theories of how the judges will behave, and these theories will owe much more to sociology than to formal statements of rules. It led to the ironic comment that a crucial decision will depend on 'what the judge had for breakfast'. Because of its strong tradition of judicial review, and a constitution that it is loosely worded in parts, it was a doctrine likely to emerge in the USA. The latter (normative) question concerns the desirability of allowing judges discretion. Were they known in advance and their incidence more or less predictable, would not the rule of law be better served if rules completely replaced discretion? This last point has relevance not only to the US Constitution but to all common-law systems. What Hart calls the 'open texture of law', the fact that legal language is necessarily uncertain, means that rules are not easy to formulate in an uncontroversial manner. Formalists hope to eliminate discretion so as to preserve the basic features of legality and the rule of law.

Hart has little difficulty in refuting the more extreme claims of the rule-sceptics. The attempt to convert all statements about rules into predictions of what the courts will do overlooks the fact that courts exist because of a secondary rule—a rule that invests their decisions with authority. The fact that difficult decisions of interpretation have to be made does not mean that rules are simply made up; it indicates that at the outer reaches of a legal system choices have to be made. A legal system would quickly become meaningless if there were no independent rules, just as a game would become incomprehensible if everything depended on the referee's discretion. A rule-governed system implies that, even though their decisions are final, officials are still fallible. If everything were a matter of discretion, they would in fact be infallible, because there would then be no independent rules by which their actions could be criticized. Of course, one cannot deny that, in the deliberations of the Supreme Court in the USA, it is useful to know the political opinions of the justices. They have indeed changed the course of US history. It would be naïve to describe the officials as disinterestedly searching for the meanings of rules. Yet even here the decisions are made in the context of rules, and reasons have to be given for them. Furthermore, large parts of social life are governed by quite uncontroversial rules which are applied almost mechanically. It would be a mistake to describe the whole of a legal system in language which is appropriate for particular aspects of it. It should also be remembered that judicial discretion is limited to cases actually brought to the courts. This is quite different from genuine legislative activity.

Hart is undoubtedly aware of the fact that a purely formal system is an impossibility. Indeed, he doubts that it is even a desirable aim. The very complexity of a modern society and the necessarily limited knowledge that is available to legislators mean that rules cannot be designed to cover all circumstances. Some issues have to be left open. There must then be judicial discretion because 'we are men, not gods'. Some writers, however, have argued that greater predictability is possible if judges are left to interpret rules in a more autonomous manner, especially as the aims of legislation are often indeterminate.

Indeed, in day-to-day law, judges interpreting traditional rules (as in the common law) may produce greater reliability than the legislatures, which can be capricious. This rationale depends upon the claim that judges *discover* law rather than make it up. Still, there is the serious problem that in common-law systems there must be an element of retrospective legislation because participants cannot know in advance of a case being settled what their legal rights and duties are. Some judicial creativity cannot be avoided.

There are perhaps no satisfactory answers to these problems within the terms of debate set by legal positivism, for we sometimes seem to be in an area where law as strictly defined seems not to apply. When judges make decisions which are not dictated by clear rules, Hart maintains that they are not completely unrestrained. There are standards which they call upon and they should 'deploy some acceptable general principle as a reasoned basis for the decision' (p. 20), but he never makes clear the relationship between these standards and the basis of the legal order itself. They are not quite part of the law (on one occasion Hart even talks of the judiciary balancing 'competing interests' (p. 126) in disputed cases, which sounds more political than legal), yet it is clear that they have an important role in the adjudicative process. It is, of course, true that the occurrence of difficult cases is infrequent, so that recourse to law is a rare phenomenon (except perhaps in the USA). For this reason it is not inaccurate to describe law as a system of rules for the guidance of conduct both in and out of court. But there is nevertheless something of a lacuna in Hart's theory. The relationship between legal standards and legal rules is not fully spelt out.

Rules and Principles

The conception of law as a system of rules has also come under attack from a rather different quarter. So far from judges having almost complete discretion, as in the realist account, there is a theory, associated mainly with Ronald Dworkin,[8]

[8] Ronald Dworkin, *Taking Rights Seriously* (2nd impression, London, 1978); *Law's Empire* (London, 1986).

that law can only be properly understood as an enterprise that necessarily involves a consideration of the *principles* that undergird society and which are called upon by judges to settle hard cases. Dworkin's theory is, in fact, a *conception* of law that concentrates specifically on the adjudicative process and is only incidentally concerned with the general features of law, or the distinction between law and other social phenomena. It is also more obviously evaluative (although not in the traditional natural-law sense). The principles that he identifies are moral and, because law necessarily involves the use of the power of the state, political. Their role in the legal process is to help judges find correct answers to hard cases. However, although judicial activity involves political theorizing, it is not the judge's own political views that are relevant to law but his *interpretation* of the prevailing community values and their application to hard cases. His view seems to be that legal activity is inconceivable if it were only a matter of finding clearly articulated rules.

Dworkin considers Hart's theory a sophisticated version of Austin's model, where law forms a neat hierarchy of rules, with the rule of recognition replacing sovereignty as the final determinant of legality. According to Dworkin, in a complex modern legal order it is impossible to identify such a rule. One suspects he regards the search for the criteria of validity as a sterile exercise. He is also particularly critical of Hart's idea that judicial discretion is unavoidable when the rules run out. But for Dworkin this means that law loses its integrity and autonomy, and also involves unwelcome retroactivity, since it is difficult to predict how the discretion will be exercised. In his view, the ideal judge exercises a very weak type of discretion.

The relationship between principles and rules is complex. While principles are for Dworkin emphatically a part of the law, they do not apply in a mechanical manner. Thus in the famous US case of *Riggs* v. *Palmer* (1889) the principle that 'no man may profit from his own wrong' was used to disallow inheritance from a victim to his murderer (even though apparently the formal rules of inheritance were satisfied). However, it need not always apply, as in cases of adverse possession. Furthermore, principles have 'weight', so that judges balance one against another in searching for a decision in a hard case.

Hart is vulnerable to this kind of criticism because of his

vagueness about the relationship between principles, or general standards of legality, and the formal delineation of rules at the edges of law. We have already seen this difficulty in attempts to determine the rule of recognition. Hart does not want to say that judges have unfettered discretion, yet he is not at all clear as to the legal status of the inhibitions that constrain them. It would surely be possible to incorporate general principles, say, of equity, into those legal standards that go to make up legality. One could even conceive of a rule that required their invocation in hard cases. This still would not require that every hard case had a definitive answer, if only the judges could discover it. In some there may be no one answer, but judges none the less have to make a decision. Even if moral principles are required here, it does not necessarily follow that judges themselves necessarily have to take a normative stance, as Dworkin seems to imply. The interpretation of a moral principle could itself be neutral. However, in Dworkin's theory the distinction between law and politics seems gradually to disappear. This is especially so when his principles turn out to consist of a radical conception of liberalism (in the American sense).

Dworkin's argument is vitiated by the fact that the moral principles that are said to underlie a community are not uncontroversial. In a pluralist society there is seldom enough agreement about them to justify their presentation as indubitable features of law. In societies characterized by a pluralism of values it is hard to imagine that there are definitively *right* answers to hard cases. The abortion debate in the USA, arising out of the controversial *Roe* v. *Wade* (1973) decision, is an instructive example, for both the 'right-to-choose' and the 'right-to-life' sides of the argument plausibly appeal to the Fourteenth Amendment to the Constitution, which prohibits the states depriving persons of 'life, liberty or property, without due process of law'. In such cases, the courts have to make decisions, but it is misleading to say that the right ones are available. In almost a direct anticipation of Dworkin's argument, Hart wrote, in *The Concept of Law*, that 'it is folly to believe that where the meaning of law is in doubt, morality always has a clear answer' (p. 200). To invoke them in the way Dworkin does compromises the core of settled meaning that, despite its obvious uncertainties at the edges, a set of rules possesses. Indeed, the distinction between hard cases and more or less routine details of adjudication would disappear if moral principles were admissible into law without the constraint provided by identifiable rules.

Law and Morality

The relationship between morals and the law has long perplexed philosophers of law. The matter extends from those who see some necessary connection between legality and morality such that the correct meaning of a legal proposition must depend on the ethical values it expresses, to more prosaic theories that detect a reflection of customary moral practices in the structure of formal rules. Legal positivists have never denied that there often is this reflexivity, but what they have been concerned to demonstrate is that the validity of a claim to law does not depend on its moral content. With perhaps one qualification, to be considered below, Hart is no exception to this way of thinking. Indeed, he makes a careful distinction between positive morality, those informal rules that partly govern a society, and critical morality, that set of values which we use to appraise positive law. Indeed, with regard to the former, he sees a considerable overlap between it and law. Both morals and law make certain conduct non-optional. A breach of either is regarded as *serious*, to be followed by various forms of social pressure. Moral and legal rules frequently compel us to act against our interests. Overall, there are interesting similarities between legal and moral obligation. Perhaps officials may be said ultimately to be under a *moral* duty to enforce primary rules.

However, significant differences between law and positive morality (pp. 169–76) are important enough to dampen the enthusiasm of old-fashioned common lawyers. Most obvious is the lack of physical sanctions to enforce moral obligation. Perhaps a clearer distinction between law and morality is that the latter is concerned with the preservation of values whereas the former can often be about rules of mere convenience. It does, for example, matter whether adultery is right or wrong, but as long as one particular rule is obligatory it is morally irrelevant whether we drive on the right or the left. Similarly, some offences are regarded by people as trivial and so frequently breached that the penalty imposed is treated as a mere tax. A more important distinction is that the role of intention differs in law and morals. Lack of deliberate intention is always an excuse for the commission of a moral wrong, but this is not always so in the law. Hence the phenomenon of strict liability.

The final distinction discussed by Hart is that morality is immune from deliberate change, whereas law can be changed almost immediately. This may not be quite as decisive as he supposed. The twentieth century has seen some remarkable transformations in behaviour, especially in sexual morality. The whole ethos of a community may be rigid but particular aspects of it can be quite fluid. Again, the law itself can be influential in changing moral attitudes. Difficulties do arise when law appears to be 'ahead' of popular opinion and this may produce unwelcome disjunctures between legal and moral obligation.

A major aim of *The Concept of Law* is to discuss whether morality is necessary to an account of the meaning of law. As a legal positivist Hart considers the validity of law is a function not of its aims and purposes but of the rules and procedures that create genuine legal obligations. In this he is firmly in the tradition of Bentham and Austin, who argued that natural law led either to the conservatism of the common lawyers or anarchy, produced when everyone has their own opinion of what law is.

For Hart, traditional teleological, and allegedly objective, natural law rests on the error of supposing that laws of society are as rigorous and compelling of those of the physical world, and that reason can give us knowledge of both. This he considers mistaken because social laws are normative; they tell us what we ought to do, while physical laws are descriptive and predictive. If a physical law is falsified we simply find a new theory that explains the phenomena better, but if a social rule is breached it does not lose its status as a law. Following Hume, Hart denies that reason can give us knowledge of those rules that are apparently objectively and universally necessary for us as human beings. Human purposes are too multifarious to constitute a compelling moral foundation for law.

However, it does not follow from this that law can have any

content. Certain true, but logically contingent, features of the human condition dictate that for genuine law to exist it must satisfy them (pp. 189–95). These truisms are, first, that human vulnerability requires that there should be limitations on the use of violence. Second, approximate equality means that forms of government (however elementary) are essential in the absence of a natural superiority of some over others. Third, the presence of limited altruism makes it necessary for some formalized and compulsory rules. Fourth, more or less permanent scarcity entails that property rules be established. Whether they are public or private, or some mixture of the two, is of less importance as long as some limitations are imposed on use. Fifth, limited understanding and strength of will require that not only must some rules exist to cope with our inevitable ignorance but also the overwhelming majority who follow rules should not be exploited by a minority of recalcitrants. Sanctions are needed to prevent free-riding on other people's obedience. Such is the necessity of these rules that Hart calls them 'natural law with minimum content'. The whole methodology is redolent of Hume's claim that the rules of justice are so necessary, and so constantly recurring through human interaction, that they might just as well be called natural laws, despite his logical refutation of that notion.

It is clear that Hart is offering a very weakened form of teleology, which has been rejected by almost all contemporary natural-law theorists. He openly concedes that his natural law is consistent with a great deal of iniquity, and that the protection it offers may not extend to all members of a community. It certainly seems to drain law of its traditional association with the basic principles of justice. At most it relates law to survival, but without indicating the moral qualities of that survival. On this issue, Hart's most insistent critic, Lon Fuller,[9] claimed that law has a kind of 'inner morality' which necessitates the existence of certain procedural rules (embodying minimum notions of equality, publicity, non-retrospectiveness, and so on). These are needed if genuine law is to be distinguished from mere arbitrariness. Indeed, he accuses Hart of defining law in terms of a kind of coercive administration.

Perhaps the distinction between natural law and positive law

[9] Lon Fuller, *The Morality of Law* (rev. edn., Connecticut, 1972).

that Hart makes is too sharp. The whole notion of law, especially in its administration, implies a certain kind of regularity
and predictability which marks it off from arbitrariness. Law
also involves a certain type of reasoning which is not dissimilar
from moral reasoning: justifications for decisions are produced,
precedents are sought, and argument is conducted with an eye
to generality (treating 'like cases alike'). These features are
characteristic of proper legal discourse even when iniquitous
laws are under consideration. The point here is that there is,
after all, a conceptual connection between law and morality
which invites us to distinguish between legal rules and those
social practices that manage to ensure the mere survival of a
group. Furthermore, we would hesitate to call a system lawful
that wilfully excluded certain groups from its protection, however well it satisfied, for example, criteria of regularity and
predictability in other respects.

These brief considerations do not help us answer the perennial question posed to positivists: 'was Nazi law really law?' In
some respects it may have satisfied positivist criteria, but in
others it is doubtful whether it met even these.

However, it seems that a consideration even of its formal
lawfulness would turn on factors that go beyond Hart's natural
law with minimum content. We answer questions of lawfulness not merely in terms of survival but also by reference to
criteria not unlike Fuller's points about the inner morality of
law. To this extent considerations drawn from natural law are
relevant not only to moral standards to which positive law
ought to conform: they are also highly apposite to an understanding of the concept of law itself. Societies can surely sur-
vive by means not normally described as lawful.

Criticism such as Fuller's derives from the close connection
between justice and law in both ordinary speech and political
theory. Hart in *The Concept of Law* (ch. VIII) readily concedes
this but does not draw typical natural-law conclusions. He
argues that there is a distinction between justice and morality
in general. Justice is a distributive concept concerned with the
ways in which people are treated under the rules of a practice.
It is intimately connected with fairness. Other aspects of morality, however, are about the desirability of various goals and
may have nothing to do with the way in which rewards and

penalties are distributed. To the extent that people are treated fairly under a rule, and only *relevant* differences and resemblances are taken into account in the application of rules, a legal system may be said to be just.

But, as Hart points out, this is only a formal account of justice. Many grossly immoral rules are fairly applied and societies differ widely in their understanding of what are relevant resemblances and differences. The rules of justice tend to apply to *classes*, so that the crucial point is what features of individuals lead to their assignment to particular categories. Historically, arbitrary classifications based on race, gender, or religion have been administered fairly in the procedural sense of justice.

It is also the case that Hart makes a distinction between justice and *social* justice or the general welfare (p. 162). He argues that few rules advance the general interest and that the implementation of desirable social policies often involves harm to certain individuals. This important point illustrates clearly Hart's pluralism with regard to moral values. He does concede, however, that all interests must be impartially considered (p. 163) if the implementation of social policies that potentially harm some people can be called just and fair. The conclusion is, though, that Hart sees little possibility of finding sufficient agreement among people on the question of substantive justice to validate the claims of traditional natural lawyers.

The major thrust of Hart's argument is that a conceptual distinction between law and morality is necessary to ensure clarity in legal discourse. Before we can appraise law we need some coherent criteria of identity, and if the range of natural law is extended too widely that coherence may be lost. Since the use of the word 'law' is invested with a certain amount of prestige, and since legal obligation is a crucially important feature of a society, too close an association between law and morality may introduce an unwelcome quietism or conservatism in the face of unjust laws. If officials comply with unjust rules, which nevertheless meet with some substantive moral standards, their actions become associated with the moral authority of law and not just its procedural requirements. In other words, if rules are to be enforced as law *because* they satisfy some minimal standards, this may give dubious orders some respectability. Indeed, as has often been pointed out, even apartheid law in

South Africa seemed to satisfy Fuller's account of the inner morality of law. Hart is, however, quite insistent on the distinction between legal obligation and moral obligation. The fact that an official is faced with a procedurally correct rule does not imply that there is an ethical duty to enforce it. Yet this would follow if law and morality were somehow necessarily fused.

Ultimately, then, Hart makes the distinction between law and morality for a moral reason. As he says: 'What surely is most needed in order to make men clear sighted in confronting the official abuse of power, is that they should preserve the sense that the certification of something as legally valid is not conclusive of the question of obedience . . .' (p. 206). There is a *historical* question as to whether or not the rise of legal positivism in Europe discouraged resistance to tyrannical laws or so-called laws. Of course, positivists deny any such connection. But irrespective of history it would be grossly misleading to suggest that the conceptual distinction between law and morality that positivists make had anything to do with the decline in legality that occurred in the first half of this century in Europe. This is never more apposite than in Hart's legal philosophy.

Bibliographical Note

The only edition of *The Concept of Law* published in Hart's lifetime appeared in 1961. A second edition, edited by Penelope A. Bulloch and Joseph Raz, was published in 1994. This reproduced the original text with a Postscript constructed from Hart's notes. It consists mainly of a reply to Dworkin's criticisms.

Although Hart made some modifications to the jurisprudence expounded in the *Concept or Law*, these were contained in essays and occasional pieces. The most important of them are collected in *Essays on Bentham, Jurisprudence and Political Theory* (Oxford, 1982) and *Essays in Jurisprudence and Philosophy* (Oxford, 1983).

Much of the critical material on Hart is concerned with highly technical matters in linguistic philosophy and jurisprudence, with very little of it to do with politics. Much of it is in specialist journals. The most comprehensive survey of Hart's work—Michael Bayles, *Hart's Legal*

Philosophy: An Examination (London, 1992)—is in this mode. This is a very detailed and thorough book that covers all aspects of Hart's work, including, in addition to the pure jurisprudence, discussions of Hart on law, liberty, and morality, and his theory of punishment, of rights, of criminal responsibility, and of causality in the law. It also provides very good accounts of the disputes between Hart and his major critics, especially Ronald Dworkin on the role of principles, and Lon Fuller on natural law. Although it is critical of some aspects of Hart's jurisprudence, notably the account of secondary rules and the rule of recognition, the general tone of the book is favourable. It is unlikely to be matched in its rigour and comprehensiveness.

Perhaps the most accessible introductory book is still Neil Mac-Cormick's *H. L. A. Hart* (London, 1981). This contains an excellent account of the foundations of law, and MacCormick interprets Hart's theory of the internal aspects of rule-following in the light of modern hermeneutics. It is critical of certain elements of Hart's jurisprudence, most notably his failure to explain the role of principles and general standards as necessary supplements to the idea of law as a system of rules. While arguing that a legal system cannot be described exhaustively in terms of rules, MacCormick is still a long way from Dworkin's claim that moral and political principles should be the main focus of an interpretive jurisprudence.

Although Dworkin has been Hart's great rival in contemporary jurisprudence, he has never published a full-scale critique. His most considered arguments appear in *Taking Rights Seriously* (London, 1978). In this and in *Law's Empire* (London, 1986) he seems to regard Hart as little more than a sophisticated exponent of the Austinian tradition of English legal positivism. This does not do justice to the richness of his thought. His emphasis on the role of moral and political principles in the interpretation of law in hard cases ultimately makes it difficult to distinguish law from politics. At least Hart's positivism enables us to discern the general features of law independently of any overtly normative predilections. The Hart–Dworkin dispute is well summarized in Bayles and also in Stephen Ball, 'Bibliographical Essay: Legal Positivism, Natural Law and the Hart–Dworkin Debate', *Criminal Justice Ethics*, 3 (1984), 68–85.

The Hart–Fuller debate on natural law and legal positivism began with Hart's essay 'Positivism and the Separation of Law and Morals', *Harvard Law Review*, 71 (1958), 593–629, and Fuller's rejoinder, 'Positivism and Fidelity to Law—a Reply to Professor Hart', 630–72, in the same issue of the journal. Both later revised, and defended, their respective positions, Hart in the *Concept of Law* and Fuller in *The Morality of Law*, without giving significant ground. It is a very important debate, not only for its foundational significance but also for the clues it gives us as to how Hart would deal with problems arising out of Nazi law that occurred in post-war (West) German courts. Rather than giving judges the authority to apply natural law, he recommended that retrospective legislation be passed to deal with cases of injustice which had arisen when individuals had wilfully used Nazi statutes to secure some private advantage. Although retrospective legislation is unjust, Hart argued that it was less bad than the uncertainty that would be created if judges could, in effect, invent law.

A very useful book of essays is Ruth Gavison (ed.), *Issues in Contemporary Legal Philosophy: The Influence of H. L. A. Hart* (Oxford, 1987). There are original contributions by Rolf Sartorius, Gerald Postema, Gavison, Neil MacCormick, and David Lyons. Unfortunately the pieces by Dworkin and Hart do not add much to the debate.

A volume celebrating Hart's work—P. M. S. Hacker and J. Raz (eds.), *Law, Morality and Society: Essays in Honour of H. L. A. Hart* (Oxford, 1977)—contains important critical essays, especially Hacker's 'Hart's Philosophy of Law'. However, most of the essays are about subjects raised by Hart's work rather than about the work itself. It is, though, an excellent tribute and illustrates just how deep his influence has been in many areas of legal, moral, and social philosophy.

Hart's analysis is applied to the British Constitution, and the changes to it brought about by the country's membership of the European Union, in Norman Barry's 'Sovereignty, the Rule of Recognition and Constitutional Stability in Britain', *Hume Papers*, 2 (1994), 10–37.

10

John Rawls: *A Theory of Justice*

JOHN DAY

IN the 1950s and 1960s political philosophers in the English-speaking world debated whether their academic discipline was dead. The ground for such pessimism was partly that increasing specialization in political philosophy seemed to have made traditional theorizing in the grand manner both superfluous and overambitious. Furthermore, linguistic analysis, then the dominant mode of philosophical investigation, argued that the task of moral and political philosophy was merely to clarify the language used in moral and political discourse, not, as had been done in the past, to offer moral and political prescriptions. The philosopher was said to have no special qualifications that entitled him to tell people what they should do. He could clear away some of the confusions and misunderstandings in political arguments, but should then leave moral and political decisions, which depended ultimately on each person's subjective values, to the individual. The classics of political philosophy that made strong political recommendations, like Plato's *Republic* and Hobbes's *Leviathan*, were thought to be phenomena of a past that had muddled true, that is, analytical, philosophy with moral advice.

Then, in 1971, John Rawls published *A Theory of Justice*,[1] which vigorously challenged his contemporaries' conception of what was possible and desirable in moral and political philosophy. Although employing the analytical skills honed by the linguistic analysts, Rawls did not accept the limitations that they had tried to impose on political philosophy. Not content to illuminate merely corners of the subject, he elaborated a sophisticated argument for an extensive and complex theory of social justice, which has made his book a modern classic. While

[1] John Rawls, *A Theory of Justice* (Cambridge, Mass., 1971; Oxford, 1972). References in the text are to this edition.

recognizing that people have different notions of what constitutes their own good, Rawls nevertheless tried to demonstrate,
in the tradition of Plato and Kant, that rational men could by
the use of their reason reach agreed, objective conclusions
about what constituted social justice. The argument, while
highly abstract in form, was intended to provide standards of
social justice that could and should be applied to actual societies. Politicians, as well as philosophers, have in practice taken
Rawls seriously. In the USA and Britain some liberal politicians to the left of centre have used ideas from his *Theory of
Justice* in formulating the theoretical justifications of their practical policies.

For over twenty years evaluation and criticism of Rawls's
Theory of Justice have dominated discussion in moral and political philosophy. Just as Isaiah Berlin's *Two Concepts of Liberty*[2]
tends to be the starting-point of modern discussions of liberty,
so philosophers examining the nature of justice cannot ignore
Rawls's *Theory of Justice*. Some critics have concluded that
Rawls's idiosyncratic method and his original conclusions are
fundamentally misconceived, but most of his opponents believe
that his arguments have to be taken seriously. One of the most
radical attacks upon Rawls's position was made by his Harvard
colleague, Robert Nozick, in *Anarchy, State, and Utopia*.[3] Yet
he wrote in appreciation of Rawls:

A Theory of Justice is a powerful, deep, subtle, wide-ranging, systematic
work in political and moral philosophy which has not seen its like since
the writings of John Stuart Mill, if then. It is a fountain of illuminating
ideas, integrated together into a lovely whole. Political philosophers
now must either work within Rawls' theory or explain why not.[4]

---

[2] Isaiah Berlin, *Two Concepts of Liberty* (Oxford, 1958), which is discussed above
in ch. 6.
[3] Robert Nozick, *Anarchy, State, and Utopia* (New York, 1974). This book is
discussed in ch. 11.
[4] Ibid. 183; cf. Michael Walzer's acknowledgement in his *Spheres of Justice* (New
York, 1983), p. xviii. 'No one writing about justice these days can fail to recognize
and admire the achievement of John Rawls. In the text, I have mostly disagreed with
A Theory of Justice . . . [but my enterprise] might not have taken shape at all—
without his work.'

The Subject of the Book

The rest of the chapter discusses the text of *A Theory of Justice*. In his Preface Rawls, recognizing that the book is long, tells the reader which sections, amounting to about a third of the book, provide most of the essentials of the theory. In addition, he recommends certain other sections without which the theory might be misunderstood (pp. viii–ix). The exposition in this chapter concentrates on these two sets of passages. The modifications that Rawls has made to his theory since the publication of *A Theory of Justice* are not discussed here.

Rawls is precise about the kind of justice that he is concerned with: his aim is not to construct a general theory that covers all kinds of justice, but to formulate the principles of *social* justice. Social justice, as he understands it, is concerned with the distribution of rights, duties, and advantages within a society. However, he is not absolutely clear about what constitutes a society. He assumes rather vaguely that a society is 'a more or less self-sufficient association of persons' (p. 4) that has a 'political constitution' (p. 7), which perhaps suggests that he has states in mind, although he does not positively disqualify communities without sovereigns. Hopefully we shall not seriously misunderstand him if we imagine him to be thinking primarily of societies like Britain or the USA.

His concentration on justice within societies means that he does not consider justice within small groups like the family, nor, except incidentally, justice between states. He leaves it an open question how justice in these other cases might differ from social justice (pp. 7–8). Another form of justice which Rawls does not discuss in the book is that which deals with people who break the rules of society (pp. 8–9). Social justice, as he defines it, is not concerned with that, but with the distribution of what people value in society, like wealth, and of what they regard as burdens, like taxes.

Rawls points out that, 'although society is a cooperative venture for mutual advantage', there are likely to be conflicts of interest between its members about the distribution of the benefits produced by social co-operation (p. 4). Invariably there will be insufficient amounts of these benefits, like wealth and power, to satisfy those who seek them. Hence competition for larger shares of what is available is inevitable. The principles of social justice lay down the right ways for the political, economic, and social institutions of a society to make distributions of the resources for which people compete. In doing so, they assign rights and duties to members of the society (pp. 4, 6–7).

The Original Position

One of the most original and most controversial parts of Rawls's theory is the method by which he works out the principles of social justice, although, with excessive modesty, he disclaims any originality for his method (p. viii). Rawls first outlines his method and the principles of justice that result from it (pp. 11–17). Later in the book, the main explanation of the principles of justice (in ch. II, pp. 54–117) precedes, somewhat curiously, the main explanation of the method which generates them (in ch. III, pp. 118–92). The exposition in this chapter explains first the method and then how the method produces the principles of justice.

Rawls imagines people coming together in certain very specific conditions, which he calls the 'original position' (pp. 11–12, 17–19, 118–50), in order to discover what these principles should be. These persons would be free, in that they could make decisions without any constraint. Also, they would be rational in the narrow sense of seeking the most effective means to their ends (pp. 14, 142–5). Each in the special circumstances of the original position would be 'mutually disinterested' (pp. 13, 127–8), considering only his own interests in the process of deciding what should be the principles of justice that would regulate societies.

The particularly distinctive, and at first sight, strange feature of the original position is that people in it choose the principles of justice behind a 'veil of ignorance' (pp. 12, 136–42). No one knows the nature of his own society, whether it is slave-owning, or capitalist, or socialist. Nor does he know his own position within a society, whether king or serf, factory owner or factory worker, master baker or apprentice candlestick maker. Those behind the veil of ignorance do not even know what their own abilities are, whether intellectual or manual, great or small. Furthermore, they are ignorant of their own psychologies, not knowing whether they are brave or cowardly, with or without common sense, extrovert or introvert. Finally, persons in the original position do not know their own conceptions of the good: they are ignorant whether, outside the original position, they prefer, for example, wealth or power, whether they are ascetic or hedonist, religious or atheist.

However, although they know nothing about their own individual characteristics or their places in society, they do have some general knowledge (pp. 137–8). This is necessary if they are to make sensible choices about the principles of justice. They do, therefore, know general facts about the workings of human minds, societies, and governments.

These people in the original position, knowledgeable about human beings in general, but ignorant of their own individual characteristics and social positions, are imagined choosing principles of justice that should regulate all societies. The purpose of the original position is to ensure that the choice of these principles is made with impartiality, which is the essence of justice. None of the persons behind the veil of ignorance could know whether he would benefit or not from any principles that might be chosen to shape societies. From the equality of ignorance of those in the original position emerges automatically what Rawls calls 'justice as fairness'.

Rawls claims that his method of determining social justice is a form of the traditional argument from an original contract (p. 11). The original position resembles a convention of individuals in a state of nature deciding the conditions on which they are prepared to form a society. However, in the original position the persons are not setting up a particular society, but working out the principles that should govern any society. Both in the traditional model of an original contract and in Rawls's original position, the individuals wish to secure the benefits of cooperation that a society brings, but also to safeguard themselves against the dangers that certain kinds of society might impose on them. One of Rawls's achievements is to show how the idea of social contract can be developed so as to produce a theory of social justice at a time when many thinkers believed that contractual theory was of merely historical interest in political philosophy.

Rawls removes the ambiguities that existed in some theories

of social contract about whether a social contract had existed in the past or might exist in the future. The original position is purely hypothetical, a device that Rawls invents to argue for a particular theory of justice. He is inviting his readers to take part in a thought experiment. He is not suggesting that the original position might have existed at some point in history, nor is he recommending that some people set it up at some stage in the future.

When Rawls says that the people in the original position do not know their own personalities or their own positions in society, he is speaking as if they are historical persons abstracted from concrete historical social situations, rather than unknown people existing before the creation of society, as in traditional contractual theories. It is as if a number of people with varying characters and abilities, from different types of society, have been lifted from their historical settings and inflicted with selective amnesia. Then, in this condition they are asked to choose principles of justice that should regulate all societies, which they do in ignorance of how these principles would affect them in their situations back home. Afterwards they might be supposed to be returned by the philosophical sorcerer to their full personalities in their actual societies, where they would feel obliged to apply the principles of justice that they had impartially agreed to in the original position.

The decision on the principles of justice in the original position is in one significant respect unlike most actual, historical agreements. The people in the original position do not have different views about what constitutes social justice. Their agreement consequently does not follow bargaining from different positions and does not represent a compromise between competing ideas (p. 139). This is because each person behind the veil of ignorance is identical to every other. He has the same general knowledge and the same ignorance of who he is and where he has come from. Each person in the original position acts rationally and in pursuit of his own self-interest. Hence, the arguments for certain principles of social justice appeal equally to all those in the original position. In one sense, therefore, all that Rawls needs in the original position is one hypothetical person. However, the way in which he sets up the original position is valuable, because it both acknowledges that people have an infinite variety of personal characteristics and social positions and shows how the impartiality that is intrinsic to justice insists that these differences are ignored.

In working out the principles of justice Rawls does not wish to rely entirely on arguments from the original position, although these arguments form the core of his theory. He proposes checking the conclusions that are derived from the original position against our intuitively held moral beliefs, which he calls 'considered convictions' (pp. 19–20, 47–8). If the original position leads to principles at variance with these convictions, there are two alternatives: either to modify the convictions, or to change the conditions of the original position so that it yields principles that no longer conflict with these convictions. Rawls expects to do a little of each, holding on to strongly felt convictions when they seem incontrovertible, but changing them if their correctness seems open to question and the original position leads to a firm principle. Rawls claims, for example, that the considered conviction that religious intolerance is wrong is beyond question. Therefore, it would be necessary to change any model of the original position that led to a different conclusion. However, considered convictions are less likely to provide certainty about the correct distribution of wealth and here the original position provides positive guidance (pp. 19–20). Rawls recommends going back and forth between considered convictions and conclusions from the original position, making adjustments in each where necessary, until the discrepancies are ironed out. This state he calls 'reflective equilibrium' (pp. 20, 48–50). As he acknowledges, he does not work through this process in the book, but he seems to say that what he does present in the book is the result of such a process (p. 21).

This section of Rawls's argument may be said to introduce a kind of moral common sense into an otherwise rigorously rational argument. However, it risks opening the floodgates to subjective moral judgements and undermining the strong argument from the original position, since different people are likely to have different 'considered convictions'. Rawls is content with the reflective equilibrium that he has reached, but are others, on checking the conclusions from the original position against their own considered convictions, likely to come up with different reflective equilibria? Clearly, Rawls

TABLE 1. *The maximin rule*

Decisions	Circumstances		
	C_1	C_2	C_3
d_1	−7	8	12
d_2	−8	7	14
d_3	5	6	8

wants to avoid presenting an abstract argument for certain principles of justice that contradicts intuitively held convictions about justice, but his advocacy of working towards reflective equilibrium seems to throw some doubt on the validity of the argument from the original position. It is difficult not to feel uncomfortable with the idea that Rawls recommends of tampering with the conditions of the original position if that is necessary to ensure that its conclusions do not violate considered convictions. However, it should be emphasized that Rawls is prepared to modify the conditions of the original position only if its conclusions fly in the face of convictions that have been well considered, that clearly do not result from prejudice, and that are held with the greatest confidence.

The Choice of Principles from the Original Position

Rawls's main concern in *A Theory of Justice* is, of course, to derive principles of justice from the original position (pp. 150–92). A crucial stage of the argument occurs when he demonstrates that the persons rationally considering their own interests behind the veil of ignorance would choose principles of social justice by adopting the 'maximin rule' (pp. 152–8). This 'tells us to rank alternatives by their worst possible outcome: we are to adopt the alternative the worst outcome of which is superior to the worst outcomes of the others' (pp. 152–3). The significance of this rule can be illustrated with the help of Table 1, which Rawls uses (p. 153).

A person has the choice of three alternative decisions, and he knows that for each decision there are three possible outcomes, depending on which set of possible circumstances actually occurs. Perhaps he is making an investment and has the opportunity of buying shares in one of three companies. An unusually prescient financial adviser is able to predict how each company will do in each of three sets of economic circumstances, and also has, miraculously, reliable inside knowledge that one of these three sets of circumstances will actually occur. If the investor makes decision d_1, he may lose £7,000 (if the units in the table are thousands of pounds) or gain either £8,000 or £12,000; if he makes decision d_2, he may lose £8,000, or gain either £7,000 or £14,000; if he makes decision d_3, he may gain either £5,000 or £6,000 or £8,000.

The attraction of decision d_2 is that, if he is lucky, he will gain more than is possible from either of the other decisions, although he also risks losing more. Decision d_1 has its own advantages, because it offers the chance of gaining only £2,000 less than d_2 if the most favourable circumstances come up, while the loss, if the worst circumstances happen, is £1,000 less. Decision d_3 offers distinctly less reward if the best circumstances crop up, but its appeal lies in the fact that even in the worst possible circumstances there is, unlike the other two cases, no loss, but a small gain, £5,000. If the investor takes decision d_3, he is acting in conformity with the maximin rule.

Which is the best decision for an individual in this sort of case may depend on his personality—for example, whether he is adventurous or cautious—or upon his personal circumstances—for example, whether he can afford to lose money, or whether a member of his family is desperately in need of the money that he might win. However, there are very special features of the original position that make following the maximin rule the only rational choice. Behind the veil of ignorance no one knows whether he will be, once he is out of the original position and in a concrete historical situation, at the top, or at the bottom, or in the middle of the social heap. He could be a slave on a sugar plantation, or a Russian serf tied to the land, or a factory worker in nineteenth-century England working twelve hours a day, or a subsistence farmer in contemporary Africa on the verge of starvation. Consequently, it is sensible to take no risks, but to ensure the best possible outcome for the worst-off in society. That entails establishing principles of justice that guarantee the improvement of whoever is most disadvantaged.

At first sight it might appear attractive to gamble and to work out principles of justice that would protect your power and wealth if you are lucky enough in real life to find that you are a millionaire monarch. However, it is not rational to count on being a slave owner when you might turn out to be a slave, or to set up principles of justice that would advantage you if you find that you are Queen Elizabeth I or Blackadder, but push you further into the mire if you end up as a pauper or Baldrick. In the original position it is not rational to accept, for example, Nozick's entitlement theory of justice,[5] which entitles a person to property if he has legitimately acquired it, as this does nothing for those who, for whatever reason, have no property.

Rawls shows the power of his argument by comparing the appeal to those in the original position of the maximin rule and of the principle of average utility, which he believes is the strongest rival to his own theory of justice (pp. 161–6, 167–75). At first sight, it might appear that those in the original position would choose the principle of average utility as the basis of social justice. The society would, according to this principle, aim to increase the average amount *per capita* of whatever people enjoyed. Justice would include, for example, increasing the wealth of the country so that, on average, everyone was better off. However, there would be no guarantee that any particular individual would get an average share of the increased wealth: he might get more than the average, but he might get less. He might even lose some wealth that he previously had, even though the average wealth per head increased. Yet, someone arguing against Rawls might say that it would be rational for people in the original position to prefer the principle of average utility. They would gamble on receiving the average increase or better, although risking getting less than the average.

Rawls, however, argues that it would not be rational in the original position to choose the principle of average utility to regulate distribution of what is valued in society. His argument

---

[5] *Anarchy, State, and Utopia*, 150–3.

is that those in the original position would not be sensible to take the risks that accepting the principle of average utility entails. Those behind the veil of ignorance have no basis for knowing their propensity to take risks (p. 172), so social justice cannot be formulated on the assumption that temperamentally they are gamblers. Nevertheless, there are some situations where non-gamblers are sensible to take a chance, because there is no certainty which course of action will be the most advantageous. In that case it is rational to weigh probabilities. For example, if there is a danger of aerial bombing, the evidence may point to people having a greater chance of survival if they shelter in a cellar, although there is a risk of their being buried alive there. In order to calculate probabilities, however, you need evidence, and this, according to Rawls, is what those behind the veil of ignorance lack (pp. 172–3). In those particular conditions they have no idea of the probabilities, if they accept the principle of average utility, of their ending up as a winner or a loser (p. 168). In these circumstances of ignorance it is not rational to risk becoming a loser, when the alternative strategy of acting on the maximin principle safeguards your position if you turn out to be a disadvantaged or unlucky member of society.

The clinching argument against people in the original position choosing the principle of average utility is that it gives no guarantee that individuals will not be used for others' ends (pp. 177–83). There might be circumstances where the greatest average utility could be achieved only by the institution of slavery. So those in the original position would not choose the principle of average utility in case they were to lose their liberty in order to benefit others in the society. In general, people would not want to risk any form of long-term social, economic, or political subordination for the sake of improving the average utility, from which they did not personally benefit.

The Two Principles of Justice

The purpose of constructing the original position is to explain which principles of social justice would be chosen by anyone who did not know his own position in society and who, therefore, would be absolutely impartial. Rawls argues that such a person would want to ensure that the position of the worst-off in any society would always be improved, irrespective of desert. Acting according to the maximin rule, those in the original position behind the veil of ignorance would, according to Rawls, choose two principles of justice to ensure the fair distribution by societies of the 'primary goods' that those societies help to produce.

Primary goods are the things that people specially value, that they want more of, and about whose distribution they are consequently particularly concerned. The primary goods that social justice is concerned with are those over whose distribution society has some control. Wealth and income are clearly important among these socially controllable primary goods, but by no means the only ones. People also want rights and liberties, opportunities for self-development and self-advancement, and power (pp. 62, 92). The most important primary good, Rawls argues, is self-respect, which 'includes a person's sense of his own value, his secure conviction that his good, his plan of life, is worth carrying out' (p. 440). Self-respect depends, paradoxically, partly on appreciation by others.

Some goods, such as vigour and imagination, Rawls says, are 'natural' in the sense of not being under the control of society (p. 62). Consequently, their distribution is not the concern of social justice. Among the things that Rawls regards as influenced by society, but not under its control, is health. However, although diseases are biological and therefore 'natural', society can, of course, do much to limit their effects. Counting health as a natural rather than a social primary good leads Rawls to ignore questions of social justice that arise in discussing the distribution of health care.

One further point needs to be made about the primary goods, the distribution of which social justice seeks to regulate. Rawls does not assume that all people in fact will be interested in all these primary goods in the same ways and to the same extent (p. 93). He is aware that there are some who despise wealth and others who are uninterested in power. In the original position the principles of justice provide for the fair distribution of the social primary goods that most people in most societies want, without assuming that everyone in all societies always wishes to take up his fair share of them all.

The first of the two principles that emerges from the original position states that each person is to have an equal right to as much liberty as possible provided that it does not prevent others having the same liberty (p. 60). The similarity with John Stuart Mill's argument in *On Liberty* that the only justification for restricting anyone's liberty is to prevent harm to others is immediately obvious. It is also interesting and significant that Rawls speaks of *rights* to liberty in his crucial first principle, since he does not in his theory of justice discuss at length, or emphasize the importance of, the concept of rights in the sense of moral entitlements, as many other philosophers of justice do, especially those in the Lockean tradition. Nozick, for example, opens his book with the declaration: 'Individuals have rights, and there are things no person or group may do to them (without violating their rights). So strong and far-reaching are these rights that they raise the question of what, if anything, the state and its officials may do.'[6] It is important to notice that Rawls, although not exploring the concept of rights,[7] as Nozick does, nevertheless has this concept at the centre of his theory of justice.

In his first, provisional formulation of the first principle Rawls speaks of the right to liberty, but later changes 'liberty' into the more cumbersome but more precise 'total system of equal basic liberties' (p. 302). He is here acknowledging that it makes more sense to talk of liberties than liberty[8] and recognizing that one liberty may come into conflict with another. For example, in some historical circumstances, political liberty, where all are free to participate in political affairs, may produce governments that infringe civil liberties such as freedom of thought (p. 201). So, the liberties to which people are entitled have to be balanced against each other in a complex system of liberties.

The right to equal liberties, which the first principle prescribes, would be chosen in the original position because no

---

[6] *Anarchy, State, and Utopia*, ix; cf. Ronald Dworkin, *Taking Rights Seriously* (2nd impression, London, 1978).

[7] As distinct, of course, from *the right*, which is of central concern to Rawls, particularly where he contrasts it with the good (e.g. pp. 446–452). For a full study of Rawls on rights, see Rex Martin, *Rawls and Rights* (Lawrence, Kan., 1985).

[8] Cf. the argument against the existence of a right to liberty in Ronald Dworkin, *Taking Rights Seriously*, 266–72.

one behind the veil of ignorance would want to risk finding himself in a society where he was deprived of liberty and where the principles of social justice said nothing about the necessity to give him liberty. Rawls believes that those in the original position fear above all else discovering when they re-enter the real world that they are slaves denied all basic liberties. Consequently they would regard it as their first priority to ensure that slavery was pronounced unjust. People need liberties because without them they cannot seek whatever ends they have chosen for themselves. Liberty is the necessary condition of self-fulfilment.

The heart of the first principle of justice is the protection of liberty, but equality is also prominent, both in the origins and the substance of the principle. Those in the original position are equal in their ignorance of their own societies and their positions within them. It follows that they are equally concerned to safeguard the least advantaged in society whom they may turn out to be. They consequently support a principle of justice that prescribes reform of any society in which the greater liberty of the rich and the powerful is enjoyed at the cost of the liberty of the poor and the weak. Equality of liberty is vital to a just society. So all must have equal rights to equal systems of liberties.

The second of the two principles of justice, which has two subprinciples, regulates social and economic inequalities. These are to be arranged so that they are, first, attached to positions and offices equally open to all, and, secondly, to the greatest benefit of the least advantaged (pp. 60–1, 83, 302). The second principle, then, does not demand that societies should move towards absolute social and economic equality. There is not, therefore, an exact parallel with the first principle, where equality of people's ignorance in the original position about their social positions leads to the prescription of equal liberty within a society.[9]

What is immediately obvious about the second principle is the effect of arguing according to the maximin rule. Just as it leads in the first principle to the provision of safeguards for those who are worst off in terms of liberty, so in the second

[9] Why this is so is explained below, pp. 236–7.

principle it results in special treatment for those who are worst off in terms of wealth and power.

Before closer scrutiny of the second principle, it is important to understand the priority that those in the original position would give the first principle over the second. A central part of Rawls's theory consists in his placing the principles of justice in what he calls a 'lexical order' (pp. 34–45, esp. pp. 42–3). This arranges the principles in order of moral importance, ranking the first principle that establishes equal liberty before the second principle that regulates social and economic inequalities. It follows from this lexical ordering that the first principle must be satisfied before the second principle. In practical terms, governments must take whatever measures are necessary to move towards equal liberty before they introduce policies to modify social and economic inequalities.

Those in the original position would choose to give priority to liberty because they would not, in historical situations, want to sacrifice liberty in order to obtain more wealth or power (pp. 151–2, 542–8). Since liberty is a necessary condition of people obtaining their ends, and thus fulfilling their human potentialities, they are not prepared to trade it in for any other benefits. In the original condition they would not accept principles of justice that endorsed sacrificing some liberties in order to secure a more equitable distribution of wealth.

Rawls recognizes only one exception to the priority of liberty: at a very early stage of social development, when people are very poor, they would accept a temporary denial of equal liberty, 'if it is necessary to enhance the quality of civilization so that in due course the equal freedoms can be enjoyed by all' (p. 542; see also p. 152). Presumably Rawls means that people in abject poverty cannot enjoy liberties, so it is necessary to build up wealth in a society to a point where they can. Then they can function as full human beings.

Although it is never right for a society to sacrifice liberty to achieve some other end (except in circumstances of dire poverty), it is sometimes necessary to restrict one liberty in order to protect another. 'The precedence of liberty means that liberty can be restricted only for the sake of liberty itself' (p. 244, see also pp. 243–50). For example, in some historical circumstances it would be best to restrict the franchise, and hence restrict political freedom, in order to prevent a popularly elected government suppressing the more fundamental civil liberties, such as liberty of conscience and freedom of the person (pp. 228–34, especially pp. 229–30, and 246–7). Another situation where liberty may have to be limited to defend liberty is where an intolerant group endangers the liberties of others (pp. 216–21). Lexical ordering is necessary in order to decide priorities between competing liberties, but the aim remains to increase the overall enjoyment of liberty.

The significance of those in the original position choosing a lexical order of principles can be seen very clearly when this method of arbitrating between independent and potentially conflicting moral principles is contrasted with alternative approaches. One way of dealing with conflicting principles of justice is that recommended by Mill in *Utilitarianism*: to use an overriding criterion—in his case, utility—to decide between them. In trying to decide whether it is just to reward skill more than effort in a factory worker, Mill claims that the only way to reconcile the competing arguments is by calculating social utility.[10] A totally contrasting way of dealing with conflicts between moral principles forms the conclusion of Isaiah Berlin's *Two Concepts of Liberty*. There Berlin argues that the essence of individual liberty is being able to choose which moral value should have priority in which circumstances: 'human goals are many . . . and in perpetual rivalry with one another. To assume that all values can be graded on one scale, so that it is a mere matter of inspection to determine the highest, is to falsify our knowledge of men as free agents.'[11] So, there is no fixed, rationally agreed hierarchy of moral values, as there is in Rawls's theory of justice. Rawls, in arguing for lexical ordering, is rejecting both the moral relativism, which Berlin positively praises, and the belief in a superior moral criterion to be used as an arbitrator between competing lower level moral principles, in which Mill has faith.

Rawls proposes a lexical order not only between the first and second principles of justice, but also between the two parts of the second principle. Just as some forms of liberty have

[10] J. S. Mill, *Utilitarianism* (Everyman edition, London, 1991), 60.
[11] *Two Concepts of Liberty* (Oxford, 1958), 56.

priority over others, so, in arranging social and economic inequalities, Rawls's particular version of equality of opportunity
has priority over increasing the benefits of the least advantaged.
Those in the original position would regard the establishment
of the fair distribution of positions of power in a society as
having moral priority over the redistribution of wealth.[12]

Rawls believes that those in the original position would
insist on some form of equality of opportunity as an integral
part of social justice. However, he argues that they would not
be content with a simple 'career open to talents' (p. 72). This
would merely ensure that the limited number of positions and
offices available in a society would go to whoever performed
best in open competitions. However, what Rawls calls 'fair
equality of opportunity' (pp. 73–4) demands more than allot-
ting positions of power on grounds of ability and not according to personal contacts. In addition, no one should be
disadvantaged in the competition for places by a defective
education resulting from an inferior social position. In some
way, those with such a handicap should receive compensation
to put them on an equal footing in the competition with those
who have no such handicap. In effect, fair equality of opportunity embraces positive discrimination. Significantly, those in
the original position are, once again, looking after the interests
of whoever is at the bottom of the pile—in this case, those
people whose education has suffered because of their social
position.

The other part of the second principle of justice, dealing
with the distribution of social and economic benefits, has probably aroused more interest and controversy than any other
element in Rawls's theory except the veil of ignorance. One
method by which he reaches what he calls the 'difference
principle' is to consider an alternative way of distributing social
and economic benefits that at first sight might seem attractive
to those in the original position. This approach is similar to the
one used in the search for the general principle that those in
the original position would adopt in working out the principles

---

[12] Curiously, Rawls calls his version of equality of opportunity the *second* part of
the second principle (e.g. p. 83), although in lexical order it has priority over the
other part about increasing the benefits of the worst off (e.g. pp. 302–3).

of justice, where the superficially persuasive theory of average utility is rejected in favour of the maximin rule.

Rawls considers whether those in the original position would prefer the principle of efficiency, known in economic theory as Pareto optimality, as the just way to distribute benefits such as wealth within societies (pp. 65–72). This would recommend as social policy that everyone should be made better off, provided that no one is consequently made worse off. However, this proves unacceptable as a principle of justice, since it provides the worst off with no guarantees of escaping from permanent poverty. For example, the principle of efficiency would justify one person holding all the wealth in a community, since there is no rearrangement that would make some better off, but none worse off. The owner of all the wealth is bound to be a loser in any rearrangement. Similarly, in certain circumstances, serfdom would be justified, when there was no way of improving the lot of the serfs without worsening the position of their lord.

In place of the efficiency principle Rawls proposes as a basis for the fair distribution of social and economic benefits his original and controversial 'difference principle' (pp. 75–80). This states that 'the higher expectations of those better situated are just if and only if they work as part of a scheme which improves the expectations of the least advantaged members of society' (p. 75). This part of the second principle of justice requires, then, that, once equal liberty and fair equality of opportunity have been secured, as the first principle and the lexically prior part of the second principle demand, rearrangements in the distribution of social goods such as wealth should normally benefit the worst off. This would often entail some form of taking from the rich and giving to the poor.

The important and interesting exception is when improving the lot of the best off also improves the lot of the worst off. If, for example, paying a senior member of the government a larger salary enables or encourages him to evolve an economic plan that increases the dole of the unemployed or provides them with better job prospects, this is justified by the difference principle. What is distinctive about this principle is that, although it tends to greater social and economic equality, it positively endorses inequality if that is the best method of improving the conditions of the most deprived. Consistently, Rawls's form of social justice has as its priority the advancement of the least advantaged, which the maximin rule that was adopted in the original position requires.

Self-Interest and Justice

Rawls's theory of social justice contains a central paradox which may look like an inherent and fatal contradiction. In order to deduce principles of justice the essence of which is impartiality, he initially supposes that people in the original position argue from self-interest. It may seem at first sight that Rawls sets himself the impossible task of deriving justice from self-interest.

To some thinkers, of course, there is no problem in moving from self-interest to justice. Acting justly to others, on the understanding that they act justly to you, is what self-interest dictates as the most efficient way of dealing with other self-interested people. Glaucon in Plato's *Republic* and Hobbes in *Leviathan* both take this line of argument. However, since Rawls does not regard justice as a branch of self-interest in this way, the problem remains of how in his theory justice can emerge out of self-interest.

The problem would never arise for Rawls, it might be thought, if he did not start by making the false, Hobbesian assumption that human beings can only have self-interested motives. However, the answer to this criticism is that, in fact, he is not denying that people can be altruistic. If people were always unavoidably self-interested, there would be no chance that his principles of justice would be implemented, except when they happened to coincide with powerful people's self-interest; but he does not make this pessimistic assumption. It is only when he is constructing the purely hypothetical original position that he posits the existence of persons arguing solely from their own self-interest. He expects, or at least hopes, that in real life, by contrast, people will try to implement the principles of justice because they are right, whether or not they personally stand to gain from their implementation (pp. 147–8). Rawls's theory of justice, far from claiming that human beings are irrevocably self-interested, assumes that they have the moral potentiality to act justly.

The question then arises as to why he sets up the original position in such a way that people within it consider only their own interests. The explanation starts from the fact that the function of social justice is to arbitrate between conflicting interests: 'A society . . . is typically marked by a conflict as well as by an identity of interests' (p. 4). If there were no conflicts of interest between individuals, there would be no need for social justice. Individuals are sometimes benevolent towards each other, but in those circumstances the issue of social justice does not arise. Social justice comes into play on those occasions when people do have conflicts of personal interest. The original position is hence established to deal with those conflicts of interest over which social justice presides.

Rawls is keen to emphasize the important role of justice in protecting the separate interests of individuals. His original position is set up with individuals seeking principles of justice that safeguard their own interests in order to rule out any principle, like average utility, that would justify sacrificing one individual's good for the sake of another's. Those in the original position find a safe form of justice in the two Rawlsian principles, which in effect elaborate Kant's categorical imperative to 'act in such a way that you always treat humanity . . . never simply as a means, but always at the same time as an end'.[13] This Kantian principle insists on respect for the individual and, therefore, reinforces the individual's respect for himself, which Rawls regards as his chief good.

In the original position each individual knows that in a real society he has a distinct and particular self-interest, although he does not, behind the veil of ignorance, know what it is. In the original position the individual self-interestedly chooses principles of social justice that will improve his conditions in a real society if he happens to be one of the most disadvantaged in that society. Thus, he chooses the principles of equal liberty, fair equality of opportunity, and the difference principle. These principles, emanating from the self-interest of people in the hypothetical original position, should be adopted in real societies

---

[13] As formulated by Nozick in *Anarchy, State, and Utopia*, 32. See *Theory of Justice*, 178–83. Interestingly, this principle is central to both Rawls's and Nozick's theories, in spite of their fundamental differences about how it should be interpreted.

because they are just. The veil of ignorance in the original position is intended to produce principles of justice that are not the product of any particular social group arguing on its own behalf. In their impartiality lies their fairness. So it is a paradox and not a contradiction that self-interested behaviour in the original condition leads to principles of justice in real societies.

Conclusion

A Theory of Justice contains and engenders a host of paradoxes. It derives practical altruistic principles from arguments about the choices of hypothetical egoistic persons. Rawls produced a classic of egalitarianism that denies the value of absolute equality. Some of his critics believe that Rawls's arguments for the priority of liberty merely rationalize the prejudices of late-twentieth-century American liberals, but ostensibly his book is a work of pure philosophy seeking through reason to discover eternal moral truths. While Rawls himself, with characteristically liberal open-mindedness, has moved on and modified the ideas of his *Theory of Justice*, this work still commands attention as a modern classic, provocative in both its methods and its conclusions.

Bibliographical Note

The work discussed in this chapter is John Rawls, *A Theory of Justice* (Cambridge, Mass., 1971; Oxford, 1972). Since the publication of this book, on which Rawls's extensive reputation was built, he has developed and modified his ideas. His most recent thoughts on political philosophy are contained in John Rawls, *Political Liberalism* (New York, 1993).

No contemporary political philosopher has stimulated more philosophical discussion than Rawls. The extensive debate in philosophical journals soon after the publication of his *Theory of Justice* is reflected in a comprehensive collection of journal articles: Norman Daniels (ed.), *Reading Rawls: Critical Studies of 'A Theory of Justice'* (Oxford, 1975). A few years later two other editors invited scholars to write essays for a book on various aspects of Rawls's theory: H. G. Blocker and E. H. Smith (eds.), *John Rawls' Theory of Social Justice* (Athens, Oh., 1980).

Three books that are devoted wholly to analysis of Rawls's theory of justice regard his book as a major work, but disagree with many of his arguments: Brian Barry, *The Liberal Theory of Justice: A Critical Explanation of the Principal Doctrines in 'A Theory of Justice' by John Rawls* (Oxford, 1973); David Schaefer, *Justice or Tyranny? A Critique of John Rawls's 'A Theory of Justice'* (Port Washington, NY, 1979); Robert P. Wolff, *Understanding Rawls* (Princeton, 1977). A critical but more sympathetic exegesis of Rawls's theory is contained in Rex Martin, *Rawls and Rights* (Lawrence, Kan., 1985).

For those seeking an easily understood and relatively short book on Rawls and his critics, Chandran Kukathas and Philip Pettit, *Rawls: 'A Theory of Justice' and its Critics* (Cambridge, 1990), may be recommended. Good chapter-length introductions can be found in the chapter by Samuel Gorovitz, 'John Rawls, "A Theory of Justice"', in Anthony de Crespigny and Kenneth Minogue (eds.), *Contemporary Political Philosophers* (London, 1976), and in Bhikhu Parekh, *Contemporary Political Thinkers* (Oxford, 1982).

Three years after the publication of *A Theory of Justice*, a colleague of Rawls at Harvard University produced a classic refutation of Rawls's arguments about justice: Robert Nozick, *Anarchy, State, and Utopia* (Oxford, 1974), especially chapter 7, section 2. Since Nozick's book appeared, discussions of justice often treat the theories of Rawls and Nozick together as of major importance (for example, Brown and Kymlicka, whose books are mentioned below). One book contains articles about both Rawls and Nozick: J. Angelo Corlett (ed.), *Equality and Liberty: Analyzing Rawls and Nozick* (London, 1991).

Special attention should be paid to two other major philosophical works, besides Nozick's, that incorporate discussions of Rawls's ideas on justice: Ronald Dworkin, *Taking Rights Seriously* (second corrected impression with appendix, London, 1978), ch. 6; Alasdair MacIntyre, *After Virtue: A Study in Moral Theory* (second (corrected) edn. with postscript, London, 1985), ch. 17.

Interesting sections on Rawls's theory of justice may be found in some books on the general theme of justice: Brian Barry, *Theories of Justice* (London, 1989); Tom D. Campbell, *Justice* (Basingstoke, 1988); David Miller, *Social Justice* (Oxford, 1976), ch. 1, sect. 4; Philip Pettit, *Judging Justice* (London, 1980), pt. 5; Michael J. Sandel, *Liberalism and the Limits of Justice* (Cambridge, 1982).

There are also useful discussions of Rawls in works on political philosophy that regard justice as the central theme: Alan Brown, *Modern Political Philosophy: Theories of the Just State* (Harmondsworth, 1986), ch. 3; Will Kymlicka, *Contemporary Political Philosophy: An Introduction* (Oxford, 1990), ch. 4.

For a full bibliography, see J. H. Wellbank, Denis Snook, and David T. Mason (eds.), *John Rawls and his Critics: An Annotated Bibliography* (New York, 1982).

II

Robert Nozick: *Anarchy, State, and Utopia*

MICHAEL LESSNOFF

ROBERT NOZICK's *Anarchy, State, and Utopia* was published in 1974,[1] three years after his colleague at Harvard University, John Rawls, published *A Theory of Justice*, and the two books have been bracketed together ever since. Politically they are sharply opposed. While Rawls's 'liberal' theory calls on governments to undertake extensive economic transfers to the poor, the 'libertarian' Nozick defends the 'minimal state', a state 'limited to the narrow functions of protection against force, theft, fraud, enforcement of contracts and so on' (p. ix) —a state forbidden to engage in any economic redistribution whatever. Such an extreme position shocked many; but all have been forced to pay careful attention to Nozick's arguments.

These arguments can be considered in four stages, as follows. (1) Nozick's fundamental moral philosophy; (2) his justification of the minimal state; (3) his theory of economic justice, which forbids any more-than-minimal, or redistributive state; (4) his argument that the minimal state provides a framework for utopia.

Nozick's Fundamental Moral Philosophy

Nozick's moral philosophy is a particular version of the priority of the right over the good (a very particular version—for Rawls also asserts this priority). As Nozick himself puts it, moral goals are subordinate to moral 'side constraints' (p. 29), which forbid *absolutely* the violation of individual rights. This

---

[1] Robert, Nozick, *Anarchy, State, and Utopia* (Oxford, 1974). References in the text are to this edition.

side-constraints morality, Nozick stresses, is *not* an injunction to minimize the total amount of rights violation (which he calls a 'utilitarianism of rights'). There is, for example, a well-known objection to the utilitarian theory of punishment that if, in certain circumstances, framing and punishing an innocent person would effectively deter crime, utilitarianism would then prescribe punishing the innocent person. In Nozick's terms this would be violating one person's rights in order to minimize rights violations overall. Such actions are absolutely ruled out by his side-constraints morality.

As Nozick explains, his side-constraints morality rests on a fundamental moral principle—the 'Kantian imperative', that is, 'the Kantian principle that individuals are ends and not merely means' (pp. 30–1). Individuals, therefore, 'may not be sacrificed or used for the achieving of other ends without their consent'. ('Other ends' means the ends of other persons.) Side constraints, Nozick says, reflect the separateness and inviolability of individual persons: harm to one individual cannot be justified by greater gain to another or others, for there is no overall 'social good' advanced thereby, only the separate individuals enjoying goods or suffering evils. 'There is no justified sacrifice of some of us for others' (p. 33).

Since states and governments, just like any other agent, are bound by Kantian moral side constraints, their power of coercion must not be used to force some persons to serve the ends of others. This 'libertarian side constraint' is fundamental to Nozick's political philosophy.

Why must persons be treated in accordance with the 'Kantian' side constraints? Because, according to Nozick, a person is a being with the ability to regulate and guide its life in accordance with some overall conception it chooses to accept. And why is this so morally crucial? Nozick suggests that the answer has to do with an 'elusive and difficult notion: the meaning of life' (p. 50). A person gives meaning to his or her life by shaping it in the way indicated: only so can a life be meaningful. Here we arrive at the very bedrock of Nozick's moral and political philosophy, the presumed premiss of all his conclusions. Whether they are really derivable from it is an important question.

Let us return to politics. Given Nozick's Kantian imperative, one might wonder whether the existence of the state—an intrinsically coercive institution—can be justified. Nozick's answer is yes—but only the minimal state.

Nozick's Justification of the Minimal State

In seeking to justify even the minimal state Nozick is, he says, taking seriously the anarchist view that the state, of necessity, 'must violate individuals' rights and hence is intrinsically immoral' (p. xi). He therefore begins his argument by considering an anarchic, or stateless, situation—the traditional 'state of nature'. Nozick does not claim to know what this anarchic state of nature would be like, but it is, he maintains, possible to frame a theoretically appropriate description. This should be neither absurdly optimistic, nor excessively pessimistic (like Hobbes's version). Given that the aim of the argument is to convince the anarchist, the appropriate starting-point is a state of nature corresponding to 'the best anarchic situation one reasonably could hope for' (p. 5), namely, one in which people generally, though not always, act as they should. Anarchism would be refuted, says Nozick, 'if one could show that the state would be superior even to this most favoured situation of anarchy . . . or would arise [from it] by a process involving no morally impermissible step'. Since Nozick in fact adopts the second strategy, the (relevant) state of nature must be subject to moral constraints. A state of nature subject to moral constraints, and in which people generally, though not always, act as they should, is, approximately, Locke's state of nature. A Lockean state of nature, therefore, is the starting-point of the argument.

Nozick claims that he takes seriously the position of the anarchist, but it would be more accurate to say that he responds to one particular kind of anarchism, individualist anarchism (as Nozick sometimes puts it) or (as it is often called) anarcho-capitalism.[2] This, I believe, is a further reason why

---

[2] Some anarcho-capitalist works referred to by Nozick are M. W. Rothbard, *Power and Market* (Menlo Park, 1970); D. Friedman, *The Machinery of Freedom* (New York, 1973); J. Hospers, *Libertarianism* (Los Angeles, 1971); and J. J. Martin, *Men against the State: The Expositors of Individualist Anarchism in America, 1827–1908* (Colorado Springs, Colo., 1970). See *Anarchy, State, and Utopia*, ch. 2, n. 4.

Nozick's argument begins from a Lockean state of nature. The anarcho-capitalist objection to the state needs to be precisely defined. It does *not* rest on any general objection to coercion. On the contrary, like Locke, the anarcho-capitalists take for granted a 'natural' right, not only to self-defence, but of self-protection by *punishing* those who have violated rights. Their objection to the state is that it (seeks to) *monopolize* (or at least to regulate) the right to punish, and that it forcibly extracts property from its citizens by taxation. According to the anarcho-capitalists, protection against invasions of person, property, and so on should be, like other goods and services, supplied and purchased voluntarily through the free market. As we shall shortly see, Nozick's argument for the state is, to a considerable extent, a response to such arguments.

Nozick's justification of the minimal state starts from the Lockean state of nature, which 'has a law of nature to govern it' (because human beings were not 'made for one another's uses').[3] In Nozickian terms, the law of nature imposes moral side constraints protecting individual rights. But the law is not always obeyed. Therefore, every person also has a right of self-defence against transgressors, a right to punish them to a degree appropriate to the transgression, and a right, if injured, to exact compensation. Such a situation, Locke says, is subject to serious inconveniences. For example, many people will lack the power to enforce their rights effectively. Also, the right of men to be judges in their own cases leads to biased judgment, and to unjustified or excessive punishment (or punishment so considered by its victims). This in turn leads to violent feuding ('war', as Locke calls it) between the parties involved.

According to Nozick, Locke's conclusion that 'civil government' is the appropriate remedy for these 'inconveniences' is too quick. We need first to explore what resources are available to deal with them in the state of nature itself—namely, 'all those voluntary arrangements and agreements persons might reach' (p. 11). First of all, Nozick says, individuals could (or would?) strengthen their power to enforce their rights by

---

[3] J. Locke, *The Second Treatise of Government and A Letter Concerning Toleration*, ed. J. W. Gough (Oxford, 1957), 5.

establishing mutual-protection associations, in which 'all will answer the call of any member' for defence against and punishment of rights violators. But such simple associations would not be satisfactory. For one thing, Nozick says, they would need to set up procedures of adjudication to handle disputes between members (where one member accuses another of violating his rights). Also, it would be highly inconvenient for all members to be constantly on call to carry out 'protective functions' for all other members. To deal with this problem, they would have recourse to 'division of labor and exchange': 'Some people will be *hired* to perform protective functions, and some entrepreneurs will go into the business of selling protective services' (p. 13). In other words, protective functions will now be performed by commercial firms ('protective agencies') selling their services on the market. This is, of course, the solution favoured by the anarcho-capitalists.

According to Nozick, however, it is not yet a satisfactory solution. 'Initially, several different protective associations or companies will offer their services in the same geographical area. What will occur when there is a conflict between clients of different agencies [and] they reach different decisions as to the merits of the case?' (p. 15). There is a conflict, as one agency tries to protect its client while the other attempts to punish him. The problem of 'war' between individuals in the state of nature seems to have been replaced by one of war between protective agencies.

However, the situation is not, according to Nozick, as bad as it seems. The forces of the opposed protective agencies may well 'do battle' (p. 16). But the outcome will be the establishment, in each geographical area, of a single 'dominant protective association'—either because one association always wins its battles in the area, and thus puts its rivals out of business there; or else (if this is not so), to avoid the wasteful costs of war, the rival agencies

agree to resolve peacefully those cases about which they reach differing judgments. They agree to set up, and abide by the decisions of, some third judge or court [in these cases] . . . Thus emerges a system of appeals courts and agreed upon rules about jurisdiction . . . Though different agencies operate, there is one federal judicial system of which they are all components. (p 16)

Nozick now asks, 'Is the dominant protective association a state?' (p. 22). His answer is that it appears not to be, but 'appearances are deceptive' (p. 25). (This is rather misleading. It would be more accurate to say that the dominant protective agency is not yet quite a state, but is poised to become one.) The association appears not to be a state because, although dominant in its area, it does not include *everyone* therein. A small number of 'independents' coexist with it, but are not protected by it, because they have chosen not to buy its protective services but instead to enforce their own rights. To turn the dominant protective association into an indubitable state, the independents must be incorporated into it. Nozick argues that this will happen, that it will be accomplished *by force*, and that this exercise of force is morally justified. Why so?

Nozick's argument is long and complex, but in essentials is as follows. The independents who enforce their own rights, unlike the dominant protective association, do not have a relatively reliable and impartial judicial procedure for determining guilt and appropriate punishment. Given individuals' tendency to partiality in their own favour when they are judges in their own case, right-enforcement by independents creates a serious risk of unjust punishment of the association's clients. Therefore, the association, on behalf of its clients, is entitled to prohibit right-enforcements by independents against them. Furthermore, it has the power to enforce this prohibition, and will do so (chs. 4, 5).

At this stage, the dominant protective agency has become what Nozick calls an 'ultraminimal state' (pp. 52, 113). It is a state because it monopolizes right-enforcement, but not yet a 'minimal state', because it is not willing to protect the rights of all—only of those who buy its protection services. Although Nozick, rather strangely, argues that the move to the ultraminimal state is morally justified in itself, he also (and surely correctly) states that it is morally obligatory to move from the ultraminimal to the minimal state. If this were not done, the former independents would be left without any means of protecting their rights. There is, however, a further issue—the *redistributive* (or apparently redistributive) nature of (even) the minimal state. For (even) the minimal state is obliged to protect the rights, not only of those in its territory who can and do pay the 'economic' price of such protection, but also of those who cannot (p. 141). As Nozick asks (alluding to the transition from dominant protective association to minimal state): 'How can a protection agency, a business, charge some to provide its product to others?' (p. 25). Presumably, it cannot, but a (minimal) state can, and justly so, Nozick argues. Prohibition of 'independent' right-enforcement is justified only if substitute protective services are offered by the prohibitors, i.e. the clients of the dominant protective association. If necessary, they must subsidize those ex-independents who would otherwise be disadvantaged by their forcibly altered status—in particular, 'those of scanter resources' (p. 112). So, the upshot is that the Nozickian minimal state may and must provide protective services, uniformly and monopolistically for everyone in its territory, whether or not they wish it, and whether or not they can afford to pay for the services. Those who cannot afford them, but receive them none the less, may appear to be beneficiaries of compulsory redistribution of income from other citizens. According to Nozick, however, the apparent redistribution is not really redistribution at all, but *compensation* for coercive removal of the right of self-protection. It is part of the obligatory compensation owed to the independents for loss of rights.

Assessment of Nozick's Justification of the Minimal State

Many commentators have been puzzled by Nozick's justification of the minimal state. No state, minimal or other, has ever been established via the sequence of events described in Nozick's story, as he must know. What, then, is the significance of the fact that this sequence can be imagined as a bare possibility? But Nozick's claim is more than this. It is that, if men began in the most favourable state of anarchy that can reasonably be expected, they would, through the promptings of self-interest but without violating any moral side constraint, eventually move into a state in the way described (pp. xi, 7, 114, 118). The argument is framed thus because it is aimed at anarchists, a fact which is particularly clear in the move from the dominant protection association to the minimal state: in effect, this says to anarchists (independents) that the (minimal) state is entitled to impose its authority on them without their consent. In these terms, does Nozick's argument succeed? I believe it is deeply flawed, because Nozick grossly underrates the differences between the state and commercial firms selling protective services. It is not possible to derive the former as an extension or modification of the latter. The fault-line between the two shows up in many ways in Nozick's argument. For example, Nozick has to admit that he can give no reason why the dominant protective association would be entitled to force independents to accept its jurisdiction *in relation to disputes with other independents* (p. 109). Thus, the Nozickian 'state' has not actually achieved a monopoly over right-enforcement and (despite Nozick's protestations) is only dubiously a state. Again, Nozick notes that independents not wishing to pay the price charged by the dominant protective agency would be entitled to refuse to do so, at the cost of forgoing protective services (p. 113). Real states, however, would prosecute such people for tax evasion, but would nevertheless otherwise protect their rights on the same basis as anyone else's. Yet again, Nozick notes that private protection agencies, including a 'dominant' one, would (in line with normal commercial practice) offer clients a variety of protective packages, at different prices, to cater to demand for more or less extensive or elaborate protection (p. 13): states, however, are supposed to provide the same protection of rights to all citizens.

Nozick's dominant protection association is, we see, much less like a state than he claims. In fact, it is in some respects a very strange animal, in so far as it is (or may be) the result of an amalgamation between a number of different commercial protection agencies competing with one another in the same geographical area. Nozick calls this outcome 'federal' but it is *not*, like a federal state, a federation of geographical units, but rather one of (competing) protection agencies, which continue to operate (and presumably to compete) in the same territory. The so-called federation is only a system of 'higher' courts set up to avoid conflict between protective agencies in cases 'about which they reach [or might reach] differing judgments' (p. 16). Such a system is nothing like a federal state or any kind of state. Yet when Nozick describes the dominant protection association turning into the minimal state, it has mysteriously become a unified organization with a single body of clients. This sleight-of-hand is necessary to bridge the huge gap between a commercial protection agency and a state. In sum, Nozick's argument as to how a minimal state would evolve out of a Lockean state of nature is unpersuasive: thus, on his own terms, he has not justified the minimal state.

There is another kind of problem besetting Nozick's attempted justification of the minimal state. To see this, we must look more carefully and critically at the idea of a commercial protective agency. What services, exactly, do such agencies sell? According to Nozick, they perform the functions of detection, apprehension, judicial determination of guilt, punishment, and exaction of compensation (p. 13). Presumably they have at their disposal detectives, police forces, judges, and prisons. A client buys their services by paying, say, an annual premium, and calls on his agency when he considers his rights to have been violated. It is rather difficult to envisage these agencies working in a satisfactory way. For one thing, one characteristic police function—the routine patrolling of neighbourhoods, in order to discourage and detect crime—would not be offered by them, since this is not a service that can be sold to individuals (it is what economists call a 'public good'). Nor is it at all clear that a system of commercial protective agencies would be an effective deterrent to crime (or rights violation). Providing the full panoply of services described by Nozick would probably be extremely expensive, and might well be beyond the means of many, perhaps most, private citizens. If so, there would be no deterrent to violating the rights of the relatively poor (perhaps the majority) but only of the rich. Nozick, therefore, has no right to assume that his 'dominant protection association' is faced with only a small number of 'independents'. The association would in fact confront *two* categories of non-members: genuine independents, or anarchists, who have chosen not to join, but to enforce their own rights; and reluctant independents, who are simply too poor to buy the association's protective services, but would if they could. Incorporation-plus-subsidization, as prescribed by Nozick, is thus *not* coercion for the latter, but a bargain they would freely accept; hence the subsidization is *not*, as

Nozick argues, compensation for forced incorporation, but genuine redistribution. This makes it all the more difficult for him to justify the 'minimal' state, but not the more-than-minimal state.

Nozick's attempted justification of the minimal state underrates both the difference between the state and a commercial protective agency, and also the inadequacies of a regime of the latter type. In this sense, he takes the arguments of the anarcho-capitalists too seriously, and concedes too much to them. What he *should* have argued is, not that the state would evolve legitimately out of a Lockean state of nature, but rather that what would evolve, short of the state, would be so unsatisfactory that it would be justified to establish the state, if necessary imposing it by force on anarchists, so long as it provides equal protection of the rights of all. This conclusion, incidentally, is unaffected by the number of anarchists so coerced.

Nozick's Theory of Economic Justice

Nozick's theory of economic justice—'justice in holdings'—is the most discussed, and the most iconoclastic, part of his political philosophy. It is called by him the 'entitlement theory', and is contrasted with two types of (allegedly) erroneous theories. One such type consists of 'end-state' principles, which 'hold that the justice of a distribution [of wealth] is determined by how things are distributed . . . as judged by some *structural* principle(s)' (p. 153). From this point of view, two distributions are to be judged equally just as if they have the same structure, or 'profile', but different persons occupy different positions in the structure. Thus, 'my having ten and your having five, and my having five and your having ten are structurally identical distributions' (p. 154). Nozick's objection to end-state principles (such as Rawls's difference principle, or a principle limiting inequality) is that they are *non-historical*, i.e. they treat as irrelevant to the justice of a distribution *how it came about*, how individuals acquired the holdings they have. Nozick's entitlement theory consists of historical principles of justice.

Nozick's second class of erroneous theories is made up of what he calls 'patterned' principles of justice. Such a principle 'specifies that a distribution is to vary along with some natural dimension(s)'. It has the form, 'to each according to his—', where the blank is filled in by 'moral merit, or needs, or marginal product', or whatever (p. 156). Patterned principles, though they may or may not be historical, are rejected because they are incompatible with any freedom whatever for individuals to use their wealth as they choose. If at a given moment a patterned distribution were established, it would of necessity be destroyed if persons could freely (and hence unpredictably) transfer some of their holdings in purchases, gifts, loans, and so on. As Nozick sums up: 'Liberty upsets patterns' (p. 160). Nozick's entitlement theory prescribes no pattern.

What does it prescribe? First, a principle of justice in *acquisition*, which specifies how unowned things may be appropriated (for the first time) by persons. Second, a principle of justice in *transfer*, which specifies how things already owned may become (legitimately) the property of other persons. According to the entitlement theory, a person is entitled to what he has if and only if he acquired it in accordance with the principle of justice in acquisition, or has acquired it in accordance with the principle of justice in transfer from someone entitled to it. (The complication created by the issue of *rectification* of injustice is ignored for the time being, though it will later be seen to be important.)

What exactly are Nozick's principles of justice in acquisition and transfer? To the bewilderment of many commentators, Nozick declines to specify them in any detail (p. 153). Despite this, it is possible to give some account of them. Thus, it seems clear that, according to Nozick's principle of justice in transfer, a person becomes the (new) legitimate owner of something already legitimately owned by another owner, if and only if the latter freely conveys it to that person. This transfer may take the form of a gift (charitable or otherwise), a bequest, a market exchange, etc. It follows, of course, that taxation by the state to provide welfare services, etc.—a forced transfer—is unjust. According to Nozick, such forced redistribution violates the Kantian imperative: it uses some persons for the benefit of others. It is morally on a par with theft.

It is harder to specify Nozick's principle of justice in acquisition, but not impossible. Notoriously, and to the perplexity of many, Nozick discusses Locke's labour theory of acquisition at length, only to reject it, without putting anything definite in its place. However, there is no doubt that for Nozick, as a general principle, labour creates entitlement. When *new* goods are *produced*, entitlement to them depends on how they were made. 'Whoever makes something, having bought or contracted for all other held resources used in the process . . . is entitled to it' (p. 160). If he uses no held (already owned) resources, he must then be entitled to what he makes out of unheld resources.

A similar conclusion is implied by Nozick's famous argument that 'taxation of earnings from labor is on a par with forced labor' (p. 169). Such taxation is 'seizing the results of someone's labor [which] is equivalent to seizing hours from him'; it forces him to devote some of his hours of labour to ends not his own. Those who so force him, says Nozick, treat him as if (during these hours) they *owned* his person and abilities. They flout 'the classical liberal notion of self-ownership' and embrace 'a notion of (partial) property rights in *other* people' (p. 172). Taxation of earnings from labour is not only like theft; it is like (partial) enslavement.

But taxation of earnings from labour is not the only way of 'seizing the results of someone's labor'. The result of a person's labour may be something he has made out of *unheld* resources. If that thing did *not* become his property, other persons would be entitled to seize it, and, in effect, become part-owner (by Nozick's argument) of its maker. His position would be like that of a (partial) slave. Presumably, therefore, the maker must in such cases become the rightful owner.

This principle of just acquisition is also implied by an argument of Nozick against Rawls. Whereas Rawls conceives of justice as the right distribution of the fruits of social cooperation, Nozick asks us to imagine 'ten Robinson Crusoes, each working alone for two years on separate islands' (p. 185), a scenario neglected by Rawls, he thinks, because it constitutes 'a clear case of application of the correct theory of justice: the entitlement theory' (p. 186). Nozick's point is that each Robinson Crusoe is the rightful owner of what, working alone, he has produced (none has any claim on the product of another). All in all, it seems almost certain that Nozick believes that a person who makes something out of unheld resources is entitled to appropriate it. Presumably, this implies a right to appropriate unheld natural resources in order to make something. And in that case, it would seem illogical not to admit also a right to appropriate unheld natural resources simply in order to use them. Nozick's principle(s) of just acquisition do not, after all, seem to be so very different from Locke's.

It need hardly be said that Nozick's assertion of the property rights created by labour has nothing in common with socialism, or with any critique of capitalism. For one thing, he would undoubtedly include within 'labour' all forms of economic activity, including management. For another, it is obvious from his principle of just transfer that the 'earnings' to which labour creates an inviolable title are whatever others are prepared to pay for it, in the market. Furthermore, Nozick thinks it feasible and desirable to extend his argument against taxation of earnings from labour to 'interest, entrepreneurial profits, and so on' (p. 170)—that is, to the specifically capitalist sources of income. Although he does not give this extended argument, he nevertheless assumes it when he objects to principles of justice that 'give each citizen an enforceable claim to some portion of the total social product' (p. 171). No matter the kind of income or wealth taxed for this purpose, the redistribution involved amounts to partial ownership of some people by others.

As is already clear, Nozick denies that there exists a right to life, in the sense of a right to what is necessary in order to live. Such a 'right' would be a right to resources that may be justly held by others, according to the entitlement theory, and of which they cannot justly be deprived. Nevertheless, Nozick's entitlement theory is not—quite—a licence for unlimited appropriation without regard to the interests of others. The right of appropriation is limited by what Nozick calls the 'Lockean proviso' (p. 179). Locke imposed, as a condition on appropriation, that 'enough and as good' be left for others. This Nozick interprets to mean that appropriation must not worsen the situation of others. He then poses the question: 'Is the situation of persons who are unable to appropriate . . . worsened by a system allowing appropriation and permanent property?', and answers it by pointing to the numerous ways in which private property 'increases the social product' and also provides 'sources of employment' (p. 177). He thus concludes that in a free-market system the proviso '(almost?) never will come into effect' (p. 179). Not quite never, however. No one is allowed to appropriate the world's total supply of drinkable water, for example, presumably because it is a natural resource necessary to human life. Monopolistic ownership of such a resource would confer on its owner a degree of power which, if misused, could bring about what Nozick calls a 'catastrophe'. It is only in such cases of catastrophe, he says, 'that the question of the Lockean proviso being violated arises' (p. 181). And this is so because, in judging the effects of a private property system, the decisive point is that 'the baseline for comparison is so low as compared to the productiveness of a society with private appropriation'. If private property had not arisen, Nozick thinks, men would be so wretchedly poor that their situation would be little better than catastrophic. But Nozick does not think that, in practice, private property in accordance with the entitlement theory is likely to produce catastrophes. He concludes that 'the free operations of a market system will not actually run afoul of the Lockean proviso' (p. 182).

Assessment of Nozick's Theory of Economic Justice

One difficulty in appraising Nozick's theory of economic justice is that one may find it unacceptable simply because one's ultimate value-judgements differ from his. About such matters not much can be said, except to register disagreement. There are, however, many points at which Nozick is open to criticism on purely logical grounds. But before criticizing Nozick I shall mention one point on which he should, I believe, be defended against his critics.

This is his argument against 'patterned' principles of distributive justice. Nozick's argument shows conclusively, in my opinion, that all such principles must be rejected because they would destroy *all* freedom to dispose of one's wealth as one chooses. Some critics of Nozick have denied this. G. A. Cohen, for example, argues against Nozick that 'patterns preserve liberty'.[4] However, his argument does not show this. The gist of

[4] G. A. Cohen, Robert Nozick and Wilt Chamberlain, 'How Patterns Preserve Liberty', in J. Arthur and W. H. Shaw (eds.) *Justice and Economic Distribution* (Englewood Cliffs, NJ, 1978), 246–62.

it is that untrammelled market exchanges in a capitalist economy lead to inequalities of wealth and therefore of power between social classes so great that subsequent market transactions cannot be described as free (the workers, who need access to the means of production in order to live, are forced to work for the capitalists, who own and control access to the means of production). This, if true, is an argument against untrammelled free-market capitalism, but not an argument for any patterned principle of justice.

It is essential, in this connection, to keep firmly in mind the difference between patterned and end-state principles of justice (Nozick himself is extremely careless in this regard).[5] A principle that outlaws extreme inequalities, or one that calls for any 'social minimum' (for example, Rawls's difference principle, or one that requires provision for the basic needs of all) is an end-state principle, not a patterned principle. These end-state principles require state redistribution, of course, but they do not destroy *all* freedom to dispose of one's wealth as one chooses. The success of Nozick's argument against patterned principles does not mean that his argument against all state welfare transfers is likewise successful. That remains to be considered.

One peculiarity of Nozick's argument is that, most of the time, it seems to presuppose a world consisting entirely of adults. The rights of children are not separately considered. Nozick's philosophy might be summed up as follows: no one has any (enforceable) obligation to help anyone else, no matter their need, unless they voluntarily consent to do so. Can Nozick apply this to children? Do parents not have an (enforceable) obligation, if they can, to look after their children? (The act of begetting children is *not* consenting to look after them.) If the parents are unable to look after their children, or are dead, do the children have no rights to be looked after? Does no one—their other relations, if any, or the wider community— have any (enforceable) obligation to ensure that orphans are looked after? Nozick has to say that there is no such obligation. If he were to make an exception for children or orphans,

---

[5] See *Anarchy, State, and Utopia*, 156, where Nozick 'extend(s) the use of "pattern" to include the overall designs put forth by combinations of end-state principles'; and p. 209, where Rawls's difference principle, incomprehensibly, is called a 'patterned end-state principle'.

he would be hard-pressed to resist extending his concession to adults who are equally unable to look after themselves—for example, the chronic sick and disabled. But he is, we know, quite unwilling to have the state use its taxation powers to help such people.

These are matters of value-judgements. Let us turn to logical problems related to Nozick's argument against (welfarist) redistribution. These begin right at the beginning. Nozick, we recall, bases his entire moral and political philosophy on his notion of a 'meaningful life': a person's life is meaningful if and only if he or she is able to shape it in accordance with his or her own choices. Is it necessary to point out that extreme poverty inhibits and may even destroy the ability to lead a meaningful life, thus defined? Despite the high *value* Nozick places on the living of a meaningful life, he does not believe there is any *right* to its material preconditions, or even to the preconditions of life itself. Yet meaningful life is certainly impossible without life. Does it then make sense to give private property rights absolute priority over life itself? It would be quite absurd to argue that a wealthy person, taxed as part of a redistributive scheme to help the poor, is thereby prevented from living a meaningful life. Although the value of living a meaningful life is supposed to ground Nozick's side-constraints morality, it cannot do so. That morality, therefore, is left ungrounded.

Another problem, noted by many of Nozick's critics, is the implications of the so-called Lockean proviso. In Nozick's view, as we saw, it has, in practice, virtually no implications at all, because the 'baseline' against which the entitlement system of private property has to be compared is a situation of such miserable poverty. What assumptions is Nozick making here? What (hypothetical?) situation provides the appropriate baseline, and why? Nozick, as often, admits he cannot give a fully adequate answer ('[The] question of fixing the baseline needs more detailed investigation than we are able to give it here' (p. 177)), but it looks as if his conception of the relevant baseline is one where no property rights whatever are recognized, where, in other words, everyone is considered free to use everything. No doubt such a state of affairs would be, as Hume argued, little short of catastrophic: but it is not clear why this is the appropriate baseline for comparison. It appears that Nozick thinks so, because of the historical nature of his entitlement theory. He conceives of the world's resources as being *initially* unowned by human beings, then becoming owned in accordance with his entitlement theory, and then asks if this makes things worse. But surely this story is *un*historical. It is not very likely that the world's resources were first appropriated by individuals, working alone. The human race, in its earliest days, was not organized on capitalist or even individualist principles. If, as seems not unlikely, acts of original acquisition were carried out by groups—clans, tribes, or whatever—recognizing a right of all members of the group to some share of the product, then—so long as no coercion was involved—Nozick would have no reason to object to such an arrangement. And, if individual private property was preceded by some such system, should not the latter be the baseline for comparison? Notwithstanding the admittedly far greater productivity of a private property economy, the Lockean proviso might not then appear so nugatory as it does to Nozick. Despite its great productivity, the private property, free-market economy almost never produces a situation of full employment, and occasionally generates mass unemployment. Under Nozick's entitlement theory, the unemployed would (charity apart) have no income. They could starve to death. Is this not a 'catastrophe'? Can one be sure that persons starving to death in a wealthy Nozickian society are not worse off than they would be in a poor society differently organized? Of course, one can be sure of nothing where such counter-factuals are involved. Still, if one wants to be reasonably sure of satisfying the Lockean proviso, one should, as several commentators have argued, provide, out of taxation, at least a basic social minimum.

Discussion of the Lockean proviso illustrates what is perhaps the most fundamental problem with Nozick's theory of economic justice. It is very hard to see how, in practice, to apply it. According to Nozick, a distribution is just if and only if everyone is entitled to what they own, and this is the case now if the *entire history* of appropriation has conformed to Nozick's principles of justice in acquisition and transfer. As everyone (including Nozick) knows, this has not happened. Apart from theft, fraud, and coercive redistribution by governments, current ownership has been much affected by past acts of military violence, warfare, invasions, and so on. According to some commentators, the establishment of capitalist private property itself depended, to no small degree, on the violent or fraudulent expropriation of previous, often collective, owners. To cope with such problems, Nozick adds to his principles of just acquisition and just transfer a third principle—the principle of rectification of injustice. This principle is at once important, and problematic in the extreme. To apply it, Nozick says, one must use 'historical information about previous situations and injustices done in them' (p. 152) to estimate the difference between the existing distribution of holdings and the (probable) distribution that would now exist if no injustice had taken place. If there is a difference, the best estimate of the latter distribution 'must be realized' (p. 153). As Nozick probably realizes, this is a hopeless enterprise. He is thus led to a quite surprising conclusion: 'One *cannot* use the analysis and theory presented here to condemn any particular scheme of transfer payments, unless it is clear that no consideration of rectification of injustice could apply to justify it' (p. 231).

But it can never be clear what should be done *now* to rectify the accumulated effects of centuries of past injustices. It thus turns out that Nozick's theory of economic justice is, indeed, purely a theory, without any practical application. If we agree with it, we learn from it what the human race, throughout its history, ought to have done, but not what we should do now.

The Minimal State and Utopia

In view of the conclusion of the previous section, it is perhaps not surprising that the last part of Nozick's book portrays the minimal state as a utopia (or, more accurately, a framework for utopia). However, this is not an admission of its unrealizability or lack of practical relevance. Rather, Nozick wishes to show that 'the minimal state is inspiring as well as right' (p. ix).

Nozick writes that the subject of this last section of his book is 'the best of all possible worlds' (p. 298). He notes, rightly, that not all goods—not all desires—can be simultaneously realized. 'The best of all possible worlds for me will not be that for you.' Utopia, therefore, must be, in some sense, 'best for all of us; the best world imaginable, for each of us'. What sort of society does this imply? Accoding to Nozick, one which has 'a wide and diverse range of communities which people can enter if they are admitted, leave if they wish to, shape according to their wishes; a society in which utopian experimentation can be tried, different styles of life can be lived, and alternative visions of the good can be individually or jointly pursued' (p. 307). The more diverse the range of communities available, the more people will be able to live (nearly) as they wish to live. As Nozick puts it, 'utopia will consist of utopias' (p. 312)—'no one can *impose* his own utopian vision on others'. The minimal state, Nozick claims, provides a framework for this utopian society.

However, I cannot see why the minimal state is a better framework for Nozick's utopia than a state which imposes taxes to provide a basic social minimum. Formal freedom, perhaps, is greater in the minimal state: but the capacity to live as one chooses, or in the type of community one would wish to live in, depends also on economic resources. If, as Nozick says, the aim is to create a world which is 'best for *all* of us' (emphasis added), this creates a strong argument *against* the minimal state, and for extensive redistribution, perhaps along the lines of Rawls's difference principle.

Nozick, however, makes a striking (and perhaps surprising) claim for his minimal state utopia. It 'has many of the virtues, and few of the defects [that] people find in the libertarian vision': 'For though there is great liberty to choose among communities, many particular communities internally may have many restrictions . . . which libertarians would condemn if they were enforced by a central state apparatus' (p. 320). Thus 'communities' (though not the state) may ban capitalism, or enforce economic redistribution among their members, refusing to allow individual members of the community to opt out of their arrangements. Why? Nozick cannot, and does not, argue that the relevant difference between communities and states is that people have joined communities voluntarily, since it is obviously possible to be born into a community, as into a state. Nor does he argue that one is free to leave a community —perhaps because he would then have to allow redistributive states so long as they too leave this freedom to their citizens.

So what is (are) the relevant difference(s)? After wrestling with this problem for about a page, Nozick concludes, with great candour: 'I do not see my way clearly through these issues' (p. 323). Nevertheless, he does not withdraw his previous claims about communities.

Conclusion

One of the great virtues of *Anarchy, State, and Utopia* has just been illustrated—Nozick's disarming honesty. Few political philosophers—probably few philosophers, or intellectuals of any kind—are as explicit and open as Nozick is in acknowledging the gaps and weaknesses in his arguments. This makes the job of a critic that much easier, and I have not scrupled to take advantage. Very early in his book, Nozick frankly tells the reader that it will not present 'a finished, complete and elegant whole', with all details thought through (p. xii). He adds: 'I believe there is also a place for a less complete work containing unfinished presentations, conjectures, open questions and problems . . .'. One can only agree. *Anarchy, State, and Utopia* is a book written in an unusual style, remarkable not only for its intellectual verve, but for the very high proportion of sentences which take the form of questions—questions which are often not answered, but are (almost always) good questions. It also includes many interesting discussions not mentioned in this survey, because peripheral to the main argument (the most famous and brilliant of these is probably on the 'experience machine' (pp. 42–5)).

But what, finally, is the value of Nozick's political philosophy? In my opinion the most valuable part is also the least acceptable, namely the theory of economic justice set out in part II. The reasons why it is not (in my opinion) acceptable have been stated above. But its value is to present a strong and impressive case for private property rights. One need not agree with Nozick that (in an ideal world) these would take precedence over every other consideration; none the less, one may be convinced by Nozick's arguments that there have to be *very good reasons* for overriding them. Vague and implausible goals like 'equality' are not enough; nor is the realization of some 'patterned' principle of distribution. Nevertheless, good reasons

—such as the relief of suffering, and provision for the needy— do exist.

Nozick's iconoclasm is also useful. He forces us to face up to such questions as, for example, what the (moral) difference is between theft and state redistribution. Why is state redistribution not theft by means of a powerful third party? Or would theft sometimes be morally justified? Arguably it would, in cases where it is necessary to prevent starvation or great suffering and does relatively little harm to the person stolen from. Can state redistribution be justified in cases where theft cannot? If so, why? *Anarchy, State, and Utopia* provokes us into asking, and trying to answer, questions such as these.

Bibliographical Note

Anarchy, State, and Utopia has attracted at least one book-length commentary, Jonathan Wolff's *Robert Nozick* (London, 1991). This is an excellent discussion of the whole of Nozick's political philosophy, sympathetic but ultimately sceptical. Other commentaries are briefer— articles, chapters, and reviews—and (except for the reviews) usually concentrate on only one aspect of Nozick's theory, either the justification of the minimal state, or (much more commonly) his libertarian theory of economic justice. However, twenty of these briefer discussions have been usefully collected between two covers by Jeffrey Paul in *Reading Nozick: Essays on Anarchy, State, and Utopia* (Totowa, NJ, 1981), to provide a general overview.

Most of the essays in *Reading Nozick* are respectfully critical and most are on the theory of economic justice. Perhaps the best is Samuel Scheffler, 'Natural Rights, Equality, and the Minimal State', which presents a careful argument deriving universal rights (and duties) from Nozick's premiss of meaningful life. Thomas Nagel, in 'Liberalism without Foundations', gives reasons why a rational person would welcome legislation to compel him to fulfil such duties. Cheney Ryan, in 'Yours, Mine and Ours: Property Rights and Individual Liberty', presents an interesting but, I think, unsuccessful counter-argument to Nozick's attack on patterned principles of distribution. A careful consideration of the circumstances in which invasion of property rights is and is not justified is in Judith Jarvis Thomson's 'Some Ruminations on Rights', while Onora O'Neill, in 'Nozick's Entitlements', argues convincingly that Lockean premisses do not yield Nozickian conclusions on absolute property rights. David Lyons, in 'The New Indian Claims and Original Rights to Land', provides a rare discussion of Nozick's principle of rectification of injustice. An attempt to provide a grounding for Nozickian property rights is Eric Mack, 'How to Derive Libertarian Rights'. Quite a number of books on political philosophy devote a chapter to *Anarchy, State, and Utopia*. For example, Chapter 10 of Tony Honoré's *Making Law Bind* (Oxford, 1987) takes Nozick to task for the parochiality of his 'liberal Western' conception of private property rights. Gordon Graham, in chapter 3 of *Contemporary Social Philosophy* (Oxford, 1988), is generally sympathetic to Nozick's theory of economic justice, but doubts whether market transactions between extremely unequal parties are genuinely free. Less sympathetic to Nozick is Jeremy Waldron, chapter 7 of whose *The Right to Private Property* (Oxford, 1988) contains a penetrating critique of Nozick's principle of just acquisition of unowned resources—namely, that it involves loss of rights by others consequent on unilateral action of the appropriator, on terms they would not accept.

Some more articles critical of Nozick may be mentioned. J. Exdell, in 'Distributive Justice: Nozick on Property Rights' (*Ethics*, 87 (1976–7), 142–9, challenges Nozick's assumption that prior to their private appropriation resources are (morally) unowned—perhaps individuals generally have a human right to benefit from them, which private property rights should respect. J. R. Kearl ('Do Entitlements Imply that Taxation is Theft?', *Philosophy and Public Affairs*, 7 (Fall 1977), 74–81, suggests that the advantages to property owners from the state's protection of property rights entitles it to tax them for redistributive purposes; while M. H. Lessnoff castigates Nozick for his confusion of patterned and end-state principles in 'Capitalism, Socialism and Justice' (in J. Arthur and W. H. Shaw (eds.), *Justice and Economic Distribution*, Englewood Cliffs, NJ, 1978). Finally, Charles Sayward and Wayne Wasserman, in 'Has Nozick Justified the State?' (in J. A. Corlett's (ed.), *Equality and Liberty: Analyzing Rawls and Nozick* (Basingstoke, 1991), 261–7), conclude that he has not. Corlett's collection also contains another five articles on Nozick.

Ronald Dworkin: *Taking Rights Seriously*

PAUL KELLY

JOHN RAWLS, Robert Nozick, and Ronald Dworkin together form the trinity of American liberal political philosophers which has dominated much Anglo-American political thought since the 1970s. Dworkin made his reputation with his book *Taking Rights Seriously*, which was published in 1977. Unlike Rawls's *A Theory of Justice* or Nozick's *Anarchy, State, and Utopia*, it was not written as a book. Although the arguments of each chapter are intricately connected, most of the chapters were first published elsewhere. In this sense Dworkin's book is much closer in style to Oakeshott's *Rationalism in Politics and Other Essays* or Berlin's *Four Essays on Liberty* than it is to the works of his American colleagues. As with Berlin and Oakeshott, Dworkin's adoption of the essay style allows him to develop an argument that is more than merely the sum of the individual chapters.

The philosophical position developed in Dworkin's book has provided the base for a host of subsequent books and articles which have further enhanced his reputation as one of the foremost theorists of a right-based liberal political order, and, in jurisprudence, as one of the most influential critics of legal positivism. Nevertheless, *Taking Rights Seriously* remains Dworkin's most important book. This is in part due to its style, in part due to its direct engagement with practical issues. Although Dworkin holds prestigious chairs in Jurisprudence at Oxford University and New York University, and although five chapters of the book first appeared in law journals, he was not writing for a purely academic audience. Instead his concerns were often unambiguously political, showing how certain theses about law or constitutional interpretation or the theory of rights have a direct bearing on our understanding of the values inherent in a liberal democratic society. An important element of his rejection of legal positivism is precisely that it separates legal philosophy from other aspects of political theory. For Dworkin, being a political philosopher or a philosopher of law involves engagement with practical life and, given the centrality of law to modern liberal democratic societies, it is, in his view, quite proper for the philospher of law to contribute to debate in the public realm of political activity. It is this willingness to connect philosophical questions with matters of public concern that makes his book important as a conception of what a political philosophy can do. In it Dworkin outlines a public philosophy for a society that takes rights seriously—that is, he outlines a genuinely *liberal* theory of law.

A Liberal Theory of Law in Place of the Ruling Theory

Dworkin brings together the varied themes and arguments of each chapter of *Taking Rights Seriously* under the heading of 'a liberal theory of law'. In his introduction he claims that his liberal theory of law was developed at a time when liberalism as a tradition of political thought was facing considerable hostility. The liberal theory of law that Dworkin develops forms part of the wider dissatisfaction with the received liberal tradition of utilitarian ethics and legal positivism. His own position is 'sharply critical' of legal positivism, which is conventionally seen as the paradigmatic liberal theory of law. Legal positivism has its roots in the philosophy of the eighteenth-century English legal philosopher Jeremy Bentham (1748–1832), and has had such a pervasive influence on modern legal theory and liberal political ideas that Dworkin dubs it the 'ruling theory of law'. As he goes on to argue throughout the rest of this book, much of the dissatisfaction that liberalism has engendered has been a result of the theoretical inadequacy of the 'ruling theory'.

The 'ruling theory' has two parts: first, a theory about the necessary and sufficient conditions for the truth of propositions about law—that is, a theory of what the law is; secondly, a theory of what the law ought to be. As Bentham argued in *A Fragment on Government* (1776), jurisprudence can be divided into *the expository* and *the censorial*. *Expository* jurisprudence is concerned with identifying what the law is, which is a straightforward scientific enterprise that does not appeal to moral standards. For Bentham and subsequent legal positivist philosophers, it is possible to identify true propositions about English law by appealing to certain institutional facts about the authoritative source of legal commands. The second task of jurisprudence, for Bentham, is that of the *censor*, whose job it is to argue for the reform or transformation of the law, and whose tool for identifying what the law ought to be is the principle of utility. These two tasks are logically distinct and, according to Bentham, the confusion of these two goals has dangerous consequences.

Dworkin's theory challenges both parts of this 'ruling theory', not only in its Benthamite guise, but also in its later manifestations such as H. L. A. Hart's legal positivism and modern utilitarian theories of political morality. He contests the logical separation of legal, political, and moral theory which underlies Bentham's distinction. Whilst propositions about the law are not the same as propositions about morality, there are nevertheless significant connections which are derived from the role of rights in both legal and political or moral argument. If we take the role of rights seriously, and reject Bentham's view of. them as merely 'nonsense upon stilts', then, according to Dworkin, we will see that an adequate theory of law is an extension of political and moral theory rather than logically distinct from it. Given the centrality of rights to Dworkin's argument, he also rejects the utilitarian view that the general welfare can override individuals' basic interests. Instead he is concerned with restoring the concept of rights within liberal political thought, by defending a view of rights as 'political trumps' which individuals hold against the pursuit of collective goals which impose loss or injury upon them.

The success of Dworkin's enterprise, and his claims for the continuity of legal, political, and moral philosophy, depends on his being able to defend a conception of rights which bridges the divide between the logical and normative components of law. Traditionally, arguments which have attempted to bridge this gap have appealed to pre-political moral or natural rights, precisely the sorts of rights that Bentham, Burke, Marx, and a host of other philosophers dismissed as metaphysical nonsense. According to positivists, the problem with such natural-rights arguments is that one can engage in meaningful discourse about law without appeal to metaphysical entities. Dworkin's argument is interesting and influential because he challenges this point in the positivist critique. Rather than constructing a full theory of rights that is external to our existing moral and legal practices, as traditional natural-law theorists did, he is concerned with constructing a theory which makes sense of the concept of rights which is employed in our moral and legal practices. Dworkin's argument is right-based, but it is significantly different from traditional natural-rights theory. It is also significant that Dworkin turns the positivist critique of natural rights against legal positivism. To the positivist argument that natural-rights theory complicates matters by incorporating external moral considerations into an account of the nature of law, which can be given solely by reference to institutional facts, he retorts that it is positivism which is trying to impose an external and hence arbitrary philosophical construction upon the law, with its denial of the significance of rights. Both traditional natural-law and modern legal positivism suffer from the same defect in constructing a particular theory of law that denies key features of our legal and moral practices. Theory construction for both of these alternatives is separate from an understanding of how law functions and connects with other moral and political practices. As a result, neither theory provides an adequate account of what law is, let alone of what it ought to be. The task of legal theorizing is not one of arguing back to first principles, whether of natural law or of utility; instead it involves drawing distinctions, and criticizing rival theories, as part of providing an interpretation of the practice of law. Dworkin's method in *Taking Rights Seriously* is precisely that which he attributes to 'Hercules', his ideal judge.

Rules, Principles and Policies: The Critique of Positivism

Dworkin's critique of legal positivism is subtle. Unlike the standard natural-law view, Dworkin's argument does not merely construct a moral conception of law, neither does it deny the positivist's claim that a satisfactory account of law must make appeals to authoritative institutional sources—that is, statutes, precedents, and legal decisions—nor, most importantly, does it deny that one can decide legal questions in clear cases by appeals to such valid rules. The rules that positivists place so much weight on do, indeed, play an essential role in any account of the law. However, he denies the positivist's claim that the idea of law as an authoritative system of rules is a sufficient account of law.

There are three basic features of legal positivism which Dworkin challenges. There is, first, the idea that law is a special set of rules for the use of public power, and that these rules can be distinguished from other social rules, such as moral rules or customs, by their 'pedigree' rather than their content. Secondly, and most importantly, there is the idea that this set of authoritative rules is exhaustive of the law, and that, if a case cannot be settled by applying any of these rules, then its settlement is an example not of applying the law, but rather of official discretion. As Hart argues in *The Concept of Law*, there are cases where the rules run out, and in such cases a judicial decision becomes a case not of applying the law but of making new law by exercising discretion. Thirdly, there is the view that in such cases it does not make sense to argue that the judge is enforcing a legal right. In other words, in cases that do not fall under a valid legal rule, neither plaintiff nor defendant has a right to a particular decision and legal rights and obligations exist only in uncontroversial cases. Thus, when a judge is trying a 'hard case', his decision will, according to the positivists, involve making new laws and extending new rights that did not previously exist.

The first part of Dworkin's assault on positivism takes the form of a philosophical account of judicial adjudication. Whereas positivists take legislation to be paradigmatic of the law, Dworkin takes adjudication, or what judges do in deciding cases, and by focusing on adjudication he argues that we can see that the model of rules provides an inadequate account of what law is like.

When judges are confronted by 'hard cases' that require adjudication, they do their utmost to appeal to rules, but they will also often appeal to standards that are not rules, standards that Dworkin calls principles and policies. The distinction between principles and policies is complex and controversial, and Dworkin gives a number of different accounts of the distinction. Basically a principle is a standard observed as a requirement of justice or morality. Later on he gives an account of principles which is connected with rights. Principles are individuated claims on behalf of groups or individual persons that can be made against the pursuit of policies or other social goals. Principles concern rights. Policies, on the other hand, concern social goals that the community wishes to achieve. Wealth maximization or the maximization of utility would constitute a policy.[1] An example that Dworkin gives of a principle is that used to decide the case of *Riggs* v. *Palmer* in 1889 in the state of New York. The case was brought to decide whether the heir to a will could inherit even though he had murdered his grandfather in order to claim the inheritance. Although the statutes regulating the making, proof, and effect of wills did not make a distinction to cover such cases, the judge decided against the plaintiff, by appealing to the principle that 'no man may profit from his own wrong' (p. 26).[2] Principles and policies are both standards used in adjudication. The difference between them is a logical one, rather than a matter of content. Principles are not special cases of rules. A principle like that given above is different in kind from a legal rule such as 'A will is invalid unless signed by three witnesses'. A rule like the latter applies in an all-or-nothing fashion. If three persons have witnessed a will, and the rule that three persons must witness a will is valid, then the answer supplied by the rule must be accepted. If the rule is not valid, then it plays no role in a decision at all. In the case of such valid rules, the judge is left with little room to exercise his judgement about the outcome. But in the case of principles, things are different. A principle has to have a weight attached to it; in adjudicating a case, therefore, it does not apply in an all-or-nothing fashion. In some cases, such as *Riggs* v. *Palmer*, the weight of the principle will outweigh adherence to the rules pertaining to the proof and effect of wills. Because rules do not have the dimension of weight or importance, it is not possible to see principles as a subset of rules. If we think of the analogy

---

[1] See R. Posner, *The Economics of Justice* (Cambridge, Mass., 1981), for the view that judges ought to maximize wealth through their decisions.

[2] R. Dworkin, *Taking Rights Seriously* (London, 1977; 2nd corrected edn., 1978). References in the text are to the second edition.

of a game, an umpire can determine whether the rules have been broken or when specified exceptions occur, but he is not generally empowered to judge whether the rule applies or not. However, in the case of principles, the judge does have to decide the weight of a principle in a given case, and on a case-by-case basis. Consequently, the positivist's argument for law as a body of rules is inadequate.

The second part of Dworkin's critique is an assault on the idea that a non-normative account of the law can be given by appeal to the source or pedigree of law. Hart, in *The Concept of Law*, had argued that the law can be divided into a system of primary and secondary rules, the primary rules being the basic rules of law prescribing actions and conferring obligations, which are identified by appeal to a secondary rule of recognition.[3] A secondary rule is identified when the 'practice conditions' of the rule are met—that is, when individuals behave in a certain way. The rule exists not because judges or functionaries believe that they have a moral obligation to recognize only certain sources of rules as sources of law, for this would thereby involve normative political questions of what sources can legitimately give rise to law. Rather Hart assumes that the mere fact that judges act in a certain way constitutes the secondary rule. This secondary rule is a 'social' rule, because it is not conferred from some external authority, but are instead constituted by a certain social practice, and it is from this alone that it derives its authority. Thus a judge behaving in a certain way exhibits through his actions that he is under an obligation to recognize only certain sources of law as authoritative. For positivists the existence of this secondary rule of recognition is simply a matter of fact exhibited by conformity to the practice conditions of the rule—that is, behaving in a certain way.

In challenging the account of the secondary rule of recognition as a 'social' rule, Dworkin draws a distinction between 'social' rules that are *constituted* by a practice and 'social' rules that are *justified* by the practice. He argues that Hart's theory works only if the content of this 'social' secondary rule of recognition is the same as the practice which gives rise to these rules. That is, the 'social' rule of recognition which specifies

[3] H. L. A. Hart, *The Concept of Law* (Oxford, 1961), 97.

that only certain authoritative sources give rise to law will only be a genuine source of obligation to recognize only those sources, if it is indeed the case that only those sources can give rise to law. But, according to Dworkin, this begs the question at issue. For this 'social' secondary rule of recognition will only be obligation-creating if it does indeed constitute the practice of law. Why should we recognize that what judges and functionaries do is both all that law is and all that it can be? For the social-rule theory to work, Hart must assume that all that law can be—that is, the full practice of law—is captured in his account of these two sets of primary and secondary rules. Hart has not provided an argument as to why the social-rule account of the secondary rule of recognition can be the only criterion of the source of law. Contrary to Hart, Dworkin argues that what legal theories do is provided contestable characterizations of what the practice of law is, each of which is justified by the practice of law. The practice cannot be fully comprehended by Hart's mechanistic social-rule account, for this would rule out the sort of argument that takes place within the practice of law over what are authoritative sources of law— that is, precisely what rule of recognition is justified by the practice. On this question Hart answers that only certain institutional sources give rise to law, whereas Dworkin argues that the resources of a community's morality are also necessary for identifying law. Both authors claim that their theory is justified by the practice of law.

The other key point to Dworkin's argument is that, if the social-rule theory is true and that genuine obligations can be inferred only from regularities of behaviour constituting social practices, then the only obligations we can have are conventional obligations constituted by such practices. The problem with this account is that it ignores an important sense in which we use the concept of obligation and duty in moral language to distinguish our moral duties from what convention tells us to do. It is often the case that appeals are made to duties and obligations in moral and political arguments for the express purpose of criticizing conventional moral rules. If Hart's social thesis is correct, then this would considerably impoverish our moral language and conduct, for his account of the authority of law could equally apply to the practice of morality.

The third component of the critique of positivism concerns the nature of judicial discretion. Positivists assert that in cases where the rules run out the judge can often be required to exercise his discretion, and, given that this is appropriate only in cases where the rules have been exhausted, it is properly understood not as applying the law, but rather as making new law and creating new legal rights.

Dworkin's response is to distinguish three senses of discretion which are confused by the positivists. In the first case a person has discretion if his 'duty is defined by standards that reasonable men can interpret in different ways' (p. 69). A person has discretion in a second sense if no higher authority may review or overturn his decision. Finally, a person can have discretion where a set of standards which impose duties on him do not impose a duty to make a particular decision. According to Dworkin a judge might regard himself as having discretion in the first and second cases whilst still considering his discretion as raising a question about what his duty as a judge is. It is only if we acknowledge that duties and obligations must be derived from 'social' rules that the judge would have a strong discretion of the sort positivists claim. But, as we have already seen, there is no good reason to believe that obligations and duties can be derived only from 'social' rules. The positivist's conception of law distorts his account of what judges actually do in adjudicating 'hard cases'. If we can have duties which are not wholly derived from 'social' rules, then there is no difficulty in claiming that, although the rules might have been exhausted, in 'hard cases' judges are nevertheless able to decide on the basis of law, and reason about legal obligations, rather than make purely arbitrary decisions.

This last point is crucial not only because it challenges the positivist account of what judges actually do in deciding such cases, but also because it has significant political consequences which the positivist ignores. If judges are to be understood as making purely arbitrary non-legal decisions in 'hard cases', by appealing simply to their own preferences, feelings, or instincts, then a question immediately arises. Why should we allow judges to make such privileged decisions rather than leave them to accountable political institutions? This is an issue for any liberal democratic community, but is perhaps most vital in the USA, where a non-elected and non-accountable Supreme Court is empowered to make very significant decisions about individual rights, the interpretation of the Constitution, and the bounds of legislation. If we consider the landmark case of *Roe* v. *Wade*, which established a woman's right to choose to have an abortion, and if, following the positivists, we interpret this as judicial legislation or the creation of a new right, then we can legitimately ask what gave those judges the authority to legislate on such a controversial moral question? Why are their opinions or moral beliefs a superior criterion for settling the issue than the political beliefs of the majority? The positivist thesis concerning judicial legislation raises the question of why unaccountable judges should be allowed to legislate, and also why individuals should regard judges' opinions as legally binding when they have based their decisions not on a matter of law but on some other standard such as their moral preferences. All the positivist can say is that it is merely a fact of our community that we do allow courts to legislate. But this will certainly not persuade those who regard abortion as a fundamental issue of morality, and who might not think convention is particularly weighty in matters of life and death.

To answer such questions we need an account of adjudication which connects with a wider moral and political theory, and is able both to ground legal rights, and justify certain decisions being confined to the courts. This leads us to Dworkin's right-based account of adjudication and political morality.

A Herculean Task: Taking Rights Seriously

Dworkin needs to provide an account of adjudication which connects with a wider moral and political theory, but in constructing such a theory he is constrained. Unlike standard natural-law theory he cannot construct and defend an external theory of moral rights which underpins the law, for he has to show that judges should appeal to right-based arguments in adjudicating hard cases, and that such a theory is the best account of how judges actually adjudicate. The theory of legal rights will be an account of the practice of law, and this is crucial because his purpose is to show that positivism mistakes what judges do. He is constrained still further by the important additional requirement of showing that arguments for legal rights are 'matters of principle' rather than 'matters of policy', for an important rival school of law—the law-and-economics movement which has grown up around the work of the American jurist Richard Posner and the British economist Ronald Coase—has attempted to show that judicial decisions in key landmark cases can be explained in terms of the policy of maximizing wealth. If the law-and-economics movement is right, then the best account of our current legal practice will be based on utilitarian policies of wealth maximization; hence their adoption of an economic model of rationality for explaining legal practice and their advocacy of judges applying a version of the utilitarian calculus in adjudicating 'hard cases'.

Alongside Dworkin's critique of positivism there are two further themes which underlie the remainder of his book, and which dominate all his subsequent writings; first, an account of how judges actually decide 'hard cases' by appeal to principle; and, second, a critique of utilitarianism as a rival account of the 'community morality' underlying the practice of law. The latter question will be addressed in the next section.

How does he show that judges appeal to principle in adjudicating hard cases? The argument is in three parts. First, Dworkin repeats his crucial distinction between principle and policy. An argument of principle 'shows that some political decision advances or protects some individual or group right', whereas an argument of policy 'advances some collective goal of the community' (p. 82). He then argues that, although the distinction is controversial, it is the 'distributional character' of arguments of principle which distinguishes them from arguments of policy. The second part of the argument focuses on principle and democracy. If judges are given strong discretion to legislate, and they do so by appeal to policy, then the following question naturally arises in a democracy: what gives unelected public officials such as judges the right to decide political questions? Unlike other political representatives, judges are neither elected, nor ordinarily politically accountable for their decisions. Decisions of policy involve the weighing and balancing of different interests in identifying the common good.

The political institutions of a democratic state provide a forum in which public discussion and debate can take place to identify these interests. Matters of principle, on the other hand, are not decided by balancing such interests, and, if the question at issue is one of determining rights, then it is not clear that democratic institutions with their reliance on compromise, bargains, and majority decisions are the best place for settling such issues. The very point of appealing to rights is that they have what Dworkin calls a 'threshold weight' against collective goals or majority decisions. If one has a right to free speech, then that right must have a 'threshold weight' sufficient to trump any consideration of collective good which might be suggested to limit free speech. It would not make sense of our use of rights to argue both that an individual has a right to freedom of speech and that the government can restrict that right whenever its exercise becomes inconvenient. This fact provides a good reason for protecting those institutions which protect and enforce rights from the vicissitudes of majoritarianism. The third part of the argument attacks a two-stage view of judicial decision-making. The standard model claims that judges enforce legal rights until the rules run out, and then appeal to their own beliefs and values. In contrast, Dworkin argues that judges are bound by a conception of political responsibility: 'This doctrine states, in its most general form, that political officials must make only such political decisions as they can justify within a political theory that also justifies the other decisions they propose to make' (p. 89). This conception underlies the practice of appealing to precedent where judges have to show how their decisions are consistent with an interpretation of other decisions already taken.

Dworkin also needs to identify the rights which the judge should appeal to in deciding such 'hard cases' as legal rights. This he does by distinguishing between 'background rights' and institutional rights, and then between institutional rights and specifically legal rights. Each has the same normative character, but they have a different specification. Background rights are general rights that justify a political decision by a society in the abstract, but do not specify who should enforce them and how. Institutional rights, on the other hand, provide a justification for a decision by some person or institution. Background

rights are abstract, whereas institutional rights are concrete—
that is, they are rights which are clearly defined so that they
can be shown to 'trump' particular political aims and decisions.
Institutions, in their turn, can be either fully or partly autonomous. The game of chess is autonomous in the sense that one
cannot appeal to morality to argue for an institutional right to
a decision in chess. Institutional rights in such a case are given
by reference to the rules which are constitutive of the game
and their authoritative interpretation. However, unlike chess
or baseball (Dworkin's favourite examples), law is only partly
autonomous, for the rules of legislation are not generally considered sufficient to decide questions of right—especially not
in 'hard cases'. An individual can appeal to wider morality to
claim that a certain right should be enacted. So law is in part
continuous with political morality and not fully autonomous.
However, it is important to recognize that institutional legal
rights are nevertheless rights, and should be enforced even
where they diverge from a political theory's background rights.
The claim that some institutions are semi-autonomous is important, as positivists claim that all institutions are autonomous,
with the corollary that questions of law are conceptually distinct from questions of morality. How we distinguish between
autonomous and semi-autonomous institutions is not, as positivists claim, a matter of conceptual analysis, but a matter of
critical reflection on the character of the practice. This involves a philosophical interpretation of the character of the
practice, which is not only a logical construction, but also an
appropriate phenomenology of adjudication recognizable to
lawyers. Although law is only a semi-autonomous institution,
it is not the case that judicial argument can arbitrarily introduce moral and political claims, so that the question of what
law is and what law should be collapses. The judge does not
appeal to external moral principles in the way that some traditional natural-law theories suggest. Dworkin does not want
to collapse the question of what rights should be enacted in
law, into the distinct but equally normative question of what
rights an individual has in a particular 'hard case'. The first case
is a matter of legislation, and consequently the appeal to moral
principle is different from that in adjudication. The judge is
concerned with what rights an individual has. Thus, when

Dworkin's fictional super-judge Hercules is deciding a 'hard case', he is not appealing to external moral principles which would change the law, but looking for a principled decision which is consistent with other key decisions, precedents, and rules in showing what the law is. When making his decision, Hercules can incorporate an appeal to background moral and political rights, but the appeal is one that applies these in giving the best account of the practice. The virtue that guides the judge in adjudicating 'hard cases' is 'integrity'. He must respect the integrity of the practice and provide the best possible account of it when making an appeal to moral principles to account for specific institutional rights. What is wrong with traditional natural-law theory is that the appeal to moral principle is not rooted in the best account of the practice. Such principles are not shown to provide a more coherent account of the practice; instead they are used to show the weaknesses of the practice. What makes Hercules' task a model of adjudication is that he is trying to show the connection between background rights and their institutional implications—that is, how they give rise to legal rights. The Herculean task of the judge is to show the continuity between the best account of law and background moral and political rights—that is, to show how they are connected and how this connection provides an account of key decisions and principles. This is a complex procedure that involves an appeal to legal history, precedent, convention, and an account of the role and function of law within a given political community. At its most complete, as practised only by the super-judge Hercules (who has both the time and the expertise to make these extremely complex decisions), the process will involve giving a full account of what law is, how the decision he makes is consistent with that general account, and how it is also consistent with the normative aspirations of that community.

In doing this the judge is doing more than exercising discretion or legislating. He is responding to an incompleteness in a particular conception of law which has to be resolved. Where the positivist claims that, when the rules run out, law ceases and discretion takes over, Dworkin argues instead that it is not law that has run out, but merely a conception of law. The positivist's rule-based conception of law is merely one contestable account of the law. The task of adjudication in 'hard cases' is to provide an alternative conception of the concept of law that will take the practice on further.[4] The implication of this view— namely, that legal argument in 'hard cases' consists of articulating alternative conceptions of law—explains why Dworkin rejects 'strict constructionist' interpretations of the law or the US Constitution. Some politicians (most notably President Richard Nixon) criticized various Supreme Court judgments for incorporating political arguments into judicial decisions and relying on 'political' philosophies of law, rather than the law itself. Dworkin's response to such arguments is that the law consists of a complex institutional structure of rules, principles, practices, and precedents, and that any coherent account of that complex practice can only be a 'conception' of law. So the 'strict constructionist' is providing a 'conception' of that practice just as much as the 'liberal'. The important difference is that Dworkin's 'liberal' is explicit about the connection between political theory and judicial decision-making in his account of law, whereas the 'strict constructionist' disguises his conservative political agenda through trying to discover the intention of the 'founders' or historical legislators. The view that we should be bound by the historical intentions of the founding fathers of the US Constitution is just as much a 'conception' of law as any other, which calls for justification as the best interpretation of the practices of law and its connection with the community's wider political and moral aspirations.

Both the positivist's theory of judicial discretion and the conservative's hostility to the liberal's use of political theory masquerading as law rely on an inadequate understanding of the function of moral reasons in arguments from principle. Their shared assumption that moral beliefs are subjective preferences gives rise to the dilemma of leaving controversial cases to courts: when it comes to abortion or desegregation, why should the moral preferences of a group of liberal Supreme Court justices have greater authority than those of the 'moral' majority? If in appealing to moral beliefs the judge were doing

---

[4] This distinction between a concept and its conceptions is derived from both W. D. Gallie, 'Essentially Contested Concepts', *Proceedings of the Aristotelian Society*, 56 (1956), pp. 167–98, and J. Rawls, *A Theory of Justice*, Oxford, Oxford University Press, 1972, pp. 3–6.

no more than saying, 'the law has run out, what do I think?', there would be some justice to the claim. But this is not how judges appeal to moral principles. The judge's appeal is not to personal preferences but to the key moral intuitions which underlie the law and society's conception of the function of law. Both sets of critics ignore the way in which moral principles function in such arguments: unlike bald assertions, they are arguments which make truth claims. Dworkin challenges the belief that moral and political assertions cannot be objects of knowledge because they are merely expressions of preference. His denial that moral assertions are expressions of preference rather than objects of knowledge connects his jurisprudence with his political philosophy and in particular with his critique of the other key component of the 'ruling theory of law'—utilitarianism.

Rights, Justice, and Utilitarianism

Utilitarianism is an essential component of the 'ruling theory of law' because it follows from the belief that all moral assertions are merely expressions of subjective preferences: the product of will not reason. Modern utilitarianism is but the most sophisticated and successful version of arguments that have their roots in David Hume's rejection of the possibility of morality being derived from reason. Dworkin's cognitivist account of judicial reasoning depends upon the view that moral reasons can be given greater weight than is provided by the emotivism or subjectivism of modern utilitarianism. However, utilitarianism poses a further and more recent problem for Dworkin, for a rival school of law, the law-and-economics movement, has argued that the best account of what judges do in deciding 'hard cases' is given in terms of policy-based arguments for wealth maximization. If Dworkin's account of right-based adjudication is to stand, he needs to show that policy-based utilitarian arguments concerning wealth maximization fail to capture the underlying public morality of law and of the wider community.

Dworkin's characterization of the right-based morality which underlies our use of the notion of rights in political and legal discourse is most clearly articulated in his extended discussion of John Rawls's conception of the social contract in his *A Theory of Justice*. Dworkin is to a large extent in agreement with Rawls, but his extended discussion of Rawls's philosophical method allows him to develop his own account of morality as right based and show how such a view can be developed and defended against critics such as utilitarians. He begins with a famous critique of Rawls's conception of the 'original position' in which individuals, deprived of important knowledge of themselves and their circumstances, agree to two principles of justice which then structure a fair society. Like many others, Dworkin points out that the 'original position' cannot provide reasons for accepting the two principles of justice, for an agreement made in such a condition of ignorance could have no binding force whatever: 'A hypothetical contract is not simply a pale form of contract; it is no contract at all' (p. 151). He then goes on to probe Rawls's argument more deeply, and it is here that he identifies the resources for his own defence of a right-based morality. He turns in particular to Rawls's method of reflective equilibrium. This method is similar to the constructivist method that Dworkin uses in the person of Hercules to justify particular decisions in 'hard cases'.

The method of reflective equilibrium starts from the common intuitions and sense of justice that individuals share. Although individuals share a sense of justice, they differ considerably in their accounts of what justice is and what it requires. Dworkin suggests that we share a belief that slavery is unjust, but we might differ significantly in our accounts of why this is so. Moral and political argument starts from these shared common intuitions. When we engage in arguments about justice we appeal to such intuitions, but we do so in complex ways. These intuitive commitments are in part constitutive of a community, and it could only abandon its core intuitions about justice by becoming significantly different. Moral argument, at least in its philosophical guise, involves the construction of theories which account for these intuitive convictions. Although these theories are developed independently of the beliefs and tested against them, in the process of articulating and developing them they undergo modification and refinement; that is why the method is described as reflective. Equilibrium is achieved when there is a match between the structure and outcome of our theory of justice and our considered intuitions about justice, and when the theory is shown to provide a better reflective account of our intuitive commitments than any rival theory does. This constructivist method of reflective equilibrium is how we justify moral and political principles. So, once again, Dworkin is rejecting a method of moral argument which presents theory as external to a particular community. Moral argument has to be grounded somewhere, and it starts not in the realm of philosophical abstraction but with these common intuitions. That said, the methodology allows for considerable philosophical abstraction and subtlety in the critique of rival theories. Dworkin then goes on to characterize Rawls's device of the 'original position' as a constructive model for public justification of moral or political principles in circumstances where individuals differ in their convictions. What underlies this device is the intuition that individuals deserve equal concern and respect, and what the 'original position' does is model a situation of choice characterized by equality of concern and respect. In such a situation equal individuals choose the principles which regulate their association. This leads Dworkin to characterize Rawls's theory as right based. He distinguishes three broad categories of moral theory: right based, duty based, and goal based. A right-based morality takes some basic right—in this case the right of individuals to equal concern and respect—as morally fundamental. Dworkin makes a good case for characterizing Rawls's argument as right based in this way, because of the priority he attaches to the individual over the maximization of welfare. However, he still has to show that our wider public morality is also right based, and show how this basic right to equality of concern and respect relates to individual rights claims.

Satisfying the first of these two requirements is easy in one sense, because all Dworkin needs to do is show that we do appeal to rights in moral and political argument. Rights certainly have an important role in public moral argument, particularly in the USA, which has a Bill of Rights and a conception of fundamental rights written into certain key constitutional amendments. However, he also needs to show that this appeal to rights is fundamental and not merely a 'short hand' for more fundamental moral principles such as utility. To overcome this challenge he needs to give a more detailed account of how institutional and basic rights used in moral, political, and constitutional argument are grounded on the fundamental right to be treated with equality of concern and respect. This he does in a discussion of 'Civil Disobedience' occasioned by demonstrations against the draft and the war in Vietnam and in the chapter entitled 'Taking Rights Seriously'. Here he identifies the point of moral and political rights as protections of certain basic human interests against the coercive power of the state. To have a right, he argues, is to enjoy protection against the coercive power of the state or community, even when the exercise of that right offends the public's sense of what is the right thing to do. Not all legally enacted rights are rights in this strong moral sense. It was not the case in the USA that individuals had an enacted legal right to dodge the draft. However, Dworkin points out that this does not entail that an individual does wrong in dodging the draft. This question depends on whether the legal enactment of the draft is constitutional—that is, whether it can be shown to be consistent with the best account of law and its function within the community. Similarly, it is not the case that an individual does wrong in protesting against the draft law, even if this runs against the grain of majority opinion, if it is the case that the legal enactment violates constitutional rights.

Dworkin's arguments about 'Civil Disobedience' are complex and controversial and deserve a much fuller treatment than space allows. What is important here is the distinction between 'rights' and 'the right thing to do'. This distinction is crucial to understanding the function of rights in public moral discourse. To have a right only when it is consistent with majority opinion about the right thing to do would undermine the idea of rights as special protections of crucial individual interests. What sort of protection would a right to freedom of expression be if it could be restricted every time the public interest required it? If we accept that rights function in this way as protections against majority tyranny and government power, then we have good grounds for rejecting any utilitarian or goal-based foundation of those rights. Any such goal-based theory would always make the enforcement of rights conditional on the achievement of the goal rather than on the principled protection of the individual irrespective of outcomes. The claim that our public morality is right based and that what underlies this right is the requirement of equal concern and respect provides a better account of the weight we attach to rights arguments than can be provided by utilitarianism. The discourse of rights which we employ in public moral and political arguments in a liberal democratic society is not merely a 'short hand' for utility, and to assume that it is fails to take seriously the function and weight of rights.

A further crucial feature of claiming that our public moral discourse is best characterized as right based is that it helps explain the complex relationship between the foundational 'background' right to equality of concern and respect and the institutional rights that are grounded on it. Dworkin's rights thesis does not give rise to a simple list of basic rights such as life, liberty, and property, such as we find in Nozick's *Anarchy, State, and Utopia*. Instead the foundational right to equality of concern and respect gives rise to a complex of rights to particular liberties, rather than to liberty as such, and to other rights which comprise equal concern and respect rather than to a right to sameness of treatment. The rejection of a crude right to sameness of treatment allows him to justify policies of reverse discrimination which on the surface at least seem to contradict a commitment to equality. The public moral argument over rights to equal treatment, reverse discrimination, and distributive justice are all, according to Dworkin, best explained in terms of articulating the full implications of this commitment to equality of concern and respect. Utilitarian arguments cannot provide an adequate account of this basic egalitarian intuition despite a commitment to 'Bentham's Dictum' of counting everyone as one and no one as more than one. The supposed egalitarianism of utilitarianism fails because it does not treat everyone as one, but actually discriminates against minorities as less than one, through its counting of external preferences. Even though preference utilitarianism seeks to satisfy as many preferences as possible, according to Dworkin it fails to satisfy strict impartiality because it includes both personal and external preferences. Personal preferences are for an individual's own enjoyment of some good or service, whereas external preferences concern the assignment of goods or benefits to third parties. If a preference utilitarian calculation is to satisfy the preferences of a group, but these are external preferences for restriction of law-school places to whites only because blacks are somehow inferior, then the simple egalitarianism of utilitarianism collapses in favour of the institutionalization of discrimination which fails to accord all individuals equality of concern and respect. Utilitarianism can be egalitarian only by excluding such external preferences, and it can only do that by ceasing to be utilitarian and instead incorporating some right-based principle which justifies this exclusion. If, however, utilitarianism seeks to abandon egalitarianism altogether as some strict act utilitarians do, then the justification of the principle is challenged by its strong incompatibility with our intuitions about rights and equality of concern and respect. And if it ignores such intuitions in its justification, there is the much more complex philosophical problem of what does ground the principle of utility and what makes it a source of moral and political obligations. Because it is wholly abstracted from even the best reflective account of our core moral and political intuitions, the argument of the radical utilitarian, like that of the traditional natural-law theorist, neither challenges nor assists us in public moral and political debate.

Conclusion

Superficially, Dworkin's arguments appear to be addressed to a political culture such as that of the USA, where rights play a significant role in public argument, and the natural implication is that his theory has little to say to a legal and political order which is not rights based. This is a familiar charge levelled against much American political philosophy—namely, that it universalizes its own political culture. Such a response fails to take seriously Dworkin's important distinction between *rights*-based conceptions of law and political community and *right*-based conceptions. In Britain and many other countries which have no written constitution, there is no basic set of rights to which all subscribe. Rights are not foundational. However, Dworkin is clearly aware of this; what he is concerned with is a conception of the moral significance of the individual as a free and equal subject. That, he rightly argues, is a view which is deeply held across very different legal and political systems. To argue that this is a peculiarly American idea would be to misunderstand the way in which this idea has its roots in modern European culture. This sort of commitment to the individual may well have its origins in historically specific communities, but it would be a mistake to see it as the peculiar property of any one community or culture. Whether we subscribe to a given set of rights as politically foundational or not, it is clear that Dworkin's right-based theory has a much wider significance and application than the USA.

In challenging the 'ruling theory of law', Dworkin set himself against some of the most cherished beliefs of modern moral and political philosophy, which denied the continuity of law, morality, and politics. His thesis is controversial enough in itself, and modern positivists have been reluctant to abandon their position when faced with his arguments. The debate between Dworkin and the 'ruling theory' goes on. However, one implication of his position has been particularly troubling, even for those who are sympathetic to his assault on positivism and utilitarianism. This is what has come to be known as the 'right-answer thesis'. If Dworkin is right in his claim that in adjudication the judge is finding law and not making it, then it follows that there is in principle a right answer to each controversial 'hard case'. Similarly, in moral and political arguments there must be a right answer to questions of justice and right. Dworkin's reasons for this thesis are complex. First, he argues that, in the case of legal and moral reasoning, the reasons never just run out. In making a moral decision about the requirements of distributive justice or law, a judge does not only argue as far as he can and then simply make arbitrary decisions like tossing a coin. This fails to capture adequately the practice of reason-giving which underlies moral and political argument. For Dworkin the practice of law is in part the institutionalization of that practice of public argument. The second reason has to do with the logic of such reasoning. The 'right-answer thesis' excludes the possibility of any middle ground between two controversial claims in law or morality. If one is true, then the other cannot also be true at the same time and must therefore be false. Such a view challenges the incommensurability which many find an irreducible feature of modern pluralist society. Traditionally, natural-rights arguments and their legacy for modern procedural theories of justice and conceptions of law have presented a picture of humans as inherently conflictual. This conflict cannot be eradicated but can be channelled into competition rather than conflict by law. Even modern procedural conceptions of the political community such as Rawls's and Dworkin's theories of justice appear to be ways of accommodating fundamental, and, at least in Rawls's case, intractable disagreements. If at the same time Dworkin wants to advance a cognitivist theory of law and adjudication, then he has the problem of reconciling this commitment with a liberal theory of justice as neutrality. After all, neutrality is usually presented as a response to an intractable disagreement over which 'right answers' are not possible. I do not wish to suggest that Dworkin cannot reconcile the cognitivism of his legal theory with his theory of justice as neutrality, but the two strands appear to pull in opposite directions, and reconciling this tension is not an easy task. In favour of Dworkin's position it can be argued that he takes seriously the practice of reason-giving which underlies legal, moral, and political decision-making. If we reject the Dworkinian view, we are left with a profound challenge: why should we trust unaccountable individuals to make such fundamentally important decisions? If their views are arbitrary rather than principled, then what place do they have in a liberal democratic society? What can legitimize a liberal democratic order is its commitment to the open public justification of political decisions, rather than the conventional acceptance of arbitrary majority will. Despite the ultimately incomplete character of his argument in *Taking Rights Seriously*, the importance of the book lies in its addressing some of the most fundamental and urgent questions of political philosophy today.

Bibliographical Note

Taking Rights Seriously was first published in 1977. In 1978 a second corrected edition appeared with the addition of a long appendix, 'Reply to Critics', originally published in an issue of the *Georgia Law Review* devoted to *Taking Rights Seriously*. The edition I have used is the second corrected edition. *Taking Rights Seriously*, although still undoubtedly Dworkin's most influential and widely read work, is very much a work in progress, an outline of a position that has been developed and expanded in a number of books published since. A further volume of essays in law and political theory, *A Matter of Principle*, was published by Oxford University Press in 1985, and in 1986 Dworkin published a complete monograph statement of his jurisprudence, *Law's Empire* (Cambridge, Mass.). *Law's Empire* develops and expands many of the arguments in *Taking Rights Seriously* and has attracted considerable attention in its own right.

Following the publication of *Law's Empire*, much of Dworkin's attention has been devoted to political philosophy rather than the philosophy of law more narrowly conceived. In particular he has been working on an egalitarian theory of justice and the foundations of liberal political theory. On the subject of justice and equality, see 'What is Equality? Part 1: Equality of Welfare', and 'What is Equality? Part 2: Equality of Resources', *Philosophy and Public Affairs*, 10 (1981), 185–246, 283–345, 'What is Equality? Part 3: The Place of Liberty', *Iowa Law Review*, 73 (1987), 1–54, and 'What is Equality? Part 4: Political Equality', *University of San Francisco Law Review*, 77 (1989), 1–30, 'In Defense of Equality', *Social Philosophy and Policy*, 1 (1983), 24–40, and 'Liberal Community', *California Law Review*, 77 (1989), 479–504. On the foundations of egalitarian liberalism, see 'Foundations of Liberal Equality', *The Tanner Lectures on Human Values*, xi, ed. Grethe B. Peterson (Salt Late City, 1990), 3–119. Dworkin is currently reworking the essays on equality for a book on egalitarian justice. His most recent book, which is a departure from these more abstract concerns, is *Life's Dominion: An Argument about Abortion and Euthanasia* (London, 1993). Although this book is a significant departure from the abstractions of contemporary political philosophy, it continues to testify to Dworkin's concern to apply his political and legal philosophy to matters of current controversy, and his view of political philosophy as contributing to the public philosophy of a modern liberal democracy.

Although there are few books on Dworkin's thought, the secondary literature is vast. The only complete guide to Dworkin's ideas so far is S. Guest, *Ronald Dworkin* (Edinburgh, 1992). This is useful but written largely from a lawyer's point of view for law students, and is thus less helpful on Dworkin's political philosophy or the wider context of philosophy of law. Other useful collections of essays are: M. Cohen (ed.), *Ronald Dworkin and Contemporary Jurisprudence* (London, 1994), and A. Hunt (ed.), *Reading Dworkin Critically* (Oxford, 1992). The latter is rather polemical. Most good studies of the philosophy of H. L. A. Hart will have a significant discussion of Dworkin's arguments. Although not devoted to Dworkin, both W. Kymlicka, *Contemporary Political Philosophy* (Oxford, 1990), and J. Waldron, *The Right to Private Property* (Oxford, 1988), are particularly useful. Both are philosophically close to Dworkin and develop some of his arguments concerning rights and equality. Dworkin's contributions on constitutional law, politics, and political philosophy appear regularly in the pages of the *New York Review of Books*.

Index